M000086717

# COURAGEOUS
# FAITH

A ONE-YEAR DAILY DEVOTIONAL

# COURAGEOUS
# FAITH

*Daily Encouragement for Life's Challenges*

# ALLEN JACKSON

# A Message from Pastor Allen Jackson

An invitation to be courageous is really an invitation to choose faith over fear. I haven't learned how to get that right every time, but I have learned that spending consistent time with God not only anchors us in how we should live, but also in who we are in His eyes. Knowing God is on our side, and that His limitless power can be found where we fall short, is one of the greatest gifts to hold onto in this turbulent world.

That's my hope for this devotional—that over the course of the coming year, your commitment to be in Scripture and prayer daily will increasingly ground you in the immovable Word of God, and that you will be able to face your days with courageous faith.

Here we go.

Allen Jackson
Pastor, World Outreach Church

## ALMOST PERSUADED

*Then Agrippa said to Paul, "You almost persuade me to become a Christian."*
ACTS 26:28 • NKJV®

I'm intrigued by the grace and mercy of God shown in Acts 26—that He would bring the most effective advocate for Jesus of his generation before the powerful Agrippa and give him an opportunity to choose Jesus as Lord. Unfortunately, Agrippa left the fateful encounter with Paul "almost" persuaded to believe. I'm quite confident that churches today are filled with people who are almost persuaded, and God graciously continues to present us with opportunities to put our trust in Him. If you are in one of those almost-persuaded places, if you are sitting in the seat of the skeptic, I invite you to find another seat. Think of the difference in Agrippa's life if he had gotten off his pompous judgment seat and said to the Apostle Paul, "Whatever happened to you on the Damascus Road, I want that too." Imagine the change in his life! It might have cost him something. He might have lost a friend or an opportunity, but his whole destiny would have been different.

### • THINK ABOUT IT •

What do you think was Agrippa's main obstacle to faith? Is it something you wrestle with too?

## *Prayer*

Heavenly Father, I want to lay down my "almost-persuaded" doubts and embrace faith in You. You are worthy of my full trust. I repent of any complacency that has kept me in the seat of the skeptic. Help me trust You more fully. In Jesus' name, amen.

## A BOLD APPROACH

*"What do you want me to do for you?" Jesus asked him. The blind man said, "Rabbi, I want to see." "Go," said Jesus, "your faith has healed you." Immediately he received his sight and followed Jesus along the road.*

MARK 10:51-52

By now Jesus had a reputation, and a crowd followed Him to see what He would say and do. A blind man named Bartimaeus was begging beside the road. He had heard of Jesus and knew that He could help him. When Bartimaeus shouted to Jesus to have mercy on him, the people tried to hush him, but Bartimaeus kept shouting. Jesus asked to have Bartimaeus brought to Him, and then He asked an intriguing question: "What do you want me to do for you?" Bartimaeus seized his opportunity and said, "I want to see!" Jesus gave him sight, and Bartimaeus followed Him down the road. Bartimaeus' attitude was not "Maybe He will notice me and help me." He shouted until He had Jesus' attention, then he asked for the impossible. Jesus is not intimidated by our problems; He wants us to bring our desperation to Him. When He blesses our persistence, we should, like Bartimaeus, follow Him eagerly.

· THINK ABOUT IT ·

Has discouragement or a lack of faith ever dampened your desire to reach out to God? Be encouraged by Jesus' willing response to Bartimaeus as you pray today.

*Prayer*

Heavenly Father, I renew my prayer to You about _____. I ask for Your grace to persevere as You intervene on my behalf. I thank You in advance for Your help and declare my confidence in Your power and love. In Jesus' name, amen.

## NEVER TOO LATE

*I trust in you, O LORD; I say, "You are my God." My times are in your hands; deliver me from my enemies and from those who pursue me.*

PSALM 31:14-15

Our enemy often uses time as a bludgeon on our hearts and minds. He whispers thoughts that make us doubtful and anxious because our life's timeline hasn't unfolded as we assumed it would. Our personal lives, careers, and material possessions are not what we imagined they would be by this point in time. Time is not your enemy, however; it does not trap you or enslave you. In Christ, you've been delivered from it. God created time, but He is not bound by it. Scripture says that with the Lord a day is like a thousand years, and a thousand years is like a day. God created you, and He has the power to redeem the days, months, and years of your life. Do not allow the enemy to hold you captive to the calendar; be faithful to say yes to the invitations the Lord puts before you today.

· THINK ABOUT IT ·

Have you given up on any dreams because you thought time had "run out"? Does knowing God's power over time re-ignite them?

*Prayer*

Heavenly Father, I rejoice that it's never too late for You to give my life meaning. With You even the old will dream dreams and the young see visions. Thank You for renewing my hope that You will fulfill Your purposes for me as I welcome Your invitations. In Jesus' name, amen.

## ROUTINE SIGNIFICANCE

*For we are God's workmanship, created in Christ Jesus to do good works, which God prepared in advance for us to do.*

EPHESIANS 2:10

"Does my life really matter?" I have asked myself this question often, and I know other people wonder the same thing. Sometimes it seems as if the daily grind is choking the significance out of our days, but if you are a person with a God-perspective you will make a difference—in your home, in your neighborhood, where you work, where you volunteer, in your classroom, at the gym. One person with a God-perspective is a game-changer because He created you with a unique personality and skill set, and He has prepared in advance when and where you would be in order to do the work He has for you. If you will say yes to the Lord, it will bring significance to your life, no matter what your daily assignments are. When you decide to live for God's purposes, and offer the most routine, mundane tasks to the Lord, they become invested with eternal purpose. Does your life really matter? Yes, it absolutely does!

### • THINK ABOUT IT •

Think about your daily routine and the people you habitually see. Intentionally give each part and person to the Lord for blessing and thank Him for the Kingdom significance of each.

### *Prayer*

Heavenly Father, through the cross You have filled me with life, gifts, and the promise of good works to accomplish. I say yes to Your design and purposes for me in Your Kingdom plan. In Jesus' name, amen.

# DAY 5

## THE SOUND OF VICTORY

*Dear friends, do not be surprised at the painful trial you are suffering, as though something strange were happening to you. But rejoice that you participate in the sufferings of Christ, so that you may be overjoyed when His glory is revealed.*

### 1 PETER 4:12-13

Why does Peter tell us not to be surprised by difficulties? Because every time one shows up, I feel unfairly singled out. Peter says that we must go through trials in order to strengthen our faith, and that we should rejoice all the while in order to prepare ourselves for Jesus' glorious return. Rejoicing through a trial isn't my first response; my first response is to complain. I have to ask the Holy Spirit to help me adopt a joyful attitude. I have found it helpful to think about what I am thankful for and say those things out loud as a praise offering to God. The sound of our voices giving thanks to the Lord in the midst of hardship is the sound of defeat to Satan and his entourage and the sound of victory to our Lord and His heavenly hosts. It's good practice for the unending praise we'll be giving in Heaven!

### • THINK ABOUT IT •

Begin to thank the Lord for His many blessings in your life. He's been good to us. Even if today it feels like you're in a hole, you can take a giant step toward contentment by choosing gratitude in your prayers.

### *Prayer*

Heavenly Father, thank You that by Your Word and Spirit You have fully provided for me. You never leave me. Your presence is my peace and security. You are faithful in the details, and I praise You for it. In Jesus' name, amen.

## REAL CHANGE

*"If my people, who are called by my name, will humble themselves and pray and seek my face and turn from their wicked ways, then will I hear from heaven and will forgive their sin and will heal their land."*

2 CHRONICLES 7:14

This well-known verse records God telling Solomon how He will respond to His people's humble prayers in the face of dire conditions: He will hear us, forgive us, and heal our land. It is time for Jesus-followers in America to stop looking for a political party or an ideology to heal our country. Real change is not going to begin on Pennsylvania Avenue or in the Congress or even in the Supreme Court. For our culture to bend toward God, we must humble ourselves before Him and plead for His mercy, and then have the courage to take the name of Jesus from our homes into our neighborhoods and schools and businesses. If you've been content to live a comfortable life but stay unconcerned about the spiritual state of our nation, I want to invite you off the fence and into the arena. Humble yourself before God and say, "I'm in. Let revival come, and let it begin with me."

### • THINK ABOUT IT •

Humility begins with acknowledging the truth. Ask the Holy Spirit to reveal and guide you in this.

*Prayer*

Heavenly Father, show me any place where I need to turn back to You. Forgive me for choosing my ways and my society's messages over Your ways and Your truth. Let revival come—to me, my family, and my nation. In Jesus' name, amen.

## CONSISTENT IN SMALL THINGS

*When Herod saw Jesus, he was greatly pleased, because for a long time he had been wanting to see him. From what he had heard about him, he hoped to see him perform some miracle.*

LUKE 23:8

Herod had wanted to see Jesus, not because he intended to honor Him as the Messiah or follow Him as a disciple, but because he wanted to see a parlor trick. We may have said to ourselves, "If I could just see a miracle, then I would have a different kind of faith." Our God does work miracles, but faith is incubated by being consistent in the small things such as Bible reading and prayer, not by exposure to the supernatural. We actually live in the midst of miracles. Each of us is a miracle of God's creative design, and the lifestyle afforded us—the blessings of abundance and freedom we experience—only God could have done that. I want to invite you to believe God for a miracle, but I don't want you to make witnessing a miracle a condition of your belief. Let's choose to cultivate a simple, persistent faith that recognizes Him and honors Him for all the daily miracles of our lives.

· THINK ABOUT IT ·

The demonstrations of God's power are all around you. Ask the Holy Spirit to help you recognize what God is doing, and choose to give Him credit for the miracles in your life.

*Prayer*

Heavenly Father, I put my faith in Your Word. Your power sustains me. Direct my heart daily into Your love and help me to persevere. I want to be steadfast in honoring You with my life. In Jesus' name, amen.

## WIPE OFF THE DUST

*All Scripture is inspired by God and is profitable for teaching, for rebuking, for correcting, for training in righteousness, so that the man of God may be complete, equipped for every good work.*

2 TIMOTHY 3:16-17 • HCSB

A Barna survey showed that fifty percent of Americans say they regularly engage their Bibles…"regularly" meaning at least four times a year. I'm glad that at least half of Americans have a Bible and that they look at it at least four times a year, but four times a year will not help us to be "complete, equipped for every good work." The Bible gives us a revelation of God—His character and His intent for us, the descendants of Adam. If you're interested in having a real relationship with Almighty God, the Bible is a necessary component. Don't settle for what the preacher tells you because you won't get to know God well enough from a few minutes on a weekend. If your Bible is sitting unopened and gathering dust, wipe it off and start reading. You'll be amazed by what you will learn and how relevant it is to the challenges of our daily lives.

### • THINK ABOUT IT •

The Bible says God's Word is "living and active." If you want to learn more about the character of God, His Word is the place to start. How could you more fully engage Scripture each day?

### *Prayer*

Heavenly Father, I want to make consistent room in my life for Your Word. Holy Spirit, please fill my heart with the knowledge, wisdom, and the truth of Scripture. I want to know You and cooperate with You more fully. In Jesus' name, amen.

# DAY 9

## A CHAMPION WARRIOR

*The LORD will march out like a champion, like a warrior he will stir up his zeal; with a shout he will raise the battle cry and will triumph over his enemies.*

ISAIAH 42:13

We are humans living in a fallen world, and we will face some expression of evil every day of our lives. The Church of Jesus Christ is not a collective effort to outsmart evil. We don't gather in our buildings and listen to teachers and meet in small groups and memorize Scripture so that we can create a battle plan for how to out-think and out-organize our adversary. We do all those things to learn about and grow closer to the God who watches over us. Our God is no coward; He is a champion, a warrior whose triumph over His enemies is assured. We stand in His strength, not our own. His power preserves us, not our own. His integrity guards us, not our own. Do not be tempted to wage the war against evil on your own. Carry His banner as you travel the journey of life, and thank Him as He tramples the enemies of His people.

### • THINK ABOUT IT •

Whether out of indignation or compassion, have you been trying to fight battles against evil in your culture on your own? Determine to find your strength and hope in the Lord—it will affect the culture around you.

### *Prayer*

Heavenly Father, You are my strength and my shield. You spread Your protection over me and fight for me. I thank You for the cross of Jesus Christ that delivers me from all evil. Draw me closer to Your heart. My trust is in You. In Jesus' name, amen.

## FAITH INCUBATORS

*"He who is faithful in a very little thing is faithful also in much; and he who is unrighteous in a very little thing is unrighteous also in much."*

LUKE 16:10 • NASB®

In my personal experience and in my observations of people across many years of ministry, I can say that big faith is not the result of dealing with the big issues of life. Big faith is generated by faithfulness in the small, private decisions of our lives—to read the Bible regularly, pray on a regular basis, be a person of integrity, and give with generosity and freedom. Those things are the incubators for faith to be demonstrated in the bigger issues of your life. People often wait until a crisis presents itself to decide that greater faith would be a good thing. If you wait for a big issue to arise to say, "I really need God's help here. I wish I had more faith," it will be hard to gain that ground as quickly as you would like. Cultivate faithfulness in the little things so that your relationship with the Lord will be strong and well established when you are faced with the big things.

### • THINK ABOUT IT •

In what areas could you increase being faithful in the "little" things? Consider asking God's Holy Spirit to help you cultivate faithfulness in these areas.

### Prayer

Heavenly Father, help me increase my faith in You today. I repent of letting busyness and the cares of life push aside diligence in things that would build up my faith. In Jesus' name, amen.

# DAY 11

## GROW FORGIVENESS

*If we walk in the light, as he is in the light, we have fellowship with one another, and the blood of Jesus, his Son, purifies us from all sin.*

1 JOHN 1:7

The verbs in this verse do not indicate actions that happen just one time; these actions are continuing. If we walk in the light and continue to walk in the light, if we have fellowship with one another and continue to have fellowship with one another, then the blood of Jesus will continually cleanse us from all sin. These are learned behaviors on our part: We have to learn how to walk in His light. We have to learn how to live in authentic fellowship with one another. We have to learn how to be washed clean of bitterness and anger and resentment and live our lives under the cleansing provision of Jesus' sacrifice. That's what the cross is about: "God, I forgive so that I can be forgiven. I release others because I need to be released. I give them freedom because I want to live in freedom."

### • THINK ABOUT IT •

Is there a place in your life where disappointment has grown into bitterness or unfairness into resentment? Disappointment and unfairness don't have to be the "potting soil" for a sin response. Ask the Lord to plant His mercy and His fruit in these areas.

### *Prayer*

Heavenly Father, I receive the continual cleansing of Your Son's blood. I want to walk and keep on walking in Your light. I forgive and release so that I can be forgiven and released. I praise You for the freedom You give me. In Jesus' name, amen.

# DAY 15

## TIMING IS EVERYTHING

*The LORD said, "I have indeed seen the misery of my people in Egypt. I have heard them crying out because of their slave drivers, and I am concerned about their suffering. So I have come down to rescue them from the hand of the Egyptians and to bring them up out of that land into a good and spacious land..."*

EXODUS 3:7

The greatest story of deliverance in the Bible, with the exception of the redemptive work of Jesus on the cross, is the rescue of the Hebrews from their Egyptian masters. In this passage we learn that God was concerned about His people during the years when they were enslaved. They had been suffering in bondage for a while—His deliverance was not immediate—so we know that God will allow us to suffer. We also know that when we are in a difficult place, God is concerned about our situation and has a plan. Throughout Scripture He willingly, consistently, and supernaturally delivers His people. I often do not understand God's plan, but I do know that our God is a God of deliverance. In His timing, and according to His plan, He will deliver us and bring us to a better place.

### • THINK ABOUT IT •

Recall a time when God's timing stretched your faith to its limit and beyond. Did this moment strengthen your faith or cause you to pull back from God? Ask God for an increased faith in His timing.

### Prayer

Heavenly Father, You are my strong, trustworthy deliverer. You delight in my well-being, and I gratefully declare my confidence in You. When my trust is tested, help me remember Your Word and works, Your power and love. In Jesus' name, amen.

# DAY 14

## OUT WITH THE OLD

*If anyone is in Christ, he is a new creation; the old has gone, the new has come!*

2 CORINTHIANS 5:17

The genetic material you inherited from previous generations of your family has a lot to do with who you are. You may have inherited something good, like a beautiful smile, or something challenging, like a genetic disease. You may not like the package you got, but that doesn't change your genetics. I believe there also is a generational impact on your spiritual life, for good or ill. Sometimes we allow ourselves to become spiritually stagnant because of negative generational holdovers, spiritual influences that come to us not so much because of our choices but because of our spiritual DNA. The good news is that through the redemptive work of Jesus on the cross, we have been delivered from the bondage of those generational holdovers. When you are tempted to fall back on old attitudes or behaviors that have a negative impact, remember that you are a new creation. You are free to take the truth about Jesus and apply it to your emotions and experiences and leave your past behind.

### • THINK ABOUT IT •

Can you think of any negative family patterns—fearfulness, quick temper, bitterness, etc.—that continue to negatively impact your own behavior and attitudes? Begin to ask the Lord for freedom in these areas.

### Prayer

Heavenly Father, thank You that through the cross, Jesus restored me and redirected my life-course. May my thoughts and conduct reflect Your character. The past is behind me, and I welcome the new day You bring. In Jesus' name, amen.

# DAY 13

## UNASHAMED AMBASSADOR

*You are a chosen people, a royal priesthood, a holy nation, a people belonging to God, that you may declare the praises of him who called you out of darkness into his wonderful light.*

1 PETER 2:9

We live in a day when it is tempting to keep our viewpoints to ourselves for fear of offending others, but this verse gives us encouraging reminders of why we should gladly proclaim our belief in God and declare His praises. I would encourage you to enthusiastically, proudly, and joyfully identify yourself as an advocate for Jesus of Nazareth. Let it be known that you are associated with Jesus and His Church. Tell others that you believe the Bible is the Word of God and that it is your rule of faith and practice. Explain that you are not ashamed of it or embarrassed by it and that you attempt to adhere to its principles and let them emerge in your home and family. The Creator of all things—who started time and placed us in it and will bring it to its culmination—is fulfilling His purposes in this generation. We have been chosen to play a part in that, and that is reason enough to share our good news.

### · THINK ABOUT IT ·

Ask the Lord how you can become a more confident and effective advocate for Jesus in your sphere of influence.

*Prayer*

Heavenly Father, there have been times I have been intimidated and silent about my faith in You. Forgive me. Give me boldness, clarity, and grace to be Your unashamed ambassador. Let Your love compel me forward. In Jesus' name, amen.

## CRAZY BLESSED

*Enter his gates with thanksgiving and his courts with praise; give thanks to him and praise his name.*

PSALM 100:4

Our lives are not always easy, but God has been exceedingly good to those of us who live in America. We have difficulties and challenges, but the blessings of God shape our life experience. We have access to the Word of God. We worship openly without fear. We meet in comfortable buildings. We have food, clothing, and shelter. Our children have schools and medical care available to them. We are blessed with freedoms, liberties, and opportunities. Our response is typically, "Well, everyone lives like this." No, they don't! God, through His grace and mercy—not through anything we have done or achieved or earned—put us in a place where those things have come to us. We are blessed! Thankfulness and gratitude for all He has done will incubate belief in your life, and I encourage you to intentionally practice those things every day.

### • THINK ABOUT IT •

God is faithful in the details. Thank Him that He's already thought of everything you need today.

*Prayer*

Heavenly Father, You are a good and gracious God. You have given me life in abundance. Thank You for every comfort I have experienced today. Most of all, thank You for sending Jesus to redeem me. In His name I pray, amen.

## TODOY IS THE DAY

*If you confess with your mouth, "Jesus is Lord," and believe in your heart that God raised Him from the dead, you will be saved.*

ROMANS 10:9

Sometimes we assume that if you attend church and even read devotionals like this that you have accepted Jesus as your Savior and Lord. I know that is not true, however. If you've never made the decision to let Jesus be Lord of your life, I'd encourage you to do that. The Bible says that if you will confess with your mouth and believe in your heart that Jesus is Lord, you will be saved. You don't need a pastor or a priest to do that; you can do that wherever you are right now. God is the only one you need to please, so don't worry about what people will say. Some of them will thank you because they have wanted to make the same decision but have been waiting for someone with courage to take the first step. You'll change your life and open doors of possibility for all kinds of people. Don't delay any longer; choose Jesus as Lord of your life.

• THINK ABOUT IT •

Today is the day of salvation. Would you like to respond to Jesus' invitation today? Or could you help some else choose Jesus as Lord?

*Prayer*

Heavenly Father, I am a sinner. I need a Savior. I believe Jesus is Your Son—that He died for my sins and was raised to life for my justification. Forgive me. I receive Jesus as both my Lord and my Savior. In His name I pray, amen.

## UNSHAKEN

*Find rest, O my soul, in God alone; my hope comes from him. He alone is my rock and my salvation; he is my fortress, I will not be shaken.*

### PSALM 62:5

In the past few years things that I thought were impossible to shake have proven unstable. Systems that I thought were well regulated have proven to be fragile. Corporations that I thought were integral to the global economy have faltered. I've had to reevaluate what is trustworthy and what is not. Those of us who fill churches and carry Bibles and quote Scripture have placed our trust in the same things that the ungodly have placed their trust in, and the instability of those things has left us unsettled and anxious. God said that He will shake everything until the only thing that cannot be shaken, His Kingdom, will remain (Hebrews 12:26-27). The world's systems are not worthy of our ultimate trust. Only the Kingdom of God merits that, and He is very graciously inviting us to reorder our thoughts and find rest in Him.

### • THINK ABOUT IT •

What have you relied on, in addition to God, to gain a sense of security? Relationships? Resources? Authority figures? How can you begin to transfer faith in those things to a faith in God's provision?

*Prayer*

Heavenly Father, You are the source of my peace. Only You are worthy and able to bring stability to my heart. Holy Spirit, help me to examine my heart and refocus my trust fully upon You. In Jesus' name, amen.

## LASTING SOLUTION

*"Your throne, O God, will last for ever and ever, and righteousness will be the scepter of your kingdom. You have loved righteousness and hated wickedness."*

HEBREWS 1:8-9

The gospel of Jesus Christ is sufficient for every challenge that confronts humanity. I don't mean the first four books of the New Testament; I mean the redemptive story of Jesus: The virgin birth. God coming to live among us. Jesus' death on a cross and His resurrection from the dead on our behalf, that we might be justified in the sight of Almighty God. The problems that plague us will not be solved through laws or rulings or cooperation among the people of the world. The world's problems will be solved by embracing the good news about Jesus Christ and giving Him His rightful place. Jesus is the only lasting solution to the challenges that face us because His is the only Kingdom that will be ruled by righteousness. I want to be on His side, don't you?

• THINK ABOUT IT •

The solutions our families and communities need are found in Jesus. Pray that when you're interacting in those places, you point them to Him with both your words and actions.

*Prayer*

Heavenly Father, I rejoice in You. I want to see Your Kingdom come. Help me be salt and light to my family and my community. I want to see Jesus exalted, lives healed, and problems solved. In His name I pray, amen.

## NEW ENTHUSIASM

*We have not stopped praying for you and asking God to fill you with the knowledge of his will through all spiritual wisdom and understanding...in order that you may live a life worthy of the Lord and may please him in every way: bearing fruit in every good work, growing in the knowledge of God, being strengthened with all power according to his glorious might...*

COLOSSIANS 1:9-11

For those of us who grew up where cultural Christianity is the norm, we might think officially "becoming a Christian" is something "everyone does." Made a profession of faith? Check. Said the sinner's prayer? Check. Got dunked in a pool? Check. Ticket to Heaven punched? Check! Following Jesus is a lifelong journey of walking with the Lord and learning to know Him better. My prayer for us is what Paul prayed for the Colossians: that the Holy Spirit will fill us with knowledge, wisdom, understanding, and power so that we will want to honor God in everything we do. Let's pray for a vibrant, increasing faith. Let's be open to all the Lord has for us, and let's say yes to Him with a new enthusiasm.

· THINK ABOUT IT ·

Consider praying Paul's prayer in Colossians 1:9-11 for yourself and your family each day. Invite God's grace in, and see what happens.

*Prayer*

Heavenly Father, thank You for sending Your Holy Spirit to guide me. Please fill me with the knowledge, wisdom, power, and passion to honor You in everything I do. In Jesus' name, amen.

## HARD SEASONS

*"I have been very zealous for the LORD God Almighty. The Israelites have rejected your covenant, torn down your altars, and put your prophets to death with the sword. I am the only one left, and now they are trying to kill me too."*

1 KINGS 19:14

The stories we read about Elijah make him seem like a grumpy old man, but we need to understand the season in which he lived. When Elijah was the prophet in Israel, the king and his wife Jezebel were the gold standard for wickedness. In that context God asked Elijah to stand publicly for His purposes. In 1 Kings 19, Elijah is literally on the run for his life after Jezebel told him she intended to kill him, and he is sharing his weariness and fear with God Almighty. Fulfilling God's purposes doesn't mean that you always get to stand in an easy place, or during an easy season. Sometimes we stand as God's ambassadors in seasons that are decidedly unpleasant. That's Elijah's story, and it may be your story too. Do not think that your hard seasons go unnoticed by the Lord. He is with you, He will strengthen you, and He will reward you in His time.

· THINK ABOUT IT ·

Can you recall a time when you felt something important to you was being threatened? Did faith play a role in your response?

*Prayer*

Heavenly Father, I put my hope in You—that You will protect, shield, and shelter me. In my hard times I will give You my sacrifice of praise. No weapon designed for my harm will overrule Your faithful care or thwart Your love. In Jesus' name, amen.

## MOMENTUM

*He did not waver through unbelief regarding the promise of God, but was strengthened in his faith and gave glory to God, being fully persuaded that God had power to do what he had promised.*

ROMANS 4:20-21

Abraham was a person of incredible faith. In Romans 4 we're told that Abraham, even though he and his wife were "as good as dead" (v. 19), chose to believe that God's promise of a child would come true. It is not hard to believe God when the momentum of your life seems to be carrying you toward His promised outcome. But to believe God when all the momentum of your life seems to be carrying you away from a God-directed outcome is very difficult. Abraham was unwavering, however. He faced the truth about his circumstances and said, "I still choose to believe God." This is not the narrative of a beginner in a life of faith. Like Abraham, we want to become people who can trust God when the momentum of our lives seems to be taking us toward God and when the circumstances seem to be saying there's no way even God could do this. Let's choose to believe in the faithfulness of God—always.

· THINK ABOUT IT ·

Abraham strengthened his faith and gained a positive outcome by consistently giving glory to God. I would submit that the momentum of your life could be enhanced in the same way. Be someone known for giving glory to God.

*Prayer*

Heavenly Father, I desire to walk by faith and not by sight. Keep me focused on Your Word always and remind me of Your promises when my circumstances urge me to give up. I choose to believe in Your faithfulness. In Jesus' name, amen.

## PERFECT WEAKNESS

*And the God of all grace, who called you to his eternal glory in Christ...will himself restore you and make you strong, firm and steadfast.*

### 1 PETER 5:10

God's intent is for Jesus to receive glory for all eternity through our lives. Have you ever thought about the enormity of that? What is there about us that would give Jesus glory for all eternity? First Corinthians 1:26-31 gives us a clue. It says that God chose lowly things like us so that through us the power of God might be displayed. It is not intellectual brilliance or bodily strength or force of character that makes us candidates to show the remarkable things of God. In fact, our most vulnerable areas are the most fertile places for the power of God to be made evident. Our weaknesses and inadequacies are so obvious that when we are "strong, firm, and steadfast" there can be no boasting because it will be plain that those qualities come from Him. We've thought as Christ-followers, we had to be perfect. The truth is that where our flaws are most evident the power of God has the greatest potential to be seen.

### • THINK ABOUT IT •

God's strength is made perfect in our weakness. We don't have to hide or pretend to be something we're not. We can be fully transparent in our prayers. He knows everything, and He still loves us with an amazing resolve.

### Prayer

Heavenly Father, forgive me for when pride drove me to either fear failure or strive to be perfect. Grant me humility to lean into Your power and grace. My confidence is in Your work in me. The glory is only Yours. In Jesus' name, amen.

## SPACE FOR JOY

*They will find gladness and joy, and sorrow and sighing will flee away.*

ISAIAH 35:10 • NASB®

Most of us have a plan for finding pleasure and happiness, but we are unaware of the significance of joy in our lives. This verse is an interesting collection of opposites: When you find gladness and joy, sorrow and sighing will run from you. If your life has too much sorrow and sighing, the antidote is not pleasure and happiness. It is gladness and joy. This is an attitude of our spirit more than the condition of our body or our emotional state. If we don't leave enough space in our hearts for joy, we have missed the contentment that could be ours. Begin to say to the Lord, "Help me understand what joy is and how I can let it emerge in my heart so that I can lead a contented life, not dependent on my physical circumstances or my emotional state, but something that transcends them." Begin to let the joy of the Lord define your life, not your circumstances or the people around you.

### • THINK ABOUT IT •

What plan could you develop to find and cultivate gladness and joy? Would you have to reprioritize other plans to make room for the things that bring God's joy?

*Prayer*

Heavenly Father, help me walk in Your joy. Set me free from any hindrances in my attitude, and help me to know true contentment by making more room for joy. In Jesus' name, amen.

## PRESS ON

*One thing I do: Forgetting what is behind and straining toward what is ahead, I press on toward the goal to win the prize for which God has called me heavenward in Christ Jesus.*

### PHILIPPIANS 3:13

Paul had one of the most dramatic "before and after" stories in the Bible. We meet him as a hater of Jesus-followers who worked to see them persecuted and even killed. Paul's encounter with Jesus turned his life around, and he became the Lord's vocal and persistent advocate. Here Paul says, "I'm going to forget what is behind me and focus on what is ahead of me." One of the challenges we have is to forget, and not be caught up in remorse over the past. None of us have perfect stories, and it is natural to feel regret and sadness over damaged relationships or wasted years. There are many ways we could revisit our lives and ponder the better choices we could have made. Certainly it is helpful to make apologies and repair what can be repaired. Beyond that we should lay the past at the feet of Jesus and "press on toward the goal to win the prize for which God has called me heavenward in Christ Jesus."

### • THINK ABOUT IT •

Don't let your past lock you in a prison cell of condemnation or regret. Release yourself from the pressure of having a perfect story, and find yourself in the perfect redemption of Jesus' resurrection.

### *Prayer*

Heavenly Father, shift my gaze to the redemptive work of Jesus, whose love pulls me forward. Help me eagerly press into the good works You have for me. I gratefully lay the weight of my past at the foot of the cross. In Jesus' name, amen.

# DAY 25

## COURAGEOUS LIVING

*"Your forefathers ate the manna in the desert, yet they died...I am the living bread that came down from heaven. If anyone eats of this bread, he will live forever. This bread is my flesh, which I will give for the life of the world."*

JOHN 6:49-51

There is something miraculous happening in the land of Israel: A generation of believers in Jesus of Nazareth is emerging. There have been little pockets of believers largely supported by Christians in other nations, but they have been marginalized by society. Today small groups of Jewish Israelis are saying publicly, without shame or embarrassment, "I believe Jesus of Nazareth is the Messiah." When I see Israelis, broadly distributed across all segments of society, following Jesus in an unprecedented way, it leads me to believe that there is a time of awakening ahead when people all over the world who have been resistant to the good news about Jesus will embrace it. It takes great courage to publicly follow Jesus in the land of Israel. Are you living courageously for Christ in your community?

· THINK ABOUT IT ·

Telling the story of God's work in your life can open doors for others to experience His grace too. Your story is part of His victorious story.

*Prayer*

Heavenly Father, forgive me for when I have been too silent, too reluctant, or too intimidated. Fill me with boldness to be Your ambassador, presenting Your grace and truth with compassion and integrity. In Jesus' name, amen.

## STEP INTO THE NEW

*"You were unwilling to go up; you rebelled against the command of the LORD your God."*

DEUTERONOMY 1:26

Most of the Israelites who had been rescued from slavery in Egypt missed their inheritance in the promised land because they were stuck in the past. God had given them a leader, rescued them from their enemy, and provided for all their physical needs. These interventions from God were miraculous and certainly worth remembering and celebrating. But the Israelites were content to stay focused on what God had done in the past rather than have the courage to obey His commands and move ahead to fulfill the plans and purposes He had created them for. We face that same temptation today. Let's remember and celebrate what God has done for us in the past, but let's also joyfully look forward to the invitations that God will extend to us in the future. Let's prepare ourselves to step into our tomorrows with the intention of doing the things that God has created us to do.

· THINK ABOUT IT ·

For some, stepping into the new is an adventure. For others, it is too big a risk. On which side do you find yourself when presented with a new God-opportunity?

*Prayer*

Heavenly Father, thank You for Your faithfulness. Help me draw faith from where You have intervened in my life in the past. Help me keep in step with Your Spirit, to accelerate—not hesitate—when You say, "Go!" In Jesus' name, amen.

## A WELCOME HELPER

*"I will ask the Father, and He will give you another Helper, that He may be with you forever."*

JOHN 14:16 • NASB®

Before Jesus left the earth He gathered His disciples and gave them some final instructions. One point stood above the rest: The Holy Spirit would come to help Jesus' followers, and He would be with us forever. If you gave me the job of undermining the effectiveness of the Church, and I knew that the Holy Spirit was here to help the Church, my main goal would be to keep the Church as far away from the Holy Spirit as I could. Few topics bring more anxiety and division to the Body of Christ than a discussion of the Holy Spirit. We'll say that we want to welcome Him, but we back away pretty quickly when it comes to practical expressions of that. I'm inviting you to welcome the Holy Spirit into your life—to acknowledge Him as your Helper, to become familiar with Him, to recognize His voice, to understand His promptings, and to heed His warnings. God's gift of the Holy Spirit is absolutely necessary to our well-being—why would we not want His help in every part of our lives?

· THINK ABOUT IT ·

Whether because of religious tradition, negative connotations, or past encounters, some have reservations about welcoming the Holy Spirit in their lives. Ask the Lord to clear up any misunderstandings you may have about His Spirit.

*Prayer*

Heavenly Father, thank You for sending Your Holy Spirit to convict, reveal, teach, empower, counsel, and comfort me. Come glorify Jesus in my heart and build His Church in the earth. In Jesus' name, amen.

## PURE AND STEADFAST

*Create in me a pure heart, O God, and renew a steadfast spirit within me.*

PSALM 51:10

Psalm 51 was written after David had been confronted about his adultery with Bathsheba. David, a wealthy and powerful king, had been reminded that the most important thing in his life was his relationship with God; and he is pleading for God's help to have a pure heart and a steadfast spirit. David is not asking God for external change; he is asking for help with his innermost being. Church people have often acted as if the objective of our lives is simply to achieve an external presentation that fits in with our church friends—choose an appropriate vocabulary with some churchy phrases thrown in, wear something similar to what they wear, and carry the right Bible. Being pure in heart and steadfast in spirit is not about creating an outward presentation; it is about creating legitimate change at the core of our being so that we become firmly anchored in our relationship with Jesus of Nazareth. David's plea should be our own: "Create in me a pure heart, O God, and renew a steadfast spirit within me."

### • THINK ABOUT IT •

Genuine purity takes much more than a veneer of religion. It requires yielding to the sanctifying work of the Holy Spirit. The Lord is inviting you to let Him complete His creative miracle in you: the creation of a pure heart.

### *Prayer*

Heavenly Father, David's prayer is mine: I want a pure heart, a steadfast spirit, and truth in my innermost being. I admit I am helpless to effect real change in my life apart from You. Work in me what's pleasing to You through Jesus. In His name I pray, amen.

## STILL A MESS

*"'I will sprinkle clean water on you, and you will be clean; I will cleanse you from all your impurities and from all your idols. I will give you a new heart and put a new spirit in you; I will remove from you your heart of stone and give you a heart of flesh.'"*

### EZEKIEL 36:25-26

Notice what God didn't say to the Israelites. He didn't say, "I'll clean you up, and then I'll do something miraculous for you." He said, "I'll take you while you're still a mess, and after I've shown you My power and My grace and My kindness, then I'll begin to clean you up. I will give you a new heart and a new future." Note who is initiating all this activity: God. He says, "I will do this, and I will do this, and I will do this." He's doing the same for you and me. He calls us out of darkness, and He begins to clean us up—bit by bit, year by year, season by season—to transform us into the image of His Son. His power continues to work within us to bring a transformation that we could never accomplish on our own.

## • THINK ABOUT IT •

Have you been uncertain about your relationship with God because you felt you couldn't be "good enough"? Read the eighth chapter of Romans. Trust in God's Word and know that His grace is sufficient for you.

## *Prayer*

Heavenly Father, I let go of my efforts to clean myself up for You. I gratefully accept Your work of grace in my life. May Your Holy Spirit work in and through me so that my life will represent Your Son well. In His name I pray, amen.

## A MERCIFUL RESPONSE

*When Jesus' followers saw what was going to happen, they said, "Lord, should we strike with our swords?" And one of them struck the servant of the high priest, cutting off his right ear. But Jesus answered, "No more of this!" And he touched the man's ear and healed him.*

LUKE 22:49-51

Judas had chosen a prayer-filled garden as the place of his betrayal, where he led soldiers and religious leaders "carrying torches, lanterns and weapons" (John 18:3) to arrest Jesus. John also tells us it was Peter, reacting with emotion in defense of His Lord, who cut off the ear of the High Priest's servant. Jesus rebuked the violence and healed the man's ear—a man who was participating in His arrest. I've often wondered about that servant and those who were watching. What did they think about this man who could heal with a touch? You would think they would fall to their knees and confess Him as Lord, but Scripture doesn't say they did. Let's not be those people who stubbornly hang on to skepticism about Jesus even when faced with evidence of His compassion and divine authority. Let's be eager to recognize His Lordship and thank Him for His compassion toward us.

### • THINK ABOUT IT •

When faced with injustice, and with unlimited power for retribution, Jesus chose to respond with mercy and compassion. Love your enemies, and know that God's truth wins.

### *Prayer*

Heavenly Father, I marvel at the compassionate ways You demonstrate Your Lordship in my life. Thank You for using Your power on my behalf. Help me respond with grateful trust and obedience to Your authority. In Jesus' name, amen.

# DAY 31

## HIS GOOD PLAN

*And we know that in all things God works for the good of those who love him,*
*who have been called according to his purpose.*

ROMANS 8:28

I think we all have dreams of how our lives will work out. Some of us have goals and plans that we have imagined and worked toward since childhood. But life can be unpredictable and difficult, and those plans are often interrupted or denied altogether. We have to make a choice: Will we be angry or filled with hate? Will we doubt God's good intentions toward us, or withdraw from Him completely? Or will we allow God to give us a new dream and begin a process that will put us in a better place? Brokenness cannot define us unless we invite it in and give it permission. The God we worship is a God who restores and delivers and heals, and His authority and power are beyond anything humans can imagine. Our God, who knows each of us better than we know ourselves, works for our good through all things and has plans and purposes for each of our lives.

### • THINK ABOUT IT •

Have unmet expectations drawn you into any bitterness or mistrust? Have confidence in God's sovereignty to fulfill His good plan for you.

### *Prayer*

Heavenly Father, Your Kingdom come, Your will be done in my life. I know "defeat" and "failure" are not the words You have spoken over me. Thank You for enlarging my outcome beyond my imagination. I welcome new beginnings in my life. In Jesus' name, amen.

## ETERNAL VALUE

*Be still before the LORD and wait patiently for him; do not fret when men succeed in their ways, when they carry out their wicked schemes...For evil men will be cut off, but those who hope in the LORD will inherit the land.*

PSALM 37:7, 9

It seems we constantly hear of people who live lives of glamour, wealth, and fame yet mock Almighty God through their words and lifestyles. Sometimes we look at them and think, "They have more opportunities than I do. They sure have a lot more fun. My life would be better if I didn't have all these constraints and boundaries." If you are following Jesus, my advice is to guard your heart when you find yourself looking at someone who is making ungodly choices and thinking, "I want to be more like that." The success and fun they appear to be having are temporary, and their eternity apart from God will be one of torment and regret. Instead, find someone whose spiritual life you trust and say, "I'm in a dangerous place with my goals and priorities. Will you help me?"

### • THINK ABOUT IT •

Don't let envy determine your definition of "blessed." If your best imaginations of blessing are all material in tone, ask the Lord to enlarge your vision to make room for His perspective.

*Prayer*

Heavenly Father, life's cares and media messages have made it too easy to focus on the world's definition of "blessed." Forgive me, and help me to set my mind and heart on the things of eternal value that truly enrich not only me but others. In Jesus' name, amen.

# DAY 33

## DIVINE WEAPONS

*For though we live in the world, we do not wage war as the world does. The weapons we fight with are not the weapons of the world. On the contrary, they have divine power to demolish strongholds.*

2 CORINTHIANS 10:3-4

We may no longer be defending walled cities as God's people once did, but the spiritual combat we are engaged in is no less real. Ephesians 6:12 describes an enemy that we dare not underestimate: "For our struggle is not against flesh and blood, but against the rulers, against the authorities, against the powers of this dark world and against the spiritual forces of evil in the heavenly realms". Thankfully, the Holy Spirit empowers us with weapons more powerful than those of any worldly army, divine weapons powerful enough to pull down and demolish the strongholds we encounter. This spiritual journey we are on is not a passive one. In order to survive, thrive, and take hold of the blessings and promises of God, we need to be aware, engaged, and ready to defend ourselves with the power of the Holy Spirit and the weapons He provides.

### • THINK ABOUT IT •

Whether through naiveté or pride, we usually try to resolve problems by resorting first to our own wits and resources. Ask the Holy Spirit to make you more aware of the kinds of opposition you are facing and how to respond with His weapons.

### Prayer

Heavenly Father, thank You for equipping me with divine weapons. Train me to use them effectively. Holy Spirit, guide and empower me to defend, not only myself, but also my family, church, and nation. All authority is Yours, Lord! In Jesus' name, amen.

## COMPLAINING OR PRAYING

*I urge, then, first of all, that requests, prayers, intercession and thanksgiving be made for everyone—for kings and all those in authority, that we may live peaceful and quiet lives in all godliness and holiness.*

1 TIMOTHY 2:1-2

I'll ask you the same tough questions I have to ask myself: Do we spend more time complaining about the leaders of our country or praying for the leaders of our country? What do our attitudes say to the young people in our lives? We have a right to hold our leaders to a high standard and expect them to lead us wisely, but for too long we have sought political solutions to our ills. The answers to our nation's problems will not come from Washington; they will come from the people of God, yielding to Him and turning our hearts and minds to Him in prayerful obedience. Paul was no stranger to politicians who were hostile to the Christian faith. Yet in this passage he does not complain about them; he simply reminds his young protégé, Timothy, that God is the source of the godliness and holiness that will lead to peaceful and quiet lives. "Requests, prayers, intercession, and thanksgiving," he advises—let us never doubt the power of prayer to bring about change in our country.

### • THINK ABOUT IT •

It's easier to pray for our leaders when we agree with them. Choose to pray for all those in authority. God can use any situation for His glory, and for the good of His people.

*Prayer*

Heavenly Father, I accept Your biblical counsel to pray for those in authority—both near to home and globally. Help me turn up Your light instead of raging against the darkness, trusting You to deliver the answer. In Jesus' name, amen.

# DAY 35

## A HERITAGE OF FAITH

*"You Samaritans worship what you do not know; we worship what we do know, for salvation is from the Jews."*

JOHN 4:22

God chose the Jewish people for a unique purpose. Through them we have the Scriptures, the prophets, the Law, and the Messiah. It's through the Jewish people that the redemptive purposes of God have been revealed. The salvation for all of humanity was delivered through the Jewish people. Today, seated at the right hand of God the Father is the man Jesus Christ—the Savior of the world, and a Jewish rabbi. The Creator of all things did not call for a vote or take a poll on the best path to provide a way of salvation and accomplish His purposes in the earth. We are indebted to the Jewish people for our heritage of faith. Some struggle with acknowledging that the roots of Christianity lie firmly within Judaism, but it is a fact that cannot be disputed. Let's commit ourselves to praying that God will shine His light on the path that He has set before His Church and the Jewish people.

### • THINK ABOUT IT •

Do you have a regular routine of praying for the Church and the Jewish people? If not, how about starting today?

*Prayer*

Heavenly Father, I "Pray for the peace of Jerusalem: 'May those who love you be secure. May there be peace within your walls and security within your citadels.' For the sake of my family and friends, I will say, 'Peace be within you.'" (Psalm 122:6-8). In Jesus' name, amen.

## A CHOICE FOR JOY

*The ransomed of the LORD will...enter Zion with singing; everlasting joy will crown their heads. Gladness and joy will overtake them, and sorrow and sighing will flee away.*

ISAIAH 35:10

You may be in a season of life that seems to be defined by sorrow and sighing. God says sadness will flee when it is overtaken by gladness and joy. We have to decide what we will believe and what path we will walk. You can welcome sorrow and sighing into your life. You can begin every response with a sigh and an awareness of what is not. Or you can begin every response with the joy of the Lord and hope in Him. We can push back on the heaviness and darkness. Begin by giving thanks to God for all He has done for you and for His watchful care over your life. Determine in your heart to trust His timing and His plan. When your heart is heavy, when your circumstances are hard, when your body is weary, if you will thank Him and recommit to His purposes, it will bring the power of God to bear in your life.

### • THINK ABOUT IT •

If you are at the bottom of your strength and resources remember, "the Lord, who remains faithful forever" (Psalm 146:6). Let gratitude and joy for what you do have fill your thoughts and your words. It will change your perspective.

### Prayer

Heavenly Father, I will choose hope because Your Word always proves true. I will choose joy because You are always faithful. The facts of my circumstances cannot nullify the power of Your promises. My confident trust is in You. In Jesus' name, amen.

# DAY 37

## WORTH THE COST

*I am not ashamed of the gospel, because it is the power of God for the salvation of everyone who believes: first for the Jew, then for the Gentile.*

ROMANS 1:16

Human history is filled with examples of how we divide ourselves into various categories, but the Bible makes it very clear that the gospel is the power of God for the salvation of everyone who will believe. At the foot of the cross, the doorway to the Kingdom of God is open to everyone. It's not about your standing in the community, your bank balance, your education, or the lack thereof. No one is excluded from God's invitation. If you will believe that Jesus of Nazareth is the Messiah, acknowledge Him as your Savior, and serve Him as your Lord and King, you can be a participant in the eternal Kingdom of God. Do not allow any message you hear or see to make you feel "less than" someone else in God's Kingdom. We are different in many ways, but God sees each of His children as uniquely valuable and precious to Him.

### • THINK ABOUT IT •

The cost paid for something indicates the value the purchaser assigns to it. The cost God paid for you is Jesus' shed blood and sacrifice on the cross. Every other standard of giving or diminishing value is not your true worth. Believe you are cherished.

### *Prayer*

Heavenly Father, thank You that You include me in Your invitation to receive Jesus as Savior, Lord, and King. Because of Jesus I am called accepted, not outcast; chosen, not rejected. Thank You for affirming my worth to You. In Jesus' name, amen.

## HEALING WAYS

*Then they cried to the LORD in their trouble, and he saved them from their distress. He sent forth his word and healed them; he rescued them from the grave.*

PSALM 107:19-20

People often ask me if I really believe God heals and if I pray for the sick. Yes! There is much I don't know, but I do know that God intends for us to be whole in body, soul, and spirit. Not only is it appropriate for us to pray for one another, we have been invited to know God as our physician. People ask me, "Do you believe in prayer or doctors?" Yes! If I am not feeling well, I'll pray and make an appointment with the doctor. I'll pray on the way to the doctor. I'll pray in the waiting room. If possible, I'll pray with the doctor. If the doctor prescribes some treatment, I'll pray before I take it. I'll thank God for His intervention, and for the skills and wisdom of the doctor, and pay the bill—gladly. It's not an either-or proposition. God can do what no doctor can, but I don't want to ignore the expertise that God has made available to me.

## • THINK ABOUT IT •

Do you need healing today? Do you know someone who does? Consider investing time today in prayer for God's perfect healing. The prayers of God's people are powerful and effective.

## *Prayer*

Heavenly Father, You are the God who heals. Work alongside doctors to bring healing and recovery to their patients. Reveal and direct when they need clarity. Replenish them when they are exhausted. Thank You for Your healing touch. In Jesus' name, amen.

# DAY 39

## SURROUNDED BY HIS GREATNESS

*"You are worthy, our Lord and God, to receive glory and honor and power, for you created all things, and by your will they were created and have their being."*

REVELATION 4:11

All around us the power and the creativity and the love of God are on display. Think of the great variety of foods He has made for our enjoyment. Think of the many plants and trees we have to admire and use in many ways. The infinite combinations of DNA that make us different people are astounding. There have never been two people who were exactly alike; even identical twins have different fingerprints. The magnitude and complexity of creation is a testimony from Almighty God: "You are important to Me. Look at the beautiful world I have created for you!" Revelation 4 describes the continual praise and worship that occurs around the throne in Heaven. Every person and creature there acknowledges the greatness of our God. Let's not wait until we get to Heaven to give Him the praise and honor He is due for all He has done for us. Let's acknowledge His many blessings today.

### · THINK ABOUT IT ·

God's power and divine nature can be clearly seen in His creation. Consider the complexities of God's work in creation. It will increase your peace about His work in you.

## *Prayer*

Heavenly Father, I worship You, in awe of Your power and wisdom so evident in Your creation. I honor You as Lord God Almighty, Maker and Ruler of Heaven and Earth. Thank You for the place and provision You have made for me. In Jesus' name, amen.

## INTERRUPTION OR INVITATION

*Trust in the LORD with all your heart and lean not on your own understanding; in all your ways acknowledge him, and he will make your paths straight.*

PROVERBS 3:5-6

Our mailboxes and inboxes often contain invitations. Some of them are from friends, and we read them carefully. Others are form letters that go straight to the trash. Throughout Scripture we see God putting invitations before people. Every invitation was given to a specific person or group at a specific time for a specific purpose—there are no form letters from God. He is still in the business of extending invitations. We are called, many times throughout our lives, to acknowledge Him and trust Him to lead us on the paths of His choosing. What will our answer be? I want us to be a generation that says yes to the Lord. I want us to experience Him in new ways and see His blessings poured over us like never before. When God puts an invitation before you, I want to encourage you to make a habit of saying, "Lord, I would be delighted to cooperate with You. I'm in!"

### • THINK ABOUT IT •

What the disciples often saw as interruptions, Jesus saw as opportunities to display the power and love of God. Ask the Lord to give you insight as to when "interruptions" are really His invitations. Don't discount small beginnings as you become more aware of His opportunities.

### Prayer

Heavenly Father, open my eyes and ears to recognize Your invitations, as Jesus always did. I acknowledge Your authority to direct my path. By Your power, fulfill every good purpose when I step out in faith and say yes to You. In Jesus' name, amen.

## RAW MATERIAL

*For no matter how many promises God has made, they are "Yes" in Christ. And so through him the "Amen" is spoken by us to the glory of God.*

2 CORINTHIANS 1:20

We all have been hurt by broken promises. I would imagine that most of us were disappointed in childhood when one of our parents gave a distracted nod or said an offhand yes just to quiet us. They may have not really heard the request that seemed so urgent to us at the time, and we were crushed when it never came to be. Perhaps you have been disappointed when a promised raise or promotion never materialized, or when a relationship that you thought was based on mutual promises turned out not to be. This beautiful verse demonstrates one of the many ways that our God is not like us: His promises, every one of them, are always kept; they are "Yes" in Christ, and through Him we say a joyous "Amen!" to the glory of God. People will disappoint us; we can count on that. But our God, who knows us, loves us, and wants the best for us, will never disappoint us.

• THINK ABOUT IT •

God keeps His promises, so it is of great benefit to know as many of them as possible. Invest time and build up your faith by studying His Word to learn more about His promises to you.

*Prayer*

Heavenly Father, increase my knowledge of Your promises. They are the raw material of my faith. I place my trust and confidence in Your Word and Your faithfulness. You never disappoint those who wait in hope for You. In Jesus' name, amen.

## UNLIMITED LIFE

*I have sought your face with all my heart; be gracious to me according to your promise. I have considered my ways and have turned my steps to your statutes. I will hasten and not delay to obey your commands.*

PSALM 119:58-60

Not all guilty feelings are bad. When the Holy Spirit illuminates something in our lives that is limiting us in some way, that is not a bad thing; that is a priceless gift that leads to repentance. Without that, we will be stuck in our limited journeys. When the Spirit of God starts to make us uncomfortable with something we could be doing differently—the way we spend our time or money, the way we treat our families, the way we act during business negotiations or on the sidelines of a sporting event—He is prompting us to take stock of our attitudes and actions. Through this process we will learn to put His priorities first and turn our steps toward Him. As we do that, we will honor Him and become people He will use and bless in new ways.

· THINK ABOUT IT ·

Sin limits us. Are there any places in your life where you have believed that the satisfaction of sin would outweigh the blessings of God?

*Prayer*

Heavenly Father, make me uncomfortable with my attitudes and actions that don't please You. Holy Spirit, reveal anything that has grieved You. I repent of it all. Align me with Your righteous ways so my life will honor You. In Jesus' name, amen.

# DAY 43

## CALLED BY NAME

*Peter replied, "Repent and be baptized, every one of you, in the name of Jesus Christ for the forgiveness of your sins. And you will receive the gift of the Holy Spirit. The promise is for you and your children and for all who are far off—for all whom the Lord our God will call."*

ACTS 2:38

Do you remember the television show Romper Room? At the end of each show, Miss Nancy would say the names of the children who were in her studio classroom. Then she would call the names of kids who were watching from home—and whose parents had sent in their names. That's the image I have of Peter on this day: I believe by the Spirit of God he could see far beyond the audience gathered in front of him. I believe he could've called our names. He had seen his friend die, and he had met the resurrected Messiah. Now the Spirit of God had been poured out upon him, and he said, "The gift of the Holy Spirit is for you, and your kids, and many more." God's promise was real for Peter and all within the sound of his voice that day, and it's real for you and me.

### • THINK ABOUT IT •

For many people, issues of acceptance are a point of pain. How does the sense of being called by name increase your awareness that you are individually known, loved, and wanted by God?

### *Prayer*

Heavenly Father, I rejoice that You have sought me and included me in Your promise. You have called me by name; I am Yours. I do humbly repent of my sins. Forgive me. Fill me with Your Holy Spirit. Thank You for this new life! In Jesus' name, amen.

## CHALLENGED TO GROW

*"I will give you shepherds after my own heart, who will lead you with knowledge and understanding."*

JEREMIAH 3:15

It is not always easy for me to admit it, but sometimes I need help. I don't mind asking for help with some piece of technology, like a computer or a telephone, but when it comes to my garden I like to think of myself as capable and competent. In hindsight I can see that I have experienced the most positive change and growth during the seasons when I have humbled myself to ask for help from people who have knowledge and experience that I don't have. This applies to my spiritual maturity as well. It has benefited me greatly when the Lord has prompted me to seek help from someone with experience and godly wisdom to share. They have invariably said, "I'll be glad to walk a season with you if you'd like." We all need help to gain spiritual wisdom and maturity, and we shouldn't allow our pride to keep us from asking for it.

• THINK ABOUT IT •

Do you have anyone in your life to help you be a more fully devoted follower of Jesus Christ? Ask the Lord to connect you to those who stand in a more mature place in Him. Their example and input will greatly enrich your faith.

*Prayer*

Heavenly Father, bring people into my life who challenge me to grow in my relationship with You. I want to walk with the wise so that I can become wise. I need help that will encourage me to persevere in my faith journey. In Jesus' name, amen.

## FULLY INVESTED

*"I know your deeds, and your love and faith and service and perseverance, and that your deeds of late are greater than at first."*

REVELATION 2:19 • NASB®

Serving others is not just a way that we sustain congregational life. In fact, that's putting the cart before the horse. One of the benefits of walking out your spiritual journey in the context of a local church is that someone goes to the effort to help you serve. You can serve in a way that suits your gifts and interests more than if you had the sole responsibility of creating and maintaining something on your own. Jesus is telling the church at Thyatira that He is aware of exactly what they have done and are doing currently, and He commends them for doing more than they have done in the past. Don't allow yourself to become the spectator who sits on the sidelines and evaluates what others are doing. Ask the Holy Spirit to show you how you can best be used to advance the Kingdom of God. There are times you will struggle with your selfishness, but get involved. It will help bring victory to your life.

### • THINK ABOUT IT •

Ephesians 2:10 tells us that the Lord has prepared good works for His people to accomplish. Have you found a place to serve the Lord?

### *Prayer*

Heavenly Father, I want to love with my actions and in truth, not just my words. I desire that the life and gifts You have given me by Your Spirit be fully invested in Your Kingdom. Help me be available to fully serve You. In Jesus' name, amen.

## BEST FRIEND

*Jesus immediately said to them: "Take courage! It is I. Don't be afraid." "Lord, if it's you," Peter replied, "tell me to come to you on the water." "Come," he said.*

MATTHEW 14:27-29

Peter was a fisherman by trade, and he was seeing something beyond his experience and imagination: Jesus was walking on the water. Peter said, "Lord, if that's You, I want to walk on the water too." Think of the things Jesus could have said: "Are you kidding, Peter? You can't take two steps without putting your foot in your mouth! A few days ago on the Mount of Transfiguration, you saw Moses and wanted to build a tabernacle. When we get to Jerusalem you're going to deny you even know me. Just sit there and be quiet." But that's not what He did, is it? He said, "Come on, Peter. You can do this." Throughout the Gospels we find Jesus saying, "I came to show you a Kingdom. In fact, what I've been doing, you can do too, in My name." The best friends share their experience and knowledge without holding anything back. That's what Jesus does. He's a great friend, and I want to be a friend to Him.

· THINK ABOUT IT ·

Friendship with Jesus can redefine adventure and break through the boundaries of what you thought was possible. He is the friend you want to have.

*Prayer*

Heavenly Father, You sent Jesus to give me abundant life. You don't let my failures determine Your view of me. By Your Spirit You include me in what You are doing. Thank You! I am humbled by the honor of being a friend of the King. In His name I pray, amen.

# DAY 47

## THE PATH FORWARD

*He determines the number of the stars and calls them each by name. Great is our Lord and mighty in power; his understanding has no limit.*

PSALM 147:4-5

We are amazed by expressions of power and intelligence. We hold our breath as a rocket fires its engines and blasts away from the Earth's surface toward a pinpoint destination in space. We are in awe of the level of intelligence and insight and skill of the people who make that happen. Yet our God transcends all of those: Almighty God, the Creator of all things, is powerful and intelligent and insightful beyond our every definition of those terms. This is not just a point of rhetoric or theology; it is helpful for us to remember that the challenges we face—difficulties and obstacles and heartbreak—do not frighten or intimidate our God. While we may be concerned about what is happening around us, God is not confused or without a plan for our deliverance. That is a wonderful truth to tuck into your heart.

### • THINK ABOUT IT •

When we can't figure out how God can possibly rescue us out of a situation, we can get shaken and discouraged. Don't let the limits of your wisdom put limits on your faith. Trust Him.

### *Prayer*

Heavenly Father, You are strong and You are loving. I put my confidence in Your wisdom, power, faithfulness, and love. Bring Your redemptive power to bear on my problem, specifically _____. Thank You that You have mapped my path forward. In Jesus' name, amen.

## SPIRITUAL TRUTHS

*Jesus said, "My kingdom is not of this world..." "You are a king, then!" said Pilate. Jesus answered, "You are right in saying I am a king. In fact, for this reason I was born, and for this I came into the world, to testify to the truth. Everyone on the side of truth listens to me." "What is truth?" Pilate asked.*

JOHN 18:36-38

Jesus is acknowledging to Pilate the truth of His authority in an unseen realm. The spiritual realm has an authority that the physical world doesn't, but that doesn't diminish the principles of the physical world; gravity is still here. The cultural pendulum tends to swing, however, and we are far on the rational side now. If scientists suggest something, we act as if it is absolute truth, even though we look back at the thoughts of the most brilliant minds from a hundred years ago and chuckle. Part of the wonder and mystery of serving the Lord is that we will never master Him. We will always be learners. In this world that has made a god out of science, let's make more room in our hearts, our lives, and our imaginations for the reality of spiritual things.

### • THINK ABOUT IT •

Over time, the presentation of science and culture will change a lot. Pray for absolute peace in your heart, knowing that the truth of God's Word cannot be shaken by either of them.

*Prayer*

Heavenly Father, I humbly admit there are things I cannot know unless You unveil them to me. Thank You for revealing spiritual truths through Your Word. Help me make more room for Your truth, and protect me from deception. In Jesus' name, amen.

# DAY 49

## KEEP GOING

*I press on toward the goal to win the prize for which God has called me heavenward in Christ Jesus.*

PHILIPPIANS 3:14

Have you ever noticed the difference between the way runners look at the beginning of a race and at the end of a race? The starting line is a photo op where everyone looks good. Everyone is wearing just the right clothes and shoes. They are excited, laughing with the other runners, and smiling for the cameras. At the finish line the runners don't look so good. Some will cross the line with the same stride they began, but many will be struggling, and some will be walking with a limp. A few will be carried across by a friend. The clothes that looked so great earlier are soggy and smelly. Between the starting line and the finish line there was discomfort and unpleasantness, but the finishers found the will to put one foot in front of the other until they crossed the line. It's true in a race, and it's true in life. The Bible acknowledges that life will be difficult and messy, but its message is always the same: Press on! Keep going! The prize will be worth it!

### • THINK ABOUT IT •

God not only promises His rewards to those who don't give up—He promises to refresh and renew and give you the means to endure as you are on your journey. Thank Him for His sustaining grace.

### Prayer

Heavenly Father, Your Word says those who wait upon You will renew their strength. Refresh me so that weariness doesn't tempt me to give up. Encourage my heart and strengthen me in every purpose and deed that aligns with You. In Jesus' name, amen.

## WELL-PLACED CONFIDENCE

*So do not throw away your confidence; it will be richly rewarded. You need to persevere so that when you have done the will of God, you will receive what he has promised.*

HEBREWS 10:35-36

If the Bible says not to throw away your confidence, you can be certain of this: We're going to be tempted to throw away our confidence. The world around us encourages us to place our confidence in everything but God: our physical appearance, our education, our career, our bank balance, our ability to influence people. Don't do it! God, the One who promised, is faithful to guide you to fulfill His purposes and reward you for it. He will see you through. I'd like to challenge you to do something every day to make an investment in the eternal Kingdom of God—Bible reading, prayer, an act of service, an invitation to the Holy Spirit. God will reveal Himself to you in new ways. You'll have a greater understanding of faith and trust. You will learn to pray with greater effectiveness. You will be a more effective servant in God's Kingdom, and you will be richly rewarded.

• THINK ABOUT IT •

Misplaced confidence can position you to be easily shaken. If "feeling shaken" by events, whether personal or national describes you, devote time to things that will strengthen your confidence in God—prayer, reading your Bible, and being in community with other believers.

*Prayer*

Heavenly Father, today I will invest in Your Kingdom. By Your Spirit, increase my understanding of Your Word. Focus me in prayer. Embolden me to tell my God-story. My confidence is in You, Lord, to fulfill Your purposes for me. In Jesus' name, amen.

## POINTS OF INFLUENCE

*"You are the salt of the earth...You are the light of the world."*

MATTHEW 5:13-14

I've never seen a greater need for leadership in our world. I used to think "leadership" was a secular word...kind of a dirty word. I thought I was too spiritual and too holy to concern myself with leadership. Then God awakened me to the reality that godly influence is a big part of the Church's assignment, which means it is our assignment. When Jesus said we are the "salt of the earth" and the "light of the world," He simply meant that we are here to make a difference. If the Holy Spirit leads you to run for office or assume a public leadership role, by all means do that. But leadership begins in the places and with the people that are already within our reach: our homes and families, our workplaces and coworkers, our neighbors and communities. These are the places that must change before we will see significant change on a bigger stage. Let's not sit on the sidelines and wait for a politician to come along and change the world. Let's get started in our homes and on our streets.

### • THINK ABOUT IT •

Would you describe your influence on the people around you as God-centered? Pray for the courage and clarity to use the platform God has given in your sphere of influence to point people toward the Lord.

### Prayer

Heavenly Father, I want to extend Your Kingdom in my places of influence. Show other people the reality of Jesus in me. Let my character demonstrate Your virtues, Lord, and my life bear witness to Your truth. Your Kingdom come. In Jesus' name, amen.

## A FIRM PLACE TO STAND

*He lifted me out of the slimy pit, out of the mud and mire; he set my feet on a rock and gave me a firm place to stand. He put a new song in my mouth, a hymn of praise to our God. Many will see and fear and put their trust in the LORD.*

PSALM 40:2-3

Perhaps you have known (or been) a person whom God miraculously delivered from something—a health crisis, an addiction, a financial catastrophe—who seemed to quickly forget the dire situation they had been in and the prayers that had been spoken on their behalf. The point of God's deliverance is not to save us from something so we can go back on our merry way, ignoring God and doing what we please. When God delivers us from something, it is with the intent of leading us into something better for His purposes and ultimately, bringing praise to our God. When God lifts you from a slimy pit and gives you a firm place to stand, praise Him publicly for what He has done for you. Allow your life and words to be a new song that will bring Him glory.

### • THINK ABOUT IT •

Recall a time God rescued you and thank Him again for it. Ask God for opportunities to tell someone else about this part of your God-story. It will encourage both their faith and yours.

*Prayer*

Heavenly Father, You have rescued me again and again. Remind me, Holy Spirit, so that I can renew my praise to You. Let Your Kingdom be extended because of the help You have given me—my life as evidence of Your faithfulness. In Jesus' name, amen.

# DAY 53

## NOOK AND CRANNY

*For there is nothing hidden that will not be disclosed, and nothing concealed that will not be known or brought out into the open.*

LUKE 8:17

We've all seen the funny television commercials where unexpected guests call to say they are dropping by in ten minutes. The unprepared family jumps up, and a whirlwind of activity begins. Dirty dishes are put in the oven, unfolded laundry is stuffed in empty suitcases, and the advertised cleaning item works a household miracle. I'll have to admit that an empty pizza box might have been found under my couch in my younger years. It's easy to push the messy parts of our lives into a hidden place and close the door. It's easy to convince ourselves that they don't matter. But they do matter. Nothing is hidden or concealed from God, so it is to our great benefit to invite the Holy Spirit into the fullness of our lives and ask Him to work in every nook and cranny. His graciousness is beyond our human understanding, and we might be surprised by the extent of His kindness and patience instead of the judgment and condemnation we were expecting.

### • THINK ABOUT IT •

The Holy Spirit desires to cleanse and heal, not shame or condemn. He can be trusted to handle your every need with compassion.

*Prayer*

Heavenly Father, thank You that You want to restore me spirit, soul, and body. Holy Spirit, I invite You to search me. Bring light to places I have kept hidden, even from myself. Thank You for the blood of Jesus that delivers me from shame. In Jesus' name, amen.

## CREEPING COMPROMISES

*"Be very careful to keep the commandment and the law that Moses the servant of the LORD gave you: to love the LORD your God, to walk in all his ways, to obey his commands, to hold fast to him and to serve him with all your heart and with all your soul."*

JOSHUA 22:5

Horseshoes is one of the few games where you can score points by "almost" hitting the target. Being world class at "almost" is an interesting distinction; there is a Horseshoe Pitchers Hall of Fame, and I can't name one person who is honored there. If the outcome matters, "almost" is not good enough: I almost made it across the train tracks. My parachute almost opened. I almost survived the surgery. It is easy to become content with the status quo and ignore the possibilities God places before us. But when it comes to our faith, "almost" is a deficit position. Note the language Joshua uses to tell the people how to guard their relationship with the Lord: "be very careful," "hold fast," and serve with "all" your heart and soul. Ask the Lord where in your life you have allowed "almost" to be good enough, and commit yourself to Him completely.

### • THINK ABOUT IT •

In what areas could you commit yourself more fully to the purposes of God? Look for one area you could take action on today.

### *Prayer*

Heavenly Father, forgive me for any way I have taken my relationship with You for granted and failed to guard it. I renounce any creeping compromise that has diluted my devotion to You. I resolve to serve You with all of my heart. In Jesus' name, amen.

## IMMEASURABLY GREAT

*And if the Spirit of him who raised Jesus from the dead is living in you, he who raised Christ from the dead will also give life to your mortal bodies through his Spirit, who lives in you.*

ROMANS 8:11

The Bible says that when you become a Christ-follower, when you acknowledge Jesus of Nazareth as Messiah and receive Him as Lord, the Spirit of God takes up residence within you. It's the great shift of the New Covenant. Prior to that the Spirit of God dwelled in identified places—a tabernacle or a temple—but now each believer is a temple of the Living God. It's impossible to overstate the significance of this: We are no longer left alone to give our best efforts toward being a good person and living a meaningful and purposeful life. The same Spirit that brought Jesus' body out of the tomb is at work in you and me to help us break every ungodly habit and establish a new course. Simply, God's power is present within us to enable us to lead triumphant lives. Now that's good news!

### • THINK ABOUT IT •

The Bible describes the power God is willing to exercise on our behalf as "immeasurably great." Ask the Holy Spirit to expand your concept of the help He wants to give you to live a triumphant life.

### *Prayer*

Heavenly Father, by Your Spirit I enjoy Your presence, understand Your truth, and overcome my challenges. I am in awe of the magnitude of Your gift to me. Holy Spirit, help me to cooperate more fully with You so that others can see Your Kingdom come. In Jesus' name, amen.

## PERSISTENT PRAYER

*Jesus told his disciples a parable to show them that they should always pray and not give up..."Will not God bring about justice for his chosen ones, who cry out to him day and night?"*

LUKE 18:1, 7

We know we should pray, yet prayer is lacking in many of our lives. There are a host of reasons why that is, but a significant one is that we have the notion that we should receive an immediate supernatural response; when that doesn't happen, we withdraw from prayer. In Luke 18:1-8, Jesus tells the parable of the woman who was so persistent in her pleas for justice that the judge granted her request just to get her out of his court. It is obvious that crying out to God day and night is a good thing, so why would we think that our requests should be "one and done"? Effective prayer is like any other skill: It requires time, intentionality, a willingness to fail and learn from what we don't know, and repetition. Let's commit ourselves to a new attitude toward prayer, one that will help us grow and deepen our relationship and our conversations with the Lord.

· THINK ABOUT IT ·

Have you ever doubted the effectiveness of your prayers? Consider Jesus' words and let faith grow in your heart. Decide to seek the Lord in prayer and not give up.

*Prayer*

Heavenly Father, help me to pray with expectation and perseverance. Teach me Your promises in Scripture; they are the substance of my confidence in prayer. Unite me with Your people with whom I can grow in prayer to honor You. In Jesus' name, amen.

## HEALING BROKEN HEARTS

*The LORD is close to the brokenhearted and saves those who are crushed in spirit. A righteous man may have many troubles, but the LORD delivers him from them all.*

### PSALM 34:18-19

Many of us know the disappointment, hopelessness, and fear that come from being brokenhearted, or "crushed in spirit." Heartbreak may be a result of our own choices or of circumstances and behaviors that are beyond our control. No matter its source, heartbreak often causes us to withdraw and isolate ourselves so that we will not be vulnerable in those ways again—but that is not the invitation of Scripture. God's Word invites us to lean into the power of Almighty God. The same God who hung the stars in the sky and calls them by name is close to His people when we are at our most vulnerable. He is watching over us and is more than able to deliver us, heal our broken hearts, and revive our spirits. You may pass through a place of despair, but God does not want you to dwell there. Trust Him to heal the wounds of your past and guide you into a future of joy and purpose.

### • THINK ABOUT IT •

Following Jesus doesn't exempt us from times of feeling crushed in spirit. Determine to tuck the immovable truths of God deep in your heart each day. In times of trouble, His Word will be a rock for you, and His peace in your heart will surpass all understanding.

### Prayer

Heavenly Father, Your promise to be near me sustains me. When a broken heart makes me want to withdraw even from You, Your compassion won't abandon me. Thank You that my troubles are temporary and Your faithful love is eternal. In Jesus' name, amen.

## TAKING TIME TO LISTEN

*Since ancient times no one has heard, no ear has perceived, no eye has seen any God besides you, who acts on behalf of those who wait for him.*

ISAIAH 64:4

If you're celebrating victories in your life today, thank God for His faithfulness. But sometime soon God is going to allow you to interact with someone who is carrying a heavy burden with no relief in sight. It's easy to feel a moment's sympathy but then turn away, because you don't think you have the time or energy to get involved. I'd ask you to be open to the leading of the Holy Spirit when this happens, because He may have chosen you to walk through this season with someone who feels very alone. You don't need to have all the answers. Just be a good listener and be honest about your own experience with the Lord. Have the integrity of heart and soul to say, "The reality is that I've had to wait on the Lord. Deliverance has come to me a piece at a time, a day at a time, until finally there was a day when that burden was a part of my past but not my present."

· THINK ABOUT IT ·

The compassion and courage to "get involved" comes from confidence in the Lord's promise to make His grace sufficient for you and the one who needs encouragement. He is eager to equip you for this.

*Prayer*

Heavenly Father, give me a greater measure of Your courageous compassion for those who are hurting. Help me to be selfless with both my strength and time, because You have promised me abundant resupply as I step into Your good works. In Jesus' name, amen.

## PROMISE OF FREEDOM

*But if we walk in the light, as he is in the light, we have fellowship with one another, and the blood of Jesus, his Son, purifies us from all sin.*

1 JOHN 1:7

The verbs in this verse are in the continuing present tense: These actions do not occur just one time; they happen repetitively. If we walk and continue to walk in the light as He is in the light, if we have fellowship and continue to have fellowship with one another, then the blood of Jesus cleanses us and continues to cleanse us from all sin. How can this continuing action be? Because one perfect sacrifice has been established so that we can be freed from the bondage of evil...now and forever. The power of evil over humanity has been broken. It's the good news that the Church of Jesus Christ holds, for our generation and every generation. It has enabled the Church to persist for two millennia through all sorts of movements and ideas. No matter how much the world changes around us, God's promise of freedom was true, is true, and will continue to be true for all who commit themselves to Jesus of Nazareth. What a miraculous gift!

### • THINK ABOUT IT •

What is impossible for you on your own is possible with God's sacrifice on your behalf. Be encouraged to live consistently in His light.

*Prayer*

Heavenly Father, I receive Your promise of a pure life and freedom from all bondage. With You is full redemption, and I worship You. Thank You that through the blood of Jesus I can live continually in fellowship with Your people. In Jesus' name, amen.

## NO MIDDLE GROUND

*Since we have these promises, dear friends, let us purify ourselves from everything that contaminates body and spirit, perfecting holiness out of reverence for God.*

2 CORINTHIANS 7:1

It was not that long ago that Jesus-followers lived with enough peace and affluence that it was possible to be content while living in the murky middle. Folks simply joined the church their family and friends were a part of without really knowing what they believed or why. Church participation was focused more on going along with the crowd and fulfilling cultural expectations than on awakening and facilitating a spiritual transformation. In this generation God is inviting us out of the middle ground to open our hearts fully to Him. He is purifying His Church and creating for Himself a holy people, a royal priesthood that reveres and worships Him in every aspect of our lives. What a privilege it is to be a part of that! Is it always easy? No. Is it always fun? No. Will there be opposition? I'm certain of it. But God is watching over us, and we should joyfully participate in His purposes in the earth.

### • THINK ABOUT IT •

Fulfilling cultural expectations will gain you the praise of people. Walking in full obedience to God will gain you the praise of God. Determining whose approval you most desire will set your life's course.

### *Prayer*

Heavenly Father, I want to be someone who stands for Jesus, even if I have to stand alone. I want Your truth represented in my life without compromise. Deliver me from fearing opposition that my life might reflect Your holiness. In Jesus' name, amen.

# DAY 61

## STABLE AND SECURE

*About Benjamin he said: "Let the beloved of the LORD rest secure in him, for he shields him all day long, and the one the LORD loves rests between his shoulders."*

DEUTERONOMY 33:12

Moses pronounced a blessing upon each of the twelve tribes of Israel, and the blessing he pronounced upon Benjamin captured my attention. He promised that the people the Lord loves can rest secure in Him and be shielded by Him. This is good news because security and stability are in short supply in our world. Things that we thought two decades ago were unshakable and could not be moved, we have found to be incredibly unstable. We have discovered that things we trusted to secure our futures are not so trustworthy after all. I would say trust is at a historic low in this season—not just in our nation, but around the world. Between natural disasters, national disasters, and human disasters, the world is a very uncertain place. Yet in the midst of that, we can lean into this remarkable promise of God's loving protection.

### • THINK ABOUT IT •

No matter how many times you see, feel, or hear chaos in these coming days, rest in these two truths: God is absolutely still in control, and He will protect those who love and follow Him.

### *Prayer*

Heavenly Father, You protect me as a good shepherd protects his sheep. Thank You for shielding me and carrying me through. May Your Word rise within me to subdue anxieties and unrest, and the peace You give me draw others to You. In Jesus' name, amen.

## WORDS INVESTED WISELY

*Pray also for me, that whenever I open my mouth, words may be given me so that I will fearlessly make known the mystery of the gospel...*

EPHESIANS 6:19

Paul had a focused perspective on his life. After his dramatic conversion from a chief persecutor of the Church to a man completely devoted to Jesus, he was determined to make up for lost time. Although in some ways he lived what we would consider a normal life—working to support himself, for example—his every word and action seem to have been filled with purpose. His greatest aims were to spread the message of Jesus of Nazareth as Messiah and to grow the fledgling Church. Paul's life should cause us to consider our lives. We probably will never be known as the greatest advocate for Christianity the world has known, but we should ask ourselves what we intend to accomplish when we open our mouths to speak. Do we spend even a fraction of the time telling people about the mysteries of the gospel and what Jesus has done for us as we do about sports, politics, and the price of gasoline? Let's make our everyday words count for the Kingdom of God.

• THINK ABOUT IT •

Idle words and conversations come easily in our communication-driven society. What percentage of your communication is invested in the Kingdom of God?

*Prayer*

Heavenly Father, I want my words to make a difference for Your Kingdom, but often less fruitful communication is easier. Help me manage my time and words in a way that they are invested into Your purposes and Your message of hope. In Jesus' name, amen.

# DAY 63

## COURAGEOUS PERSPECTIVE

*"You spoke by the Holy Spirit through the mouth of your servant, our father David: 'Why do the nations rage and the peoples plot in vain? The kings of the earth take their stand and the rulers gather together against the Lord and against his Anointed One.'...Now, Lord, consider their threats and enable your servants to speak your word with great boldness."*

ACTS 4:25-26, 29

The lives of these Jesus-followers have been threatened because of their allegiance to Him, but they realize that opposing God's purposes is not a new thing. They quote from Psalm 2, written by King David a thousand years before, and ask for supernatural support in their advocacy for Jesus. We're two thousand years later than the apostles were in this story, and rulers of the world are still taking their stands against the principles of God. We should not be shocked or surprised, and neither should we feel bullied or intimidated. It is simply time for the Church to find the strength and courage to be the Church. As we face the challenges of our generation, let us pray as these early believers did: "Lord, enable us to speak Your Word with great boldness."

### • THINK ABOUT IT •

In the face of spiritual opposition, gaining a courageous perspective that trusts God to prevail in our lives turns up His light in the midst of the darkness.

### *Prayer*

Heavenly Father, thank You for the warning that threats to Your purposes will arise. Grant me fresh courage, enabling me to speak Your Word with boldness and clarity. Help me honor You by making the most of every opportunity You extend. In Jesus' name, amen.

## THE NEXT ASSIGNMENT

*The LORD had said to Abram, "Leave your country, your people and your father's household and go to the land I will show you."...Abram was seventy-five years old when he set out from Haran.*

### GENESIS 12:1, 4

You may think you're old enough that you've done all the significant things you're going to do in your life. You may have accomplished many of your life goals and checked a few things off your bucket list. You may think that now is your time to kick back and relax. That's not what the Bible teaches. God showed up to Abram when he was past our traditional retirement age and said, "Get ready!" Abram went, and the rest is history—our history. If you have decided that it's time to sit on your good intentions, I'd invite you to push that footrest away and ask the Lord what He has for you to do. Churches and communities and individuals are in great need of the experience you have to offer. When you joyfully accept whatever assignment the Lord has for you—whether it's in your church, your community, or even in a land He will show you—you will be blessed as you bless others.

### • THINK ABOUT IT •

Increased birthdays do not limit our God-opportunities. No matter how old you are, ask the Lord what fresh and fruitful exploits He has for you. Begin to pray for whatever season is next. He will honor your prayers of preparation.

## *Prayer*

Heavenly Father, thank You that You promise older age need not diminish my service to You. Whether that is near or far off in time, by Your Spirit I will continue to live a fruitful life. Energize me for my assignment in this season. In Jesus' name, amen.

## ENDURING PROMISE

*Consider him who endured such opposition from sinful men, so that you will not grow weary and lose heart. In your struggle against sin, you have not yet resisted to the point of shedding your blood.*

HEBREWS 12:3-4

I read an article in a runner's magazine about the lie of the first mile. I didn't think the article applied to me because I think I'm done at the end of the first mile. Apparently there are some people who run more than that! The premise of the article was that during the first mile of a run, your body is going to give you all kinds of messages that you should quit: You're too tired; you're not getting enough oxygen, etc. The author of Hebrews is telling us that we should consider the One who went ahead of us so that we don't grow weary in our struggle against sin, because Jesus endured more than we are enduring. It doesn't say that you're not going to be tired; it says you should not give in to it. God will allow you to carry burdens and face opposition, but when we persevere we will grow in our knowledge and experience of His faithfulness.

### · THINK ABOUT IT ·

Perseverance produces character and hope. It's the narrow path to maturity. To gain it, keep your eyes on the promise, not on the pain. Consider Jesus.

### *Prayer*

Heavenly Father, I don't want to give in to weariness and forfeit the rewards You have promised to those who endure. I choose to keep my eyes on Jesus, trusting Him to mature my faith as I follow Him. Help me learn to rest in You. In Jesus' name, amen.

## VIGILANCE REQUIRED

*Be self-controlled and alert. Your enemy the devil prowls around like a roaring lion looking for someone to devour. Resist him, standing firm in the faith...*

1 PETER 5:8-9

You have a spiritual adversary who intends to obstruct God's purposes for your life, and he has a kingdom of associates who will join him in that task. Sometimes we think we are too sophisticated to believe in the Devil, but Jesus believed in him and knew how destructive he can be. You need a plan for shielding yourself from his activity in your life, because if you have no plan, you will be at his mercy. Commit yourself to vigilance by being self-controlled and alert. Always being on guard doesn't sound like fun, but the peace you will feel will be worth it. Make a habit of Bible reading and prayer, and you will gradually find it easier to recognize and resist evil when it touches your life. Do not give the enemy an inch when he attempts to gain a foothold. The power we have through the blood of Jesus and the wisdom available to us through the leading of the Holy Spirit are greater than any power that wants to destroy us.

### • THINK ABOUT IT •

Temptation can wear many masks, beginning as choices that are "no big deal." Ask the Holy Spirit to show you the trajectory of your choices so that you can avoid the ones that will veer you off God's path.

*Prayer*

Heavenly Father, You faithfully strengthen and protect me from evil, and there is safety in obedience to You. I choose to agree with Your counsel. Grant me the wisdom and courage to resist any scheme opposed to Your work in my life. In Jesus' name, amen.

# DAY 67

## THE BLESSING OF DISCIPLINE

*Blessed is the man you discipline, O LORD, the man you teach from your law...*

PSALM 94:12

I used to break colts. I didn't teach them to ride; I just taught them their ground manners when they were about a year old. Horses are strong, and you have to teach them how to behave so that they don't hurt people. They don't particularly like that; they would rather stay in the pasture doing what they want to do. We're a little like that. It's easy for us to keep living for our own desires, so God has to teach us how to be godly. He'll teach us new ways to think. He'll teach us new priorities. He'll teach us how to serve others, because that's not intuitive; we want others to serve us. He'll teach us how to think of others ahead of ourselves. If you're in one of those seasons where God is shining that light of discipline and instruction into your life, it's not a bad thing; it's evidence that He loves you and wants to bless you.

### • THINK ABOUT IT •

God's discipline elicits a response. It is good to remember His correction is proof of His kindness, love, and care.

*Prayer*

Heavenly Father, Your faithful discipline trains me well when I embrace it. I choose to respond with willing obedience that I might enjoy the peaceful fruit of righteousness that results. In Jesus' name, amen.

## IN ALL THINGS

*We know that in all things God works for the good of those who love him,*
*who have been called according to his purpose.*

ROMANS 8:28

God works for good in everything that happens to the people who love Him...what an extravagant promise! It would be preposterous if our God were not the Creator of the universe and everything in it, the Alpha and Omega, the Anointed One, the God Who Sees, the Messiah, our Provider, and many other things. If the One who can part the sea or raise the dead or open a blind eye or multiply loaves and fishes says He is working for our good, we should get excited about that. When trials come—and they will—do not allow your emotions to control your life. I'm not telling you your feelings are not legitimate; they are. But you have to decide what's going to control your life, and emotions are a lousy guide. When you are tempted to be led by anger, resentment, envy, fear, guilt, or shame, remember this promise from God and look forward to what He is going to do in your future.

### • THINK ABOUT IT •

While emotions are subject to the shifting perception of circumstance or self-interest, faith is led by the eternal truths of God's Word. Rely on the best evidence available: the trustworthiness of God's Word.

### Prayer

Heavenly Father, help me diligently put Your Word into my heart that my mind and emotions might be anchored in Your truth. May my faith grow and doubt starve as I trust Your promise to work all things for my good. You are able. In Jesus' name, amen.

## AN UNDIVIDED HEART

*Joshua told the people, "Consecrate yourselves, for tomorrow the LORD will do amazing things among you."*

JOSHUA 3:5

The greatest breakthroughs in our lives come when we submit ourselves to God's direction and cooperate with Him. To do that, we first have to consecrate ourselves. We have to be willing to cleanse ourselves, repent, and set ourselves apart for the purposes of God. Think about your current relationship with Him. Have you treated Him casually, acting like His commandments are mere suggestions? Have you ignored the voice of the Holy Spirit when He has led you to do or not do something? Have you doubted His love when He has not done what you want when you want it? Have you questioned His purposes when He has led you in a direction that you did not desire or understand? Consider what attitudes you need to make a course correction on, then ask His forgiveness and commit yourself to His purposes. His desire is to "do amazing things" through you!

### • THINK ABOUT IT •

Consider your perspective of God's voice in your life. Could you more fully open your heart to His opinions and listen with the intent to obey?

### *Prayer*

Heavenly Father, I repent of any place where I have disregarded, ignored, or doubted You. Help me become single-mindedly obedient to Your directions that I might honor You. I choose to serve You with an undivided heart. In Jesus' name, amen.

## DARING TO REACH OUT

*A woman who had been subject to bleeding for twelve years came up behind him and touched the edge of his cloak. She said to herself, "If I only touch his cloak, I will be healed." Jesus turned and saw her. "Take heart, daughter," he said, "your faith has healed you." And the woman was healed from that moment.*

MATTHEW 9:20-22

The redemptive work of Jesus isn't just about the "sweet by and by." It has impact on our lives in time. Our salvation includes our body, soul, and spirit—every part of our person—that we might be healed, delivered, and given a purpose in God's Kingdom. This woman had spent twelve years fighting a private battle. Her medical condition would have determined her life choices. She wouldn't have been welcome in public, but she braved the crowds that day and approached Jesus. She knew that Jesus could deliver her and change her life completely if she could just touch Him. She did, and He did, and hers is one of the most touching stories of deliverance in the Bible. Jesus wants to do for You the same thing He did for this woman. Reach out and touch Him, believing that He will deliver you.

· THINK ABOUT IT ·

Jesus is the same yesterday, today, and forever. Be confident today of Jesus' willingness and power to heal as the woman with the problem of bleeding was then.

*Prayer*

Heavenly Father, Jesus was wounded on the cross that I might be healed. Help me continually apply Jesus' finished work through His shed blood to my life— body, soul, and spirit—to deliver and restore me to health. Thank You for Your compassion. In Jesus' name, amen.

## ALL-POWERFUL SWORD

*For the word of God is living and active. Sharper than any double-edged sword, it penetrates even to dividing soul and spirit, joints and marrow; it judges the thoughts and attitudes of the heart.*

HEBREWS 4:12

It is amazing how many different kinds of Bibles we have access to today. There are multiple translations of the original languages, and those have been translated into hundreds of modern languages. Some Bibles fit in your pocket, some take up a coffee table, and some are online. But all of those Bibles are just words on a page or screen until you open your heart to the Word of God. Then the Spirit of God brings it to life, and it has the power to change you. Daily Bible reading is not just some religious exercise; we need the Word of God within us. This verse compares Scripture to the sharpest of swords that will help you evaluate the thoughts and attitudes of your heart and eliminate those that are not what the Lord desires of you. The discipline of reading your Bible on a daily basis will prepare you to hear the voice of the Holy Spirit as He calls you to accomplish the Lord's purposes in your life.

### • THINK ABOUT IT •

God has provided His Word that we might know Him and His plans for our lives and be transformed by the power it wields.

### Prayer

Heavenly Father, help me open my heart and time to Your Word, giving it daily priority. Holy Spirit, bring the Word of God to life that I might believe and be transformed by its power, stand firm in its truth, and pray with renewed hope. In Jesus' name, amen.

# DAY 72

## NEVER OUTNUMBERED

*O LORD of hosts, How blessed is the man who trusts in You!*

PSALM 84:12 • NASB®

"Lord of hosts" is the phrase typically used in English translations, but if we translated it literally from the Hebrew it would be "Lord of the armies." Not the Lord of the heavenly athletic teams or the Lord of the heavenly debate team—the Lord of the heavenly armies! God is identified as the Lord of the heavenly host hundreds of times in the Bible, and that is the God who is on our side. You don't need an army if there is no conflict, and the Bible says a time is coming when we will make war no more. I'm looking forward to it! But between here and there I'm grateful that I reside under the watchful eye of the Lord of the armies. When the enemy is taunting you with feelings of hopelessness and despair, when circumstances seem to be so overwhelming that they cannot be overcome, remember that your God commands armies of angels who are sent forth on my behalf and yours.

### • THINK ABOUT IT •

We can many times feel alone, vulnerable, and defenseless. Trusting God's care and provision brings overcoming strength.

## Prayer

Heavenly Father, there are times I am without courage and hope, even fearful. Help me cultivate trust in You that becomes a first response to circumstances and challenges. Thank You for commissioning hosts of angels to help Your people. In Jesus' name, amen.

## ACTIVE DUTY

*Endure hardship with us like a good soldier of Christ Jesus. No one serving as a soldier gets involved in civilian affairs—he wants to please his commanding officer.*

2 TIMOTHY 2:3-4

Paul equates being a Christ-follower with being a soldier. I haven't served in the military, but I've listened carefully to many who have. I've come to understand that while they have lives outside the military, all of those things become secondary concerns when they are on active duty. It's a complete realignment of your priorities, and the orders of your commanding authority are primary. If you ignore orders and pursue secondary things, you will pay a price for that. We've been a little guilty of having our priorities misaligned. We've pursued pleasure and success, and those are not evil pursuits unless they become your highest priorities. We call that idolatry, and the Lord made His feelings about that clear in the first of the commandments: "You shall have no other god before me" (Exodus 20:3). When we make pleasing the Lord, our commanding officer, our primary objective, the rest of life's assignments will fall in place.

### • THINK ABOUT IT •

To "pursue" something is more than an expression of casual interest. Pursuing implies an ongoing, dogged effort to seek and attain. Pursuit reveals priorities. Do you pursue God and the things that please Him?

*Prayer*

Heavenly Father, I want to be pleasing to You, so I choose to make You my highest priority. I acknowledge Your authority to direct my steps and want to align with You fully, pursuing first Your Kingdom and righteousness. In Jesus' name, amen.

## MAKING ROOM TO HEAR

*He said to me, "Son of man, stand up on your feet and I will speak to you." As he spoke, the Spirit came into me and raised me to my feet, and I heard him speaking to me.*

EZEKIEL 2:1-2

Scripture is full of accounts of God speaking to His people. Here He speaks to Ezekiel, filling him with His Spirit and calling him to be His prophet. God is still speaking to His people. He'll speak to you through His Word. He'll speak to you through that still, small voice inside you. He's given you a conscience to know right from wrong. If you learn to listen to it, the Spirit of God will amplify it. If you ignore it, it becomes calloused and insensitive. God will speak into your life through the most improbable people and situations. Yet we struggle with the notion of listening to God. We are excited to hear about people who are intuitive. We'll get teary watching a movie about a "horse whisperer" but make fun of people who say they've heard the voice of God. Why would we say "What a wonderful gift!" about one and "You're crazy!" about the other? The enemy will tempt us to harden our heart to spiritual things, and it would help all of us to become more intent about listening when God speaks.

• THINK ABOUT IT •

God made your heart, soul, and ears that you might hear Him when He speaks. How could you make more room for His voice today?

### Prayer

Heavenly Father, I want to learn to listen to You when You speak, no matter the delivery system. Help me recognize Your guidance and understand Your wisdom. May I be more watchful and attentive to Your voice with the grace to obey. In Jesus' name, amen.

# DAY 75

## OUTCOMES IN THE BALANCE

*Come near to God and he will come near to you...*

JAMES 4:8

If you are walking through a stormy season of life, the best solution I know is spending time with Jesus. You are engaged in spiritual warfare, and you will benefit greatly if you make it a priority to spend as much time as you can sitting at Jesus' feet. This is not overly complicated. Spend more time in prayer and thanksgiving than you usually do. Thank God, not because you like what you are going through, but for who He is and the deliverance He has promised. Pray in the Spirit. Invest yourself in the Word of God. Spend more time reading your Bible than you do scrolling through social media and watching television. Attend more worship services. Lifting your concerns and praises to the Lord along with other believers will encourage you and remind you that you are not alone in your struggles. Replace secular music with worship music, and sing along. Spiritual warfare is very real. Outcomes are in the balance, and your future is in question. This verse is beautiful in its simple advice: "Come near to God and he will come near to you."

### • THINK ABOUT IT •

Many of us medicate our troubles through entertainment. God's invitation is to find your immediate refuge in Him. How can you begin to practice drawing nearer to God?

### *Prayer*

Heavenly Father, my only hope is in You. Help me draw near to You both in times of peace and in times of spiritual warfare. You are my Refuge and Strong Tower, the God in whom I trust. In Jesus' name, amen.

## GENEROSITY SEEDS

*[Cornelius] distinctly saw an angel of God, who came to him and said, "Cornelius!" Cornelius stared at him in fear. "What is it, Lord?" he asked. The angel answered, "Your prayers and gifts to the poor have come up as a memorial offering before God. Now send men to Joppa to bring back a man named Simon who is called Peter."*

ACTS 10:3-5

Cornelius was a Roman soldier, a Gentile, who was "devout and God-fearing." His extraordinary story and its far-reaching consequences are told in Acts 10-11. The angel told Cornelius that his prayers and generosity had come to the Lord's attention, and he had been chosen to fulfill a very important task for the expansion of God's Kingdom. Generosity is an important component of being blessed and used by God. If that hasn't opened up in your heart yet, start to plant seeds of generosity. You'll plant small ones at first, because you'll be doing it begrudgingly, with gritted teeth and clenched fists. But if you'll start to practice generosity, and learn to live generously, the blessings of God will come to your life in ways far beyond monetary things.

· THINK ABOUT IT ·

We can be generous no matter the size of our wealth, even in our poverty. Start planting those seeds today with anticipation of the harvest to come.

*Prayer*

Heavenly Father, You freely gave Your Son that, through His sacrifice, I might live in Your abundance. Please deliver me from any fear, unbelief, or greed that would prevent me from extending Your generosity of heart. In His name I pray, amen.

## CHECK THE MIRROR

*Then I heard the voice of the Lord saying, "Whom shall I send? And who will go for us?" And I said, "Here am I. Send me!"*

ISAIAH 6:8

God said to Isaiah, "Whom shall I send?" and Isaiah's quick reply was, "Here am I. Send me!" If God asked us the same question, many of us would say, "I know the perfect person!" How many of us have asked God to raise up voices in our nation to make a difference for the Kingdom of God? Do you know what His answer was? "Check the mirror!" "No, God," we reply. "I meant someone important. Someone who is gifted at public speaking. Someone who has a seminary degree. Someone whose children are grown and gone. Someone who can afford to put their career path on the back burner. Someone who has enough money in the bank. Someone who is uniquely prepared." Isaiah did not argue or try to negotiate with God about his own qualifications or God's plan or timing; He simply accepted God's invitation. Like Isaiah, we have to be willing, where we are, to say, "God, here am I."

· THINK ABOUT IT ·

Sometimes it's easier to see our inadequacies than it is to see God's invitations. Even Moses originally protested God's call. When you look in the mirror, be sure to look through the corrective lens of faith and trust God's plan.

*Prayer*

Heavenly Father, You give me everything I need to serve You. Your grace is sufficient where I am weak. Relying on Your promise that the Holy Spirit can be at work in me, I am willing to say, "Yes! Send me." In Jesus' name, amen.

## THE WAY, THE TRUTH, THE LIFE

*"For God so loved the world that he gave his one and only Son, that whoever believes in him shall not perish but have eternal life. For God did not send his Son into the world to condemn the world, but to save the world through him."*

JOHN 3:16-17

The Dome of the Rock is the building with the beautiful gold dome on the Temple Mount in Jerusalem. It is actually a Muslim shrine, and inside are a series of inscriptions written in Arabic. Among the views stated there are that there is no Trinity and that God had no need of a Son, thus Jesus was simply a messenger from God. This could not be further from the truth, as we read in this passage from John. God sent His Son to the earth to live among us, die among us, and be raised to life again. Why? So that the world would be saved "through him." Do not allow yourself to be confused about the deity of Jesus. He is the way, the truth, and the life—the only way to the only God.

· THINK ABOUT IT ·

When Jesus rose from the dead, all His claims—including His deity—were verified. Today, know you can entrust your life completely into His care, and believe every word that He said.

*Prayer*

Heavenly Father, I believe Jesus is Your Son, born of the Virgin Mary, crucified, buried, and resurrected from death for my salvation. Help me bear witness to the evidence for my faith—that Jesus is the only way to the only God. In His name I pray, amen.

## AUTHENTIC FAITH

*I care very little if I am judged by you or by any human court; indeed, I do not even judge myself...It is the Lord who judges me...He will bring to light what is hidden in darkness and will expose the motives of men's hearts.*

1 CORINTHIANS 4:3-5

Film sets constructed to look like something they are not are interesting. From the outside one can look like a Wild West town or a street in Paris or a cul-de-sac in an American neighborhood. Yet in reality it is nothing more than a detailed façade built on a studio back lot. When you walk through the doors, there is nothing more than can be seen from the outside. Many of us church folk have learned to construct a façade that we put on before we walk through the doors on the weekend. For a couple of hours we look like our faith is authentic, but we shed that façade as soon as we walk out the doors. This passage reminds us that the Christian life is not about creating an image that can fool the people around us. It is about living so that the Lord will be pleased when He examines our hearts.

• THINK ABOUT IT •

Are there areas of your life where you care more about what people think than what God thinks of you? How can you begin to reprioritize?

*Prayer*

Heavenly Father, shine Your light on any area of my life that is not authentic. I am devoted to You, and I want truth to be the core of my life that I might be holy as You are holy. In Jesus' name, amen.

## AVAILABLE AND ALERT

*He who watches over you will not slumber; indeed, he who watches over Israel will neither slumber nor sleep.*

PSALM 121:3-4

Humans are hard-wired to need sleep. Newborns sleep many hours of the day, and if we are healthy that amount decreases as we grow older. Doctors say that adults need seven to nine hours of sleep each day, but many of us get by with less. One of the many astounding ways that God is different from us is that He never needs to sleep—never!—and that means He is watching us and available to us around the clock. In the morning when you open your eyes, He is with you. When you open your Bible to read His Word, He is there to illuminate it for you. As you deal with a difficult coworker, He is there to answer your pleas for patience and wisdom. When you bow to give thanks for your blessings, He is there to hear your gratitude. Remember that no matter the time of day, or the place, or the circumstances, God is with you, to hear you and help you.

• THINK ABOUT IT •

What a reassuring comfort it is to know that the Creator of Heaven and Earth never tires in His watchful care over the lives of His people. At all times, and above all else, let your greatest confidence be in the Lord.

*Prayer*

Heavenly Father, thank You for teaching me in Your Word that You are an ever-present God, ready to hear my cry and protect, provide, guide, and sustain me—even when I am asleep. Help me maintain the realization that You are near. In Jesus' name, amen.

# DAY 81

## GROWTH CHARTS

*Therefore leaving the elementary teaching about the Christ, let us press on to maturity...*

HEBREWS 6:1 • NASB®

When we look through the window of a hospital nursery at all of those bundles of joy, we understand that all they have is the equipment to begin a journey. They're going to have to learn to walk and talk, feed and clothe themselves, and read and write. At some point they'll leave the safety of home and figure out how to live in the world. These milestones are the rhythms and joys of life; we don't stand in the window at the hospital and weep for what we know is coming. The same is true with our spiritual lives. The Bible uses the images of a new birth because we begin our Christian journey as spiritual newborns who are expected to grow up. That process can be awkward and uncomfortable, and sometimes we wish we could stay childlike and avoid grown-up responsibilities. But maturity and the responsibilities that come along with it are the lifelong pursuits of people who want to be more like Jesus and fulfill His purposes in their lives.

### • THINK ABOUT IT •

Maturing is not always pleasant, but it is a necessary part of growth. Are there any places in your life you would be willing to tell the Lord, "Please, help me gain maturity in You"?

### Prayer

Heavenly Father, I turn away from any perspective that prevents Your purposes from being fulfilled in my life. I choose instead the path of spiritual growth, along with its responsibilities, that I might be conformed to the image of Christ. In Jesus' name, amen.

## NO DRESS REHEARSAL

*Now listen, you who say, "Today or tomorrow we will go to this or that city, spend a year there, carry on business and make money." Why, you do not even know what will happen tomorrow...*

JAMES 4:13-14

This Scripture passage is not condemning planning ahead or working hard to grow a business or make money; in fact, the Bible encourages those things. It is simply a reminder that while we do those things, we should seek God's guidance and depend on Him every step of the way. This lifetime is not a dress rehearsal; we only get one opportunity to live each of our days, years, and seasons. We will only have one season to honor the Lord as a teenager, young adult, mature adult, and so on. Each of those seasons will bring unique opportunities to do things for the Kingdom that you may not have in other seasons. No matter the season of life you are in, look for ways to grow and serve because there are no do-overs, and "you do not even know what will happen tomorrow."

· THINK ABOUT IT ·

We can often take for granted other God-opportunities will arise if we take a pass on the one before us. What would it look like to become more invested in God's Kingdom today?

*Prayer*

Heavenly Father, I want my life to be well-invested in Your eternal purposes. Help me be more deliberate in serving and honoring You, even in the mundane areas of my life. May I not take this season for granted but live it for You. In Jesus' name, amen.

# DAY 83

## SHARPENED FOR STRENGTH

*As iron sharpens iron, so a friend sharpens a friend.*

PROVERBS 27:17 • NLT

Each follower of Jesus needs to live in community with other people of God. We've let this myth grow in us that we can mature as believers with God alone, but we need one another too. The biggest spiritual breakthroughs in our lives are not solitary events in dark corners. There are layers to them, and there are many people who will help us as we walk along those pathways. That's why you are so valuable, and so important to what God is doing. Sitting in groups with one another. Serving each other. Serving others. Encouraging one another's gospel witness. Praying with one another. Bearing each other's burdens. Sharing each other's joys. When you are weak, someone else will be strong. When someone else is unsure, you will have Spirit-filled wisdom to share. Be a faithful participant in a caring community of believers. As you sharpen others and allow yourself to be sharpened, the community of faith and the individuals in it will be strengthened.

### • THINK ABOUT IT •

Isolation makes us more vulnerable. Spiritual maturity happens when we are in fellowship with other Christ-followers. Taking our place in the community of faith adds value both to our lives and others.

### Prayer

Heavenly Father, You desire Your people to live in fellowship with one another. Help me open my life more fully to those around me and be a devoted and consistent participant in the community of faith where You have placed me. In Jesus' name, amen.

## HIS CHOICE

*In the sixth month of Elizabeth's pregnancy, God sent the angel Gabriel to Nazareth, a village in Galilee, to a virgin named Mary. She was engaged to be married to a man named Joseph, a descendant of King David.*

LUKE 1:26-27 • NLT

In Luke 1:25-26 we read the story of the elderly priest Zechariah and his wife, Elizabeth, who were childless. Childlessness was a great burden and shame in that time, because children were a sign of blessing from God and caretakers of parents in their later years. An angel visits to tell them that God has chosen them to be parents of a son who will be called John—we know him as John the Baptist—and he will do great things for God. In this passage we see Elizabeth's young cousin Mary having her own angelic visitation and receiving her own news of playing a part in God's unfolding plan. An elderly couple who thought they had missed God's blessing and a young, unmarried couple who received perhaps the most startling news in history. God chooses people to serve Him not based on their age or social standing; He chooses whomever He wills.

### • THINK ABOUT IT •

Neither youth nor old age disqualifies you from significance in God's plan. Willingness to serve counts for more than natural talent, and humility more than status.

### Prayer

Heavenly Father, thank You that at every age, You can use those who place their trust in You and make themselves available to Your Holy Spirit. Thank You for choosing me—may I serve You well and honor Your name all the days of my life. In Jesus' name, amen.

## SET FREE INDEED

*Therefore, there is now no condemnation for those who are in Christ Jesus, because through Christ Jesus the law of the Spirit of life set me free from the law of sin and death.*

ROMANS 8:1-2

If I had to choose words that describe what Jesus represents in our lives, "freedom" would have to be included in that list. Jesus brings us spiritual freedom—freedom from our sins, freedom from our failures, freedom from the shadows of our past. He brings us physical freedom—freedom from our addictions, freedom from sickness and disease, freedom from generational curses that plague us. He brings us freedom from emotional oppression so that we can live in peace and confidence without being frightened, or threatened, or anxious. Jesus brings us freedom from demonic oppression. He brings us freedom from worry. One of the beliefs that has settled over our culture is that following Jesus will limit you, but nothing could be further from the truth. Following Jesus will bring freedom to you that nothing else will bring.

• THINK ABOUT IT •

The price for spiritual freedom from sin and death was paid for by Jesus' sacrifice on the cross. How can we best thank Him for that incomparable freedom?

*Prayer*

Heavenly Father, thank You for the freedom available through the cross of Jesus Christ. Please continue to set me free to both serve You more fully and, in thanksgiving, help others grow in that same liberty. In Jesus' name, amen.

## ALL-PURPOSE TRAVEL GUIDE

*Your word is a lamp to my feet and a light for my path.*

PSALM 119:105

Have you ever tried to take a walk in the pitch black of a moonless night? It would be hard enough to walk down your own street in complete darkness, but what about walking down a road you had never been on before? Can you imagine being on a mountainous trail with trees and rocks and dangerous drop-offs, or in a jungle with crocodiles lurking in the water and pythons watching from the trees—all without a ray of light? This is the nature of life without the guidance of Scripture. All around us there are dangerous but unseen spiritual forces at work to confuse us, trip us, trap us, and harm us. We desperately need the light of God's Word to guide our steps as we make our way on life's journey. The Bible will not tell you which college you should attend or recommend the highest-yielding mutual fund. But the overarching principles it teaches, illuminated by the understanding the Holy Spirit gives you, make it a totally sufficient guide for traveling the pathways of life.

### • THINK ABOUT IT •

Have you ever read a portion of Scripture in the morning that shed light on a circumstance later in the day? Reading our Bibles every day can bring us more hope, wisdom, guidance.

### *Prayer*

Heavenly Father, I want Your light to shine on the path before me. Help me yield time each day to take advantage of Your written Word, depending on and trusting it to teach me Your character and how to walk by Your Spirit. In Jesus' name, amen.

## MORE THAN A THEORY

*God is not unjust; he will not forget your work and the love you have shown him as you have helped his people and continue to help them.*

HEBREWS 6:10

We do not serve God theoretically; we serve God by serving God's people. We are not generous toward God theoretically; we are generous toward God by being generous toward His people. One of the ways we express our love for God is by helping His people. Our journey toward spiritual maturity is greatly impacted by how much we are willing to interact with the people He has placed in our path. Some of those people will be easy to help, and some of them will be very difficult to help. Yet that is what we are called to do. In hindsight, I can see that God has changed my heart in very significant ways as I have purposed to serve Him by serving people. It is humbling and fulfilling, and has changed me in ways that nothing else could. In addition to the great joy we find in helping others, it is good to know that He is watching and promises to remember what we have done in His name.

### • THINK ABOUT IT •

Jesus came to serve, and He has purposed our interactions with each other to be marked by acts of service. Your talents, time, and resources may seem small to you but, directed by the Lord, they could make a very big difference in someone else's life.

### *Prayer*

Heavenly Father, Your Word counsels us to take care of not only our own interests, but also the interests of others. I want to follow the example Jesus set. Make me sensitive to the ways I can be helpful to others as they serve You. In Jesus' name, amen.

## INVESTMENT GOALS

*Jesus replied, "Foxes have holes and birds of the air have nests, but the Son of Man has no place to lay his head."*

MATTHEW 8:20

We all naturally want to be successful in life. As Jesus-followers, we say we want to be more like Him every day. But how many of us really want Jesus' kind of success? As far as we know, He never owned a home, or more possessions than He could carry or wear. In His hometown, they tried to kill Him. The power brokers in Jerusalem orchestrated His execution. The Roman governor knew He was innocent but ordered Him to be condemned. Yet we would all agree that Jesus' earthly life was a success, because He was fully invested in the Kingdom of God. It's easy to compare ourselves to others and think that we are not as successful as they are. But material possessions like houses and cars are not indicators of true success, because you can lose those things in a moment. The wise person chooses to follow the example of Jesus by investing in the eternal Kingdom of God. When we do, like Jesus, we will reap rewards from the Creator of all things for all eternity.

• THINK ABOUT IT •

Investment counselors always begin by asking what your investment goals are. That's a good question for your life as a Jesus-follower too. Jesus' goal was always to advance the interests of His Heavenly Father, and He defined His life's success accordingly.

*Prayer*

Heavenly Father, help me turn my focus from the success of my own interests to the success of Yours. My goal is to be fully invested in the things You value. I want to see Your Kingdom come, Your Church growing, and Your name glorified. In Jesus' name, amen.

## PROMISE OF ABUNDANCE

*"I will surely bless you and make your descendants as numerous as the stars in the sky and as the sand on the seashore."*

GENESIS 22:17

Have you ever stopped to truly consider the generosity of God? He is generous to humanity in general—think of the beauty and bounty of our world. He is particularly generous to those who love Him—our lives are examples of that. He did not say to Abraham, "Follow me, and I'll give you a son." He said He would make Abraham's descendants as numerous as the stars in the sky and the sand on the seashore. These are not vague promises. The Bible says that God knows every star by name, so He can surely give you a tally of how many there are. He knows how many grains of sand there were yesterday and today. Our God is all-wise, all-knowing, and generous beyond what we think to ask for. His love is great, and He wants to demonstrate that love to you every day. Believe that His promises are true. Trust that His timing is perfect, and thank Him for all He has done and will do for you.

· THINK ABOUT IT ·

2 Corinthians 9:8 says, "God is able to bless you abundantly, so that in all things at all times, having all that you need, you will abound in every good work." Be confident that His love never stops short and His power on your behalf is beyond measure.

*Prayer*

Heavenly Father, I take You at Your Word that You make abundant grace available to me. You are generous to me beyond comprehension. I gratefully put my trust in Your unfailing love, confident of Your power to provide. In Jesus' name, amen.

# DAY 90

## EXTRAORDINARY INVITATION

*[Jesus] made himself nothing, taking the very nature of a servant, being made in human likeness.*

PHILIPPIANS 2:7

The nature of God's invitation to Jesus is very sobering. It's also counter to everything the world tells us our goals in life should be. God's assignment for Jesus was to lay aside the glories of Heaven, all of the power and prestige He had access to, and become a part of His earthly creation. Jesus did what His Father asked and changed the course of human history. Can you imagine that God would give you an invitation that would ask you to forfeit something? To lay something aside for a season or a lifetime? To humble yourself and take a lesser role? To make a sacrifice that would affect you and your family? It's improbable that you will be able to accept an invitation from God and maintain the status quo, but that is not a bad thing. Saying yes to Him will impact your relationships, your schedule, and your resources. Do not let that deter you, however, because He has something better for you: He is going to rewrite your future!

### • THINK ABOUT IT •

The late missionary Jim Elliot said, "He is no fool who gives what he cannot keep to gain that which he cannot lose." The Apostle Paul understood it isn't about what we can gain because of Christ. It is about gaining Christ Himself. The cost of following Him is dwarfed by the rewards.

### *Prayer*

Heavenly Father, nothing You could ever ask me to give up can compare with the surpassing value of knowing Jesus as Lord. Help me understand what that means in my life to "gain Christ and...be found in Him..." In Jesus' name, amen.

# DAY 91

## THE ONLY PATH TO PEACE

*Jesus answered, "I am the way and the truth and the life. No one comes to the Father except through me."*

JOHN 14:6

Many people believe that Jesus is "just another"—just another prophet, teacher, face in a painting, or word to express frustration—and they treat Him with casual disregard. They couldn't be further from the truth. Jesus is unique. There has never been another like Him, nor will there ever be. It isn't just that Jesus was a good person, or better than the rest of us. We are born hard-wired for sin, but He was born without sin and chose to lead a life honoring God. That's why the virgin birth was necessary for the redemptive death of Jesus Christ to be sufficient. That's why Jesus is the end of the Law as a means of righteousness. There is no set of rules that we can keep to make us good enough to earn a spot in Heaven. We needed help, and Jesus accomplished that for us. Don't ever believe the lie that Jesus is "just another." He is "the way and the truth and the life," the only path to peace and joy in this life and the next.

### • THINK ABOUT IT •

Jesus can be your personal Savior. Let your statement of belief mirror Peter's in Matthew 16:16: "You are the Christ, the Son of the living God."

*Prayer*

Heavenly Father, Your Word promises that at the name of Your Son, Jesus, every knee will bow, every tongue confess that Jesus is Lord. I bow my knees now and confess Jesus as my Lord and Savior, the only way to be reconciled to You. In Jesus' name, amen.

## DIVINE DISRUPTIONS

*O LORD, you are my God; I will exalt you and praise your name, for in perfect faithfulness you have done marvelous things, things planned long ago.*

ISAIAH 25:1

Do you ever feel like God is inviting you toward something, but the information you are given is incomplete? Me too! When I'm at the end of the process with a God-story in hand, I can look back and see that His faithfulness is absolute, complete, and undeniable. Oftentimes when I'm living it out, however, I have some questions about how His plan will work with the plan I've already made! One of the most consistent issues I've had with the Lord has to do with His sense of timing; but He has also challenged me to depend on Him regarding obstacles, finances, and my expectations of the end result. I can say with absolute certainty that every time I have put my own plans aside and said yes to the Lord, He has blessed me beyond anything I could have imagined. Yes, the Lord will disrupt your plans, but His disruptions are always good.

· THINK ABOUT IT ·

When God called Abraham, faith enabled him to obediently set out, though he did not yet know where he was going. Is there any place where you have delayed obeying God because you couldn't see how it would all work out?

*Prayer*

Heavenly Father, increase my awareness of the promptings of Your Spirit so I can obey and confidently step out in faith. Your thoughts and ways are higher than mine. I will trust Your plans, for they bring hope and healing. In Jesus' name, amen.

## HEART OF HUMILITY

*As Jesus was walking beside the Sea of Galilee, he saw two brothers, Simon called Peter and his brother Andrew. They were casting a net into the lake, for they were fishermen. "Come, follow me," Jesus said, "and I will make you fishers of men."*

MATTHEW 4:18-19

Peter and Andrew, then James and John, were fishermen who recognized that Jesus was giving them an opportunity like none they had ever had. During this time rabbis invited young people to follow them and learn from them. It was like being recruited to participate on a college athletic team. Some rabbis were like the famous coaches of our day, high profile and connected to a network of power brokers. Jesus, however, was a little-known itinerant rabbi who was not a part of any earthly network of influence. Most of God's invitations will invite you outside the normal structures of power and prestige. Occasionally you will be invited to participate in some event that will make the news. Most often your invitations will involve befriending, listening, serving, and supporting. You will miss God's invitations if you wait for them to come in fancy packages, for they are most often seen in hurting faces, empty hands, and anguished hearts.

· THINK ABOUT IT ·

Jesus responded to the ones others overlooked. He heard, He cared, He responded, and brought the blessings and power of God to each.

*Prayer*

Heavenly Father, I don't want to be found watching for "big" invitations and walk past the one who is hurting. Help me cultivate a heart of humility so that I can respond with Your power and compassion to those who need Your touch. In Jesus' name, amen.

## AVAILABLE AND COMMITTED

*He is not served by human hands, as if he needed anything, because he himself gives all men life and breath and everything else.*

ACTS 17:25

One of the first things prospective employers want to know is what education, training, skills, and experience you have to offer the organization. God is quite different when He is gathering people to Himself. How much education, training, skills, and experience is required to be a disciple? None. God will use our life experiences for His purposes when we follow Him, but He doesn't need them to put His Kingdom over the top. When I said, "Jesus, be Lord of my life," the angels didn't all say, "Whew! I'm not sure we would have made it without Allen's skill set. Now it's going to get a lot easier." God gives us different gifts and abilities and life assignments and jobs. As we make ourselves available to Him and commit ourselves to His purposes, He will allow us to participate with Him as ambassadors for the Kingdom of God. When we do that, we glorify Him and open the door for His blessings on our lives.

• THINK ABOUT IT •

The Apostle Paul boasted of his weaknesses, knowing they were the opportunity for the power of Christ to dwell in him (2 Corinthians 12:9). Jesus at the center of our lives is the story of our qualification and our call.

*Prayer*

Heavenly Father, You are my Maker and the source of all my abilities. Apart from You I can do nothing of lasting value. I want to be available to You, and I commit to making Jesus Lord of my life that all my days might be fruitful. In Jesus' name, amen.

# DAY 95

## WELL-PLACED TRUST

*"Here now is the man who did not make God his stronghold but trusted in his great wealth..."*

PSALM 52:7

Psalm 52 is David's rebuke of a man who boasted in, among other things, his great wealth. God wants us to think about our resources in the context of His provision and His faithfulness. He wants us to learn not to depend so fully on our money, because it has limits. I've been with too many people with significant resources who have problems they can't fix. That's when they call me. If money will fix it, my name doesn't come up. But when a bad diagnosis or some other scary thing comes up and they don't have a way to address it, they look for another expression of power. God loves you so much that He will invite you into a trust transfer. He will engineer it to try to get you to shift your trust from your money into Him. It's to help us learn there is a resource greater than the things we can hold. If you learn that God is our "stronghold" and begin to live with that awareness, you will gain great momentum in your relationship with the Lord.

### • THINK ABOUT IT •

Jesus taught that it's not possible to serve both God and money. Misplaced trust results in anxiety and uncertainty. Consider a trust transfer to God with the unshakable peace that can bring.

### Prayer

Heavenly Father, my anxieties reveal my misplaced trust. As Jesus trustingly thanked You for the loaves and fishes, I thank You for the supply You have given me. I will put my trust in Your faithfulness and grace to meet all my needs. In Jesus' name, amen.

## DISTINCTIVE KINDNESS

*The Lord's servant must not be quarrelsome but must be kind to everyone, able to teach, not resentful. Opponents must be gently instructed, in the hope that God will grant them repentance leading them to a knowledge of the truth, and that they will come to their senses and escape from the trap of the devil, who has taken them captive to do his will.*

2 TIMOTHY 2:24-26

It's easy to become bewildered by the array of options available in the marketplace of religious ideas today. It's easy to believe there are many paths to God—do whatever you want, and it will all work out in the end. This passage is good instruction for those of us who have friends or family who have bought into the idea that there is no Almighty God and no overarching truth. This is not a trivial matter, because Paul plainly writes "the devil...has taken them captive to do his will." We must speak and live our faith in their presence with gentleness and kindness, continually opening the doors of possibility for them to seek God and the new life they can find only in Him.

## • THINK ABOUT IT •

Representing our faith in Jesus with kindness, gentleness, and respect will distinguish us well from the tone of our current culture which seeks to destroy any opposition with angry, demeaning words and actions. It is one way we will shine like stars in the midst of our generation.

## *Prayer*

Heavenly Father, Jesus—there is no other name by which we must be saved (Acts 4:12). Open the eyes of those around me to see this truth. Help me demonstrate the reality of the risen Christ living in me with gentleness and kindness. In Jesus' name, amen.

# DAY 97

## CONFIDENT PEACE

*"As you sent me into the world, I have sent them into the world."*

JOHN 17:18

When God sent Jesus into the world, He knew it wasn't going to be an easy assignment. When Jesus sent us into the world, He likewise knew it wasn't going to be an easy assignment. That's why He said, "You can use My name. I give you My peace." It is not always easy to be a Jesus-follower. In the past we had the luxury of living in a nation where Christianity was celebrated by most but tolerated by all. That is not true today. Even people who claim to follow Jesus find it easier to keep our faith to ourselves and within our circle of friends than risk the confrontation or rejection we fear will come if we mention it to others. We need to live in His peace and stand in the authority of His name. These are gifts to us from Jesus, the Son of God, the Savior who died for our sins so that we might reap the blessings He lavishes upon us.

### • THINK ABOUT IT •

When a stand for Jesus and God's truth results in rejection, does the opposition make you angry, cause you to shut down, or motivate you to confidently stand in the gifts of Jesus' peace and authority?

*Prayer*

Heavenly Father, give me courage to stand for You, unashamed and unafraid, in the face of spiritual confrontation. Help me fix my eyes on You and stand in the power of Your name. May I guard my heart and mind and walk in Your peace. In Jesus' name, amen.

## ACTIVE FAITH

*"Be strong and do not give up, for your work will be rewarded."*

2 CHRONICLES 15:7

This is part of God's message to Judah's King Asa, who "did what was good and right in the eyes of the LORD his God." Like Asa, we will have to show great determination if we are going to see God's purposes through to the end. I believe the new birth is a miracle and a necessity. But the point of being birthed into the Kingdom of God is to complete the journey for which we were created. It will not be a passive process, nor will it happen accidentally. You will have to say, "God, I am not going to give up. I am going to finish this." Be happy that you can identify the beginning point of your spiritual journey, but make sure that your story is characterized in terms of what God is doing in your life now. Think of the steps of faith you are demonstrating in this season, of how you are growing up. When trials come, and they will, remember that your work will be rewarded in your days under the sun and in your eternity in Heaven.

### • THINK ABOUT IT •

Pursuing God's interests and purposes requires a measure of forethought and self-discipline. Endeavor to put your faith into action by spending time in God's Word, prayer, and serving His people.

*Prayer*

Heavenly Father, help me to persevere and put my faith into action. Show me how to train myself for godliness. Direct me to good instruction, people of prayer, and places to serve. I want my faith in You to be fruitful. In Jesus' name, amen.

# DAY 99

## BUILT UP AND BLESSED

*Therefore encourage one another and build each other up...*

1 THESSALONIANS 5:11

When I look across my own journey, I can tell you that God has always provided a voice of encouragement when I have needed it. It has not always come in the package I expected. I have typically wanted a massive choir singing a glorious anthem: "You are doing a great job! This is precisely the path you should be walking on! Don't stop!" I've never had a choir; but there has always been a voice, and it has often come from an unexpected person. He also has been faithful to send someone to encourage me at just the right time. I believe God is faithful to give each of us the encouragement we need, if we will be willing to listen. In the same way, we should be encouragers. It is selfish to crave encouragement yet not be willing to extend it to others. Ask the Holy Spirit to reveal to you the people who need to be encouraged and to give you the words to say. They will be blessed, and you will be too.

### • THINK ABOUT IT •

The Lord is at work in each of His followers. Ask Him for eyes to see His good work in fellow believers so that you can express thankfulness for what He is doing in them.

*Prayer*

Heavenly Father, You have so often encouraged my heart and strengthened me to accomplish good things in my life. Make me equally an encourager of Your purposes in others, helping me look for opportunities to say, "You are a blessing from God to me!" In Jesus' name, amen.

## PROOF OF IDENTITY

*Your words became for me a joy and the delight of my heart; for I have been called by Your name, O LORD God of hosts.*

JEREMIAH 15:16 • NASB®

Jeremiah was humbling himself before the Lord and reminding Him that he loved His words and was called by His name. When you believe in Jesus as the Messiah and submit to His lordship over your life, you become a new creation with a new name. What kind of name have you had? Have you been known as an angry person, a violent person, an immoral person, a self-righteous person, someone unwilling to believe? Just as certainly as you are a new creation in Christ, you are now known by His name: child of God, Jesus-follower, Christian. The power of God is present to help you become more like Him. Whatever you have done, His mercy is sufficient to forgive you. Whatever you have been, He can change you. The power of God will mean more to us and be more available to us if we will humble ourselves and lean into God's Word. Won't you commit to trust Him more fully today?

### • THINK ABOUT IT •

The only way to realize your true identity is to discover your identity in Christ Jesus. The One who made you knows exactly who He made you to be. To know who you truly are, start by knowing Him.

### *Prayer*

Heavenly Father, You can make all things new, including me. I trust Your work in me, My Creator and Redeemer. May my image increasingly reflect Your Son. I am in awe of Your workmanship in Your creation and in me. In Jesus' name, amen.

# DAY 101

## BEYOND THE COMFORT ZONE

*God, who set me apart from my mother's womb and called me by his grace, was pleased to reveal his Son in me so that I might preach him among the Gentiles...*

GALATIANS 1:15-16

We know him as Saul of Tarsus. When we meet him, he's a Pharisee, an observant Jewish man. He has been immersed in the study of Judaism since his childhood. He's a zealot who wants to persecute anyone who believes that Jesus is the Messiah. Until Acts 9, that is, when Jesus of Nazareth has a little meeting with Saul on the road to Damascus. Somewhere in the northern part of Israel, Saul is traveling and Jesus grabs him by the back of the neck—modern translation—and says, "What do you think you're doing, son? It's Me you're persecuting." Saul's a clever man, and he said, "Well, who are You, Lord?" and Saul of Tarsus becomes the Apostle Paul. There's an irony in Jesus choosing the most Jewish of His followers to be the messenger to the non-Jewish world. We shouldn't be surprised when God invites us to serve Him in a place that is out of our comfort zones. Paul, perhaps the greatest advocate for Christ the world will ever know, showed us that it can be done with great success and lasting impact.

### • THINK ABOUT IT •

Though not always comfortable, being a Christ-follower is rewarding, peace-giving, stabilizing, healing, encouraging, and empowering.

### *Prayer*

Heavenly Father, Paul set the standard for following Christ: He was "all in," no matter the cost. Help me learn what he knew—Your grace is sufficient. Holy Spirit, enable me to adapt, serve, and grow in every situation You bring me to. In Jesus' name, amen.

## UP CLOSE & PERSONAL

*You will call on me and come and pray to me, and I will listen to you. You will seek me and find me when you seek me with all your heart.*

JEREMIAH 29:12-13

I pray because I have experienced the power of prayer. Prayer is not a formal speech that we make in public religious gatherings. Prayer isn't something that professional religious people do. Prayer is opening your life, your thoughts, and your words to God in order to establish a loving relationship with Him. Many of us have used prayer as a measure of desperation: "When all else fails, pray!" What a sad way to approach God! That's like saying to your spouse, "Listen, if I can't find anyone else to love or care about, I'll talk to you. You are my response of last resort. You're okay with that, aren't you?" That's not much of a declaration of affirmation or value, yet we've acted that way toward God as if He somehow should be encouraged. Prayer is the stuff that sustains us, and not just because we feel comforted by it, but because it works. Determine in your heart to become a person of prayer. It will change your life.

### • THINK ABOUT IT •

God responds to spiritual "911" calls. But He wants to give you so much more of Himself than that. Rest assured: He who offers you His Son and His Spirit wants your relationship with Him to be close and personal.

### *Prayer*

Heavenly Father, I want to be a person of prayer. I need help, Holy Spirit, because I don't always know how to pray as I ought. Help me listen to Your heart also, as I pour out mine to You. In Jesus' name, amen.

# DAY 103

## CHANGE OF FOCUS

*Then I heard a loud voice in heaven say: "Now have come the salvation and the power and the kingdom of our God, and the authority of his Christ. For the accuser of our brothers, who accuses them before our God day and night, has been hurled down."*

### REVELATION 12:10

Satan is described here as "the accuser of the brothers." It is a role he plays throughout Scripture, and he is still actively opposing the people of God. He looks for every weakness, every flaw, every failure, every inconsistency, every ungodly thought, every ungodly activity. He will do his best to highlight those things and remind you of them in order to discredit you. You see, guilt is the key to our defeat. We will never pray with any authority, with any confidence, with any boldness, with any true faith, as long as we are more conscious of our failures than we are aware of what God has done on our behalf. Do not allow yourself to focus on your shortcomings and inadequacies. Focus on who God is, who you are in Him, and what He has promised to do in you and through you.

### • THINK ABOUT IT •

Agreeing with what God says about you—Cleansed! Justified! Chosen!—honors the finished work of Christ on your behalf. The enemy's accusations are an attempt to discredit Jesus' work on the cross. Don't buy into that. Jesus' sacrifice is effective for you!

### *Prayer*

Heavenly Father, I believe what You say about me, not what the accuser says. Teach me Your promises in Scripture so I can overcome the enemy's opposition. Thank You for working in me to complete Your good purposes for me. In Jesus' name, amen.

## WITH YOU

*Moses said to God, "Who am I, that I should go to Pharaoh and bring the Israelites out of Egypt?" And God said, "I will be with you."*

EXODUS 3:11-12

Moses had an interesting life story. As a baby, he was abandoned by his parents. While they had good intentions, he was still sent down the river—literally. Pharaoh's daughter fished him out and reared him in the palace as her son. Can you imagine the emotional pressure that brought? He knew that he was a Hebrew and that his people were enslaved while he was living with all of the advantages that came with being the son of Pharaoh's daughter. Moses was a confused and angry young man, and when he saw an Egyptian slave master mistreating a Hebrew, he murdered him. He ran for his life, and for forty years he was a sheepherder on the back side of the desert. One day God came for him, and his story began to change dramatically. No matter who you are, or where you are, or what you've done, God has a plan for your life. He can take your past, and turn it around, and give you a new future.

### • THINK ABOUT IT •

Our lives as Christ-followers are defined by the strength, mercy and wisdom of God on our behalf. His power is put on perfect display in our weakness. You can trust that God will be with you as you pursue Him.

*Prayer*

Heavenly Father, thank You that You go before me. Thank You that You are my strength. My life isn't perfect, but I choose today to put my trust in Your plans for me. Be glorified in my life. In Jesus' name, amen.

# DAY 105

## STRATEGIC TRAINING

*Though by this time you ought to be teachers, you need someone to teach you the elementary truths of God's word all over again. You need milk, not solid food!...But solid food is for the mature, who by constant use have trained themselves to distinguish good from evil.*

HEBREWS 5:12, 14

Most of us in Church World are educated far beyond our level of obedience. For most of us it's not about information; it's about our intent, our desire, and our willingness. The author of Hebrews says through constant use we train ourselves to distinguish good from evil. It's not automatic or intuitive, so if you're not in training for godliness, you will be deceived. Training is engaging in an activity today that will enable you to accomplish something in the future that you couldn't accomplish today. Unfortunately, many of us have confused training with trying. We've thought, "If I'm trying, that's enough." No, it isn't. Sincerity and trying are no substitute for training. Ask the Holy Spirit to help you learn the truths of God's Word and help you distinguish good from evil. He is a tutor like no other and is eager to respond to your desire for help.

### • THINK ABOUT IT •

Elements of physical training include repetition and resistance. Spiritual training requires the same: the repetition of making good choices informed by His Word and daily resisting temptation to do otherwise. Athletes are motivated by medals. The rewards God offers us are eternal.

### *Prayer*

Heavenly Father, resisting the urge to "skip a day" or more of Bible study or prayer requires exerting continual discipline. Holy Spirit, I invite You to put me in training. I want to progress to maturity in Christ. In Jesus' name, amen.

## YOUR FATHER SEES YOU

*"Then your Father, who sees what is done in secret, will reward you."*

MATTHEW 6:6

I have found a tremendous humility among the great prayer warriors I have known. If you are a person who is called to the ministry of prayer, you may be thinking, "I'm just a prayer person." You may think that because your ministry is not in view, that because your ministry takes place behind closed doors, you are less significant to the Kingdom than those whose callings are more public. I want to assure you that nothing could be further from the truth. I imagine that Jesus is smiling as He takes note of the hours you have spent in prayer for your brothers and sisters in Christ. I can picture the shouting in the heavenly realms when someone you have been interceding for decides to choose Jesus of Nazareth as Lord. Don't call the assignment God has given you small, and don't worry that it is done in secret. Jesus says, "Your Father sees you, and He will reward you."

· THINK ABOUT IT ·

To love the Lord and care about His agenda—to desire His Kingdom to come and His will be done—is the birthplace of prayer. If you ask Him, He will freely give you what you need to be an intercessor: an open, listening ear and His wisdom.

*Prayer*

Heavenly Father, You are working; let me labor beside You in prayer, echoing Your heart for those far from You. Your Word reveals Your intent, so I will fix my eyes on Your truth and proclaim it in hope. In Jesus' name, amen.

# DAY 107

## NOT FORSAKEN

*Then he continued, "Do not be afraid, Daniel. Since the first day that you set your mind to gain understanding and to humble yourself before your God, your words were heard, and I have come in response to them."*

DANIEL 10:12

If you want to pick a Bible character whose life should have been filled with despair, hopelessness, and resentment, it's Daniel. Most of his life was spent as a slave in a foreign country, with no hope of returning to his native land or seeing the rebirth of his people. Every external marker says Daniel's life should have been defined by bitterness, hatred, and anger—all of the things that come when your dreams have been put through the shredder—but the opposite is true of Daniel. He decided to honor the Lord no matter the cost, and he developed a relationship with the Lord that would be unique across the ages. The Bible says God is close to the brokenhearted. If you are filled with despair, if disappointment has flooded you, God has not abandoned you. He is standing there with you. I'm not diminishing your discomfort, but I'm telling you that God has not left you, and He has a wonderful plan for your life.

### • THINK ABOUT IT •

Disappointment fosters hopelessness and despair—even the idea that God has forsaken you. When emotions grow dark, choose to remember that God will never leave you nor forsake you. That is a relationship-building promise.

### Prayer

Heavenly Father, Daniel was certain of Your faithfulness and power because he devoted himself both to knowing Your Word and to prayer. Help me lift my eyes above my pain to see the promises of Your Word and open my heart to Your faithfulness. In Jesus' name, amen.

## HIS "GREATEST"

*"Anyone who breaks one of the least of these commandments and teaches others to do the same will be called least in the kingdom of heaven, but whoever practices and teaches these commands will be called great in the kingdom of heaven."*

MATTHEW 5:19

Jesus said we all are not going to receive the same reward when we step into eternity. You can be the least or the greatest, depending on what you've chosen to do with your life. People say, "Pastor, it doesn't matter to me—least, greatest—I just want to be a part." I think people are sincere, but I don't think they understand that they are showing tremendous disregard for the privilege of being a part of the Kingdom of God. When we say, "I don't care enough about it to give my best. I just want to get in the door," we're really saying that we don't attach much value to that gift. Don't allow your life to slip past you in mediocrity and lack of concern. Honor Him in difficult seasons. Turn away from evil and choose good. Serve His people. Invest in His Church. Do not be content with His "least" but strive toward His "greatest."

### • THINK ABOUT IT •

Giving our best to the Lord—in our homes, in the marketplace, in our houses of worship—requires intentionality. No matter your circumstance, look for opportunities today to honor Him both in private and in public.

### *Prayer*

Heavenly Father, loving You with all my heart means giving You my very best. May Your love spur me on to the good deeds You've prepared in advance for me to accomplish. I want my life to be marked by fruitful labor for Your Kingdom. In Jesus' name, amen.

# DAY 109

## FREE BUT NOT CHEAP

*"I tell you the truth, anyone who will not receive the kingdom of God like a little child will never enter it."*

MARK 10:15

God could have made becoming a disciple extraordinarily difficult. He could have made it so that only one percent of us would have the intellectual capacity to grasp it. A God who has the precision to put the Earth in its orbit around the sun, where the minutest variation would make life impossible on our planet, could have made the pursuit of Him—the pathway of discipleship—almost unknowable. He could have made it a complex mathematical equation that you'd spend your whole life studying just to begin to understand it. But God's not like that. It's not that He isn't all-knowing and all-powerful; it's that in order to help you and me, He has made the pathway simple. Romans 1:19-20 says that He has clearly revealed His power and glory in His creation so that every person can see Him and know Him. Following God is more about the condition of our hearts and minds and our intent. Nobody who seeks Him will miss Him. No one who truly wants to be a part of the Kingdom of God will be left out.

### • THINK ABOUT IT •

A child cannot secure his own well-being by his own efforts. He depends on and trusts the parent to do this for him. As a good father, God stands ready to extend His love, help, and guidance to you.

### Prayer

Heavenly Father, salvation from sin and reconciliation to You may be free, but it is not cheap. It cost You a great deal. Thank You that what I cannot do for myself, You have made possible through the cross of Your Son, Jesus. In His name I pray, amen.

## LET'S GET STARTED!

*Do not let this Book of the Law depart from your mouth; meditate on it day and night, so that you may be careful to do everything written in it.*

JOSHUA 1:8

How much attention do you give to reading the Bible? Personally, I intend to read my Bible every day—not just when I'm in the mood or when it's convenient—and I'm not going to read it randomly. I'm not going to open it and read wherever my finger falls. I'm going to read it intentionally, so that my mind will be focused on it. If we spend more time listening to sports talk than we do with the Word of God, that's where our hearts will be. If we follow the financial markets and spend more time with them than we do with the Word of God, that's what we will meditate on. Bible reading is a simple practice that reaps profound and transformational benefits in your life. If you spend about fifteen minutes a day reading the Bible, you'll read through the whole thing in a year. Don't worry about what day of the year you begin reading—just get started and see what the Lord will show you over the next 365 days!

• THINK ABOUT IT •

Because the Word of God is living, it is continually relevant. It is the only book that "reads" you while you are reading it. Don't miss out on the hope, insight, correction and encouragement it can give you.

*Prayer*

Heavenly Father, I need to feed my spirit even more than I need to feed my body. Encourage my heart through Your Word—may it instruct me in Your character and ways. Holy Spirit, help me to align my thoughts and actions with the Word of God. In Jesus' name, amen.

## SEEING THROUGH TEARS

*For many walk, of whom I often told you, and now tell you even weeping, that they are enemies of the cross of Christ, whose end is destruction, whose god is their appetite, and whose glory is in their shame, who set their minds on earthly things. For our citizenship is in heaven, from which also we eagerly wait for a Savior, the Lord Jesus Christ...*

PHILIPPIANS 3:18-20 • NASB®

It is a terrifying thought that Almighty God identifies people who have not accepted Jesus as Savior as "enemies" of the redemptive work of Jesus. Paul writes through tears that their god is their appetite, they glory in their shame, and they have set their minds on earthly things. The price they will pay is eternal destruction. In contrast, those who follow Jesus are strangers in this world, pilgrims who are passing through for a season but whose citizenship is elsewhere. We should, like Paul, see those without Christ through our tears. Do not ever become hardened to the condition of the unsaved people around you. Instead, commit to living in such a way that they will want to know the source of your joy and contentment.

• THINK ABOUT IT •

By God's grace, Paul changed from being a man murderously hostile to Christians to a man foremost in his devotion and service to Jesus. Never underestimate God's power to deliver and save those who seem far from God.

## Prayer

Heavenly Father, You have made Your light shine in my heart. Let my life now bring Your light into every place You assign me. Open the eyes of the lost around me to be able to see Your light and come toward You in faith. In Jesus' name, amen.

## ABSOLUTE AND STEADFAST

*Jesus answered them, "Is it not written in your Law, 'I have said you are "gods"'? If he called them 'gods,' to whom the word of God came—and Scripture cannot be set aside—what about the one whom the Father set apart as his very own and sent into the world?"*

JOHN 10:34-38

What title did Jesus give to Scripture? He called it the Word of God. It is significant that Jesus understood Scripture to be God's Word to us. He didn't say, "It was written by people. It was written over a long period of time. It's hard to understand." Instead, He revealed its authority: "It cannot be broken. It's a certainty. It's more certain than a physical law." If there are immutable spiritual principles available to you and me, it would be in our best interest to know them. It's popular these days to say the Old Testament is not relevant because we have a new covenant that has superseded it. If that were true, don't you think Jesus would have clued us in? Jesus accepted the Old Testament Scriptures without question. He accepted their authority as the inspired Word of God. He based all of His teaching on the Scriptures and spent His entire life obeying them and fulfilling them. We are Jesus-followers; because He attached tremendous authority to Scripture, we should too.

### • THINK ABOUT IT •

There will always be skeptics, but Christ-followers who trust God's Word can powerfully turn up the light of God's truth in the world.

### *Prayer*

Heavenly Father, Your Word will not pass away; not one word of Yours has ever failed. I hope in Your Word, knowing it can keep my heart strengthened and my way pure. I acknowledge its authority and receive Your Word with faith. In Jesus' name, amen.

## MINDSET MISS

*But He turned and said to Peter, "Get behind Me, Satan! You are a stumbling block to Me; for you are not setting your mind on God's interests, but man's."*

MATTHEW 16:23 • NASB®

Peter had been personally recruited by Jesus and had spent three years watching His ministry. They were on their way to Jerusalem, and Jesus began to tell the twelve who were closest to Him what would happen when they arrived—His betrayal, arrest, and passion. When Peter took Jesus aside and said, "May that never happen to you!" Jesus' rebuke was swift and harsh. Peter was a part of the inner circle, a disciple, a trusted friend of Jesus. Yet Peter missed what God was saying because of his mindset. From that we can deduce that it is possible for us to be church folks, check all the boxes, do all the things that go with being God's people, and still have our heart and mind in the wrong place. If that's your circumstance today, don't defend it or justify it. Say, "Lord, help me! I want to set my heart and mind on You."

• THINK ABOUT IT •

A mindset that obscures God's perspective can come from wanting to prevent unpleasant circumstances. Guarding our hearts and minds each day with God's Word will help us keep our eyes on His perspective.

*Prayer*

Heavenly Father, Your Word renews my mind and helps me set my heart on You. I want to put Your interests first, and I need Your help to clear out the clutter of self-interest and anxious doubts to gain single-minded focus on You. In Jesus' name, amen.

## EVER PRESENT POWER

*You know what has happened…how God anointed Jesus of Nazareth with the Holy Spirit and power, and how he went around doing good and healing all who were under the power of the devil, because God was with him.*

ACTS 10:37-38

The Bible tells us that Jesus is the same yesterday, today, and forever. Just as certainly as He was anointed with the Holy Spirit in power, and went around doing good, and healing all who were oppressed by the Devil in the first century, the Spirit of Christ is moving in the earth today—doing good, and healing those who are under the power of the Devil. That's the good news that the Church has. That's the light we hold up in a dark world: There is power present, under the direction of the Holy Spirit, to bring freedom and liberty to every human life, even those who are enslaved to evil. Do not ever underestimate the power of the Lord to move in our world and change the hearts of people. Even those who seem too far away from God to ever find redemption can believe in the Lord Jesus Christ and be saved.

### • THINK ABOUT IT •

Jesus said that the Kingdom of God was like a mustard seed that kept growing. His story didn't end in the first century nor did the work of the Holy Spirit in His Church. Ask the Lord for your assignment in His Kingdom expansion plans in your generation.

### *Prayer*

Heavenly Father, Your Church is still growing, and You are still working with us to confirm Your Word in our day. Let captives be set free and the authority of Jesus be demonstrated as we proclaim the good news to our generation. In Jesus' name, amen.

## GOD REALLY DID SAY

*Now the serpent was more crafty than any of the wild animals the LORD God had made. He said to the woman, "Did God really say...?"*

GENESIS 3:1

The Bible doesn't tell us how Satan came to be present in the Garden of Eden, but we do know his intent. He came to Eve and asked, "Did God really say?" All these millennia later, his tactics haven't changed; he is still challenging the authority of God's Word in my life and yours. How many times do you have a God-thought and the next thing that pops in your head is, "Can you really believe that? Do you really think that will bring better things to you? I have a better idea." He tempted Adam and Eve to believe that God was an oppressive force who wanted to keep them from realizing their full potential. Isn't that the same lie that percolates in your heart and mine? That seeking righteousness will somehow keep us from experiencing the best life has to offer, and if you'll rebel against God and cast off restraint, everything will be better? "Did God really say?" Yes, He really did.

### • THINK ABOUT IT •

Compare Eve's encounter with Satan to Jesus' in Matthew 4:3-11. Unlike Eve, Jesus put ultimate value and trust in the authority of God's Word: He knew it precisely, applied it accurately, obeyed it completely. His was the victorious outcome.

### *Prayer*

Heavenly Father, Your Word always proves true and gives life. Help me honor Your Word completely by obeying it. When the enemy challenges the authority and trustworthiness of Your Word, let faith in Your Word be my response. In Jesus' name, amen.

## CULTIVATING JOY

*Though you have not seen him, you love him; and even though you do not see him now, you believe in him and are filled with an inexpressible and glorious joy...*

1 PETER 1:8

I have found that contentment can be difficult to find and keep. We chase many things, but we are not content even when we attain them. The real key is understanding what brings fulfillment. The Bible says we are body, soul, and spirit. You live in a body, and your body finds fulfillment in pleasure. Pleasure was God's idea, but if you spend your life chasing it, you probably will miss the Kingdom of God. Your soul is your mind, will, and emotions. They find fulfillment in happiness, which also was God's idea. If you make every decision based on your happiness, however, you probably will miss the Kingdom of God. Your spirit is the part of you created most in God's image because it is eternal. Your spirit finds fulfillment in joy, and you can have joy in the Lord and His faithfulness even in unpleasant circumstances. When we find joy in the Lord, everything else will fall into place.

· THINK ABOUT IT ·

Jesus wants His joy to be in you and your joy to be made full (John 15:11). You can make space and preparation for this joy—sow the seeds for it—by spending time in God's Word.

*Prayer*

Heavenly Father, teach me the difference between happiness and joy. I don't want my emotions or circumstances to determine my contentment. Holy Spirit, let joy rise up in my spirit as I listen to and align with Your Word. In Jesus' name, amen.

# DAY 117

## LIFE AND PEACE

*Those who live according to the sinful nature have their minds set on what that nature desires; but those who live in accordance with the Spirit have their minds set on what the Spirit desires. The mind of sinful man is death, but the mind controlled by the Spirit is life and peace...*

ROMANS 8:5-6

I am more aware than I have ever been of my need for the Holy Spirit. The redemptive work of Jesus is an accomplished fact—nothing can be added to it, and nothing can be taken from it. But understanding that gift and implementing it fully are only possible with the help of the Holy Spirit. The thought that the Spirit of Almighty God would want to know me and participate in my life is an incredibly humbling thing. Why would He do that? I am inconsistent, even on my best day, yet He is ready to help whenever I turn to Him. He is my friend, and I want to make sure He is an everyday part of my life. I want to welcome Him into my thoughts and behaviors more than ever before.

### • THINK ABOUT IT •

Jesus promised three times to send the Holy Spirit to His disciples. The presence and work of the Holy Spirit—His help and counsel—is "mission critical" to God's purposes being established on the earth and in your life.

*Prayer*

Heavenly Father, I welcome Your Holy Spirit into my life and want to cooperate with Him. Forgive me for the times that I have either ignored or grieved Him. I need His help now more than ever. In Jesus' name, amen.

## FREEDOM LESSONS

*The LORD called to Moses and spoke to him from the Tent of Meeting. He said, "Speak to the Israelites and say to them: 'When any of you brings an offering to the LORD, bring as your offering an animal from either the herd or the flock.'"*

### LEVITICUS 1:1-2

Thus begins the book of Leviticus. The Israelites had been Egyptian slaves for hundreds of years. They knew about the Egyptian gods, the Egyptian forms of worship, and the Egyptian holy days. But they were brand new to freedom, and they had to be taught how to worship their Almighty God. He told the priests how to conduct the necessary hygiene practices, how to prepare a place of worship, and what sacrifices were acceptable. It's very clear when you read Leviticus that true worship does not come intuitively to humans; we must learn how to turn our hearts toward the Lord. That's a significant lesson for us today. We learn how to come to church and not embarrass ourselves, what to wear and say, when to sit and stand. But learning to truly worship God is something entirely different: It is an attitude of the heart.

### • THINK ABOUT IT •

The Lord is seeking those who will worship Him "in spirit and truth" (John 4:23). Learning to turn your heart toward the Lord in an attitude of honor, humility, and gratitude pleases Him and will mature you in countless ways.

### Prayer

Heavenly Father, I want to offer You a sacrifice of praise from my heart, honoring Your holiness and majesty. Holy Spirit, create true praise on my lips to the God and Father of my Lord Jesus Christ. In Jesus' name, amen.

## HIS REWARD IS WITH HIM

*He humbled himself and became obedient to death—even death on a cross!*
*Therefore God exalted him to the highest place and gave him the name that*
*is above every name...*

PHILIPPIANS 2:8-9

On the cross, Jesus was our substitute, taking the punishment we deserved. But during His days on the earth, Jesus also modeled the pathway to victorious living. Our attention is often drawn to those demonstrations of His power when He would still a storm, or cast out a demon, or heal a broken body. But Jesus also laid down His will and His comfort to fully pursue the purposes of God. His submission brought God's unique blessing, when God gave Him "the name that is above every name." We must know the cross in both of those ways. We enter the Kingdom of God by faith in the death of Jesus on our behalf. But we also accept His invitation to take up our cross and lay down our preferences in order to fully embrace God's purposes. Just as certainly as God rewarded Jesus, I believe God will reward you and me.

### • THINK ABOUT IT •

The willingness to obey God, whatever that costs and wherever it leads, brings great reward. Ask the Holy Spirit for greater clarity about what He is asking of you.

*Prayer*

Heavenly Father, I lay down my preferences in order to fully embrace Your purposes. Strengthen me in my resolve to obey You and persevere. Your eternal rewards far outweigh my troubles. In Jesus' name, amen.

## SOURCE DETERMINES CEILING

*Wealth and honor come from you; you are the ruler of all things. In your hands are strength and power to exalt and give strength to all.*

### 1 CHRONICLES 29:12

God is the source of every good thing in our lives. I want you to get that grounded in your heart because the ceiling of your potential will be determined by the source of your life. If your source is rooted in your physical strength, your intellect, your income, your education, your family, or your friends, that will set the ceiling of your life. If God is your source, then the ceiling of your potential is the ceiling set by an all-knowing, all-powerful God—and that's an upgrade over anything this world has to offer. We are the people of God, and He wants to share with us His wealth, honor, strength, and power. When you truly believe that and allow that belief to influence your daily life, it will change the whole scenario for your life story and for your children and the generations who will follow.

### • THINK ABOUT IT •

God is our everlasting Source—all others deteriorate and diminish. Are you depending on something or someone other than God and His provision? Would you be willing let Him raise your ceiling of potential?

*Prayer*

Heavenly Father, You alone can continually sustain, renew, and replenish me. Your power on my behalf is never exhausted. Your abundant grace is all-sufficient. Strengthen me to reach the full potential You have designed into me. In Jesus' name, amen.

## DOORS OF POSSIBILITY

*One of those days Jesus went out to a mountainside to pray, and spent the night praying to God. When morning came, he called his disciples to him and chose twelve of them...*

LUKE 6:12-13

This passage suggests to me that Jesus went to the mountain to pray, and one hour turned to two hours, then it just spilled over into an all-night prayer meeting with His Father. When He came back from that night in prayer, He selected the twelve men who would be His closest followers and helpers, the men who would continue His work after He was gone. This is the Son of God, who left Heaven to live among us as a man, yet even He did not make such an important decision without spending hours in prayer. Prayer matters. When we ignore God's invitations to have these intimate conversations with Him and fail to pray, we leave closed the doors of God's opportunities in our lives. When we take prayer seriously and practice it diligently, we open doors of possibility for God to work in our lives. I want to be a person of prayer.

### · THINK ABOUT IT ·

Going a long time without prayer begets isolation and cuts you off from God. Today, choose to fill the "dead air" between you and the Lord with conversation and praise.

*Prayer*

Heavenly Father, You have given me a unique voice. Deliver me from all doubt that my voice matters to You—that You eagerly wait for me to talk with You. Strengthen me to stand in Your presence, share my heart, and listen with hope. In Jesus' name, amen.

## ORDER AND BEAUTY

*In the beginning God created the heavens and the earth. Now the earth was formless and empty, darkness was over the surface of the deep, and the Spirit of God was hovering over the waters.*

GENESIS 1:1-2

The creation account in Genesis stirs my imagination about God, the world He created, and His relationship with me. A dark, formless, and empty place was brought into order and beauty and usefulness by the intelligence and creativity of God and the sheer authority of His will to bring His plan to fruition. It's very humbling to realize that the same Spirit of God that was present before time began lives within me and wants to empower me today. I'm filled with gratitude that the same power that brought order and beauty out of chaos is available to bring order and beauty out of the difficult situations of my life. Life is more complicated than we would like. When it seems confusing and chaotic, ask the Lord for a fresh vision of His ability to create something beautiful and a fresh filling of His Holy Spirit to guide you through.

### • THINK ABOUT IT •

The Holy Spirit's power to bring peace and order where there is confused disorder can transform you from being one who is overwhelmed by challenges to being one who overwhelmingly conquers (Romans 8:37). You have Someone who can and wants to help.

### *Prayer*

Heavenly Father, You bring order and beauty to my life's story. Holy Spirit, I invite You in to quell the confusion and restore peace here, specifically _____. Thank You for the grace to conquer my challenges and not be overwhelmed. In Jesus' name, amen.

# DAY 123

## WELCOME TO THE NEIGHBORHOOD!

*How can they believe in the one of whom they have not heard? And how can they hear without someone preaching to them?*

ROMANS 10:14

Do you make a habit of inviting new neighbors to church? When people move to a new community, they have broken some ties. They may have moved away from family, friends, schools, and activities. People who are new to your community are eager to form new bonds and uniquely receptive to an invitation. Whether they are believers of many years or have never sung a hymn, the most powerful, single factor in someone coming to your church is a personal invitation—not a card they get in the mail, not an invitation on social media, but a personal invitation. We have enormous potential for making a difference in people's lives by doing this one thing. I want to encourage you to begin to invite people to join you for church. If you meet someone who is new to the community, let your smile show that you're excited about extending an invitation to something good. Then simply say, "Won't you visit my church?"

### • THINK ABOUT IT •

Not waiting for us to come to Him, Jesus came to seek and to save us. Ask the Lord for fresh ideas of how you too can take the initiative in your neighborhood by extending invitations to church.

### *Prayer*

Heavenly Father, help me be a good neighbor by reaching out to those around me with friendly invitations to visit my church. Go before me and prepare their hearts. Make my conversations with them gracious, and draw them to Your Son. In Jesus' name, amen.

## PURSUING RIGHTEOUSNESS

*Righteousness exalts a nation, but sin is a disgrace to any people.*

PROVERBS 14:34

God wants to bring good things to us. The challenge is understanding how to respond to God so that we can facilitate His best in our lives. First we need to realize how serious sin is and how it affects us. There is nothing frivolous about sin and its repercussions. We tend to laugh it off and think that it is not a big deal, but that is wrong. Scripture says it is a disgrace. When we seek righteousness, which simply means right standing with God, the ability to come into the presence of God without guilt, shame, or condemnation, then we will be exalted, or promoted. This is true of a nation, but it's also true of an individual, a family, a community, and a congregation. Righteousness is not an accident; it does not occur by happenstance. Righteousness requires an intentional desire to be closer to God, and then acting on that desire. Righteousness is a worthwhile goal for anyone who wants to grow in spiritual maturity and strength, and I invite you to pursue it with your whole heart.

· THINK ABOUT IT ·

Though you cannot earn the gift of righteousness, you can pursue the practice of it. Scripture describes the results of righteousness as peace, quietness, and confidence (Isaiah 32:17), so your pursuit will be well worth it.

*Prayer*

Heavenly Father, You love righteousness and call me to pursue it wholeheartedly. Help me walk rightly before You, obeying Your commands and showing integrity, purity, and uprightness in all my dealings, thoughts, and speech. In Jesus' name, amen.

# DAY 125

## NO SUGARCOATING

*Dear friends, I urge you, as aliens and strangers in the world, to abstain from sinful desires, which war against your soul.*

### 1 PETER 2:11

Can we be honest enough to say that even though we come to church and have Bibles and give our time and money, there is still a war going on in our mind, will, and emotions? We are created by God, in the image of God, with an awareness of good and evil; that is why there is a conflict in us. Being a pastor doesn't remove me from that arena of conflict. I sincerely desire to conduct myself in such a way that the blessings of God can fill my life. Candidly, it often feels like a battle is being fought inside me. I have thoughts that don't reflect godliness at all. Peter doesn't deny or even sugarcoat this. He says very bluntly, "Abstain from sinful things, because there's a war in you." I want to be careful about which side of the battle I send ammunition to, and that's why I'm very careful about what I put in front of my eyes and what I allow to go in my ears.

### • THINK ABOUT IT •

Apostle Paul said that not all things are profitable and not all things edify. Are there behaviors, patterns of thought or entertainment in your life that aren't helpful to your life as a Christ-follower? Wisdom would counsel removing them and replacing them with what will build up your faith.

### *Prayer*

Heavenly Father, give me wisdom and self-discipline to make better choices that will sow into my life what Your Holy Spirit desires. Help me weed out what would choke my faith and make my life unfruitful. In Jesus' name, amen.

## UNRIVALED PRIVILEGE

*The LORD upholds all who fall and lifts up all who are bowed down. The eyes of all look to you, and you give them their food at the proper time.*

PSALM 145:14-15

We sometimes act as if prayer is a tedious task to be performed: "She's not going to let us eat until someone asks God to bless the food." Or we turn to it as a last-ditch effort when we're feeling desperate: "Nothing I've tried has helped my condition. I guess I might as well try praying about it." If we couldn't pray, if there was no one to pray to, if there was no one to listen, if we didn't have the hope of prayer, life would be unbearable. If I were left to my resources, my wisdom, and my strength alone with no imagination of God's provision and help, I couldn't face another day. The God of the universe has offered to have a relationship with us, and prayer is one of the ways we let that relationship unfold. Prayer is not a burden. Prayer is a privilege.

### • THINK ABOUT IT •

Think about your practice of prayer. Have you held the notion that prayer is a burden? If so, humble yourself before the Lord and ask Him to help you embrace it as the great privilege that it is.

*Prayer*

Heavenly Father, forgive me for when I have depended on other sources than You. Your Word reveals that You are attentive to the voice of Your people. Help me to call out to You first in expectant prayer, rejoicing in the privilege. In Jesus' name, amen.

# DAY 127

## PERFECTED POWER

*But he said to me, "My grace is sufficient for you, for my power is made perfect in weakness." Therefore I will boast all the more gladly about my weaknesses, so that Christ's power may rest on me.*

2 CORINTHIANS 12:9

Paul had asked the Lord three times to remove a physical problem he had, a "thorn" in his flesh (v. 7). Paul knew that he would become conceited without the imperfection, and he had come to be grateful for this enforced humility that kept him dependent on God's power. In this generation, it would be easy to think the strength of our lives resides in our intellect, our education, our financial assets, our determination, and our contact list. Those things are blessings and gifts, but the greatest challenges of our lives are the challenges that we can't outthink, that we are not physically capable of resolving, that our financial resources are inadequate for. Life presents challenges to all of us, and we need to recognize that the real power in our lives comes from the Lord.

· THINK ABOUT IT ·

Fear comes to us when our trust in the things of this world fails. Faith comes when we begin to trust God more than we trust in anything or anyone else. Where can you begin to trust God more?

*Prayer*

Heavenly Father, I am grateful that Your grace is enough for any challenge I might face. Help me to depend on Your power alone to accomplish all You desire in my life. May I rejoice even in my weaknesses, that Jesus might be exalted. In His name, amen.

## GOATS IN A TREE

*The Sovereign LORD is my strength; he makes my feet like the feet of a deer, he enables me to tread on the heights.*

HABAKKUK 3:19

Ein Gedi is one of my favorite places in Israel, and if you visit you will see acacia trees. We would call them overgrown bushes; they are just a few feet tall, and the branches are very slender. One of the amazing sights there is to see a Nubian ibex, a small mountain goat, climbing the acacia trees! They jump from the ground up onto small branches. Then, even as the branches are swaying, they catch their footing and eat the leaves. It's pretty strange to see goats standing in a tree! When the prophet says that God will make my feet like the feet of a deer and I'll be able to climb the heights, I picture those sure-footed mountain goats. God has enabled them not only to frolic along the mountain cliffs but to stand in improbable places, and He will do the same for us. He'll give us firm footing so that people will say, "Only God could have caused that to happen."

### • THINK ABOUT IT •

Can you cite a place and time in life when it would have been impossible to stand safely and securely without God's help? Did it help prepare you for the next time that happened?

### Prayer

Heavenly Father, when the ground shifts beneath my feet, You can keep my footing sure. When foundations crumble, You enable me to stand firm on our Rock, unshaken and trusting. Therefore, I need not fall headlong into fear or doubt. In Jesus' name, amen.

## CHURCH WITH A CAPITAL "C"

*"I will build my church, and the gates of Hades will not overcome it."*

MATTHEW 16:18

I grew up attending church, but church was not really a meaningful thing to me as a young person. I came to faith outside of the organized church, and I did what I could to avoid it for a season. When the Holy Spirit brought this verse alive for me, it changed the course of my life. When I realized that Jesus was in the business of building His Church, I understood that my life assignment had to be somewhere along those lines as well. Today I'm an advocate for the Church—not a particular denomination, but the Church with a capital "C." We have underestimated the role and the significance of the Church. The gathering of God's people to fulfill the purposes of God in the earth is the most powerful force for the transformation of human beings that our world has ever seen, and I am weary of hearing the Church maligned and criticized. Jesus Himself is establishing His Church in the earth, and I want to be a part of that.

### · THINK ABOUT IT ·

The Lord has given every one of His followers a gift to be used to build up His Body, the Church (Ephesians 4:7, 12-13). As a Christ-follower you have something to contribute that will help others grow up in Christ, and you are needed.

*Prayer*

Heavenly Father, Church isn't a building; it's Jesus' Body, and I want to serve Him. How can I use what You've given me to build up Your Church and help others grow up in Christ? Let Your Kingdom come and lives be transformed. In Jesus' name, amen.

## OUR SURVIVAL DEPENDS ON IT

*When the trumpets sounded, the people shouted, and at the sound of the trumpet, when the people gave a loud shout, the wall collapsed; so every man charged straight in, and they took the city.*

JOSHUA 6:20

The account of Joshua and the Israelites conquering the walled city of Jericho is a well-known Old Testament story. God had promised Abram this land back in Genesis 12. But the Israelites had a big shock when they got there: Someone was already living in their land, and the only way they could take it was to go to battle. The emphasis when we hear this story taught is usually about seeing God's power at work when we do what He says. That's certainly true, but I'd like for you to consider a different aspect of the story: In principle, all the rights and privileges of the Kingdom of God come to us when we become Christ-followers. But experientially, we must learn how to engage in spiritual warfare in order to overcome our adversary. You will not find all God created you for, all God intends you to be through the redemptive work of Jesus, until you know how to address the adversaries of the purposes of God.

· THINK ABOUT IT ·

As seriously as new military recruits train in the care and use of their weapons—because their survival in combat depends on it—we must train in the exercise of our spiritual weapons, beginning with the Word of God, which Paul called "the sword of the Spirit" (Ephesians 6:17).

*Prayer*

Heavenly Father, I need to learn how to engage wisely in spiritual warfare, beginning with knowing and rightly handling Your Word of truth. I rely on Your promise to train me for battle (Psalm 144:1), armed with Your sword, protected by Your shield. In Jesus' name, amen.

## HIS INDESCRIBABLE GIFT

*Carrying his own cross, he went out to the place of the Skull (which in Aramaic is called Golgotha). There they crucified him...*

JOHN 19:17-18

The essence of our story as Christ-followers is the cross. When I say the cross, I mean Jesus' death, burial, and resurrection. We have no message, no hope apart from that. It is the anchor of our faith and the foundation of who we are as a people. Death on a cross was a torturous ordeal intended by those who utilized the practice to intimidate their enemies into submission. The idea was that if you crucified someone in a public place, it was so horrific that it would quell any thought of rebellion. When Hollywood has attempted to depict crucifixion accurately, it has been nearly impossible to watch. The symbol of the cross has become the most identifiable symbol of our faith. It is hung on walls as home décor, worn as jewelry, and used on business cards. I have no problem with that, but my hope is that we will always see the cross for what it is—the place of our Lord's death on our behalf—and be reminded to thank Him for His indescribable gift.

· THINK ABOUT IT ·

If the depths of suffering Jesus endured on the cross on our behalf are kept in view, worship and obedience toward God will flow. Remember what it cost Him. May we "never boast except in the cross of our Lord Jesus Christ..." (Galatians 6:14).

*Prayer*

Heavenly Father, what inexpressible love You have for me that You presented Your Son, Jesus, as a sacrifice of atonement on my behalf. I receive Your gift of righteousness by faith and worship You with thanksgiving. In Jesus' name, amen.

## FINDING OUR VOICE

*"Judge for yourselves whether it is right in God's sight to obey you rather than God. For we cannot help speaking about what we have seen and heard."*

ACTS 4:19-20

Over 240 years ago, our forefathers courageously stood for a set of values and lifestyle, declaring independence from England. Today, we have to find the courage to make new choices. It is not enough for this generation to point to our heritage and say that we have been a Christian nation. It is not enough for us to point to our Constitution, or Declaration of Independence, or Bill of Rights, or our history of other godly choices. We have questions before us in this generation: What kind of people will we be? What are we going to hand to the generations who follow us? Will we stand for God's truth and against ungodly forces? Our values, and the spiritual forces shaping our lives, are being challenged. The Church of Jesus Christ has been quiet too long in the midst of many other voices growing increasingly stronger. The Church needs to find its voice. Do we have the courage to own our faith publicly the same way the generations before us did?

• THINK ABOUT IT •

Have you ever been reluctant to speak up for God and His values in an arena of opposition? Would you begin to ask the Lord for help in finding your voice and giving renewed expression to His goodness?

*Prayer*

Heavenly Father, I celebrate the freedom of the cross. Forgive me for when I have been silent about Your truth. Restore the voice of Your people, and give us the courage to consistently identify with and honor You in every arena. In Jesus' name, amen.

# DAY 133

## THE BEGINNING AND THE END

*The scepter will not depart from Judah, nor the ruler's staff from between his feet, until he comes to whom it belongs and the obedience of the nations is his.*

GENESIS 49:10

We often imagine that the Old Testament is pretty much separate from the New Testament. It's as if at the end of Malachi, God wanted a fresh start—a new brand, if you will—the creative team met in a heavenly conference room, and out of that they launched the Jesus-initiative. In reality, the Jesus-story starts in the first verses of the Bible and continues through the last page. God has always had a purpose and a plan—for His Son, and for His people. Do not allow the world to tell you that our world was a cosmic accident. Do not believe the lie that Jesus was just a good man who lived and died. Do not buy into the message that you are just another random genetic combination. God, who has known the end from the beginning, sent His Son, the Lion of Judah, in order that you could have a life of joy and purpose. The more fully we comprehend that, the more we can choose to lead victorious lives.

### • THINK ABOUT IT •

You are not irrelevant to God. Your life is purposely planned for by God and desired by Him. Through Jesus, His purposes for You can be accomplished even now, if you will follow Him.

### *Prayer*

Heavenly Father, Your eternal plan was to provide redemption to all who would receive Jesus. The failures of men and angels haven't thwarted You. Your Kingdom will come; Your will assuredly will be done on earth as it is in Heaven. In Jesus' name, amen.

## LET'S PRAY!

*"You will call upon Me and come and pray to Me, and I will listen to you. You will seek Me and find Me when you search for Me with all your heart."*

JEREMIAH 29:12-13 • NASB®

You interact with people all day, every day. You talk to the produce person at the grocery. You talk to your children's teachers. You talk to your neighbors. You ask them how they're doing, and they give you a short answer or a long one. There are an unprecedented number of God-opportunities in the communication that comes toward you every day. We have a two-word response among our congregation that helps us invite God into those conversations: "Let's pray!" When someone says, "I'm dragging today. My baby didn't sleep well last night," say, "Let's pray." Then drop your head and say, "God, help this family have a good day and sleep better tonight. In Jesus' name, amen." Then look back up and move right on with your conversation. "I'm worried about my husband. He's tired and on the road." "Let's pray. Lord, please give him a safe journey. In Jesus' name, amen." Let's be known as people who open the door of God's possibility any time someone unlocks it. Let's pray!

• THINK ABOUT IT •

Ask the Holy Spirit to enable you to listen to people in a new way and recognize where you have been given the cue to invite God's power into their lives. Jesus often asked hurting people, "What do you want me to do for you?" and then proceeded to meet their perceived needs.

*Prayer*

Heavenly Father, help me make the most of every opportunity to invite a "Let's pray!" encounter with You. Grant me the compassionate boldness I need for that. I want to see Your Kingdom draw near in the lives of people around me. In Jesus' name, amen.

# DAY 135

## COUNTED WORTHY

*They called the apostles in and had them flogged. Then they ordered them not to speak in the name of Jesus, and let them go. The apostles left the Sanhedrin, rejoicing because they had been counted worthy of suffering disgrace for the Name.*

ACTS 5:40-41

Some of the apostles had been put in jail for speaking about Jesus. An angel released them and told them to go back to the Temple and tell the story again. So they did. When the Sanhedrin discovered that they were missing, they sent soldiers to bring them in for questioning. The Sanhedrin spared them from death but had them flogged, and the apostles left rejoicing. My question is this: If the angel is capable of letting them out of prison, wouldn't you think the angel would have arranged an ending that didn't include torture? Are you prepared to walk a pathway where God supernaturally intervenes but doesn't diminish the pain of the journey? I've heard people talk about the intervention of God as if He is going to take away all the uncomfortable things. That thought can't be supported scripturally, but Scripture does give us examples of people like these, who rejoiced in being counted worthy of suffering for the name of Jesus.

### • THINK ABOUT IT •

The faith that allows us to endure hardships and suffering is built up by spending time with the Lord, His Word, and His people.

*Prayer*

Heavenly Father, it takes courage to yield to Your will in the midst of suffering. May faith-honoring courage inform my responses to pain and even persecution, and my first reaction be rejoicing in being found worthy to stand the test. In Jesus' name, amen.

## STILL SERVING AND SEEKING

*I, John, your brother and companion in the suffering and kingdom and patient endurance that are ours in Jesus, was on the island of Patmos because of the word of God and the testimony of Jesus. On the Lord's Day I was in the Spirit, and I heard behind me a loud voice like a trumpet...*

REVELATION 1:9-10

When we meet John in the book of Revelation, he is an old man on the small island of Patmos. The emperor Domitian demanded that the royal family be worshiped as gods. John would not, of course; thus we find him living in exile. On the Lord's Day, when he was in the Spirit, he heard a loud voice and turned to see his beloved Savior. The message Jesus had for John that day is thrilling as we contemplate what is to come. I love the thought of Jesus appearing to John, who had been His faithful friend and servant. Undoubtedly, the Holy Spirit had given John great insight over his many years, and he was counted worthy to receive and convey this important message. At the end of my days, I want to be like John—still serving, still seeking the Holy Spirit, and counted worthy to be called His friend.

### • THINK ABOUT IT •

Arriving to old age still full of vitality and useful work—this is one of the blessings a life-long friendship with Jesus can bring. The best is yet to be if you commit to following Him.

### *Prayer*

Heavenly Father, I desire to be still bearing fruit for Your Kingdom in my old age. Keep renewing my youth like the eagle's and let my strength equal my days. I want to finish well, still serving and seeking You. In Jesus' name, amen.

# DAY 137

## POWER TO DELIVER

*The LORD is my rock, my fortress and my deliverer; my God is my rock, in whom I take refuge. He is my shield and the horn of my salvation, my stronghold. I call to the LORD, who is worthy of praise, and I am saved from my enemies.*

PSALM 18:2-3

The fundamental presentation of the Bible is that the God we worship is a Deliverer. From the book of Genesis to the book of Revelation, the Creator of Heaven and Earth repeatedly steps into time to deliver His people. We have a tendency to reject the deliverance of God when it doesn't come in the package we are expecting or it doesn't suit our preferences. Our God is sovereign, however, and in His grace and mercy He intervenes in our lives in the way that He knows is best. This is much easier to see in hindsight than in the moment, but trusting Him during times of crisis is one of the ways we increase our faith. We have a wonderful message to tell the world: You are not left to face the challenges of life alone, in your strength and your power. The power of God is greater than any earthly power, and He wants to use it to deliver you! Hallelujah!

### · THINK ABOUT IT ·

Whom can you help experience God's deliverance by praying for them or helping them to persevere until they receive their rescue?

*Prayer*

Heavenly Father, thank You for being a God of deliverance—deliverance from fears within and troubles without. I resist the bitterness that would displace hope with my anxious demands, and I declare my trust in Your timing and plan. In Jesus' name, amen.

## GOOD MESSAGING

*I am not ashamed of the gospel, because it is the power of God for the salvation of everyone who believes: first for the Jew, then for the Gentile.*

ROMANS 1:16

I suspect you know that the word gospel means "good news," and more than just "good news" as opposed to "bad news." The gospel is the message of salvation found in Jesus of Nazareth—"the power of God for the salvation of everyone who believes." Before we had all the means of communication we have today, when we still communicated verbally, people would send a messenger from town to town with important news, both good and bad: "We have a new king!" "A new tax will be collected!" "A plague is spreading across the countryside!" That is the intent behind the word of the gospels—that we have a message that is so important that it needs to be delivered personally to every person and gathering of people we can find. It is tempting to be complacent about the gospel and keep it to ourselves. But that is not God's desire; just as someone shared the good news with us, we are to share the good news with others.

### • THINK ABOUT IT •

Make it personal; tell your God-story. Your life is a letter others can read testifying to the reality of Jesus' death and resurrection.

*Prayer*

Heavenly Father, thank You that someone honored You and loved me enough to share the gospel with me. Now it's my turn. Help me to tell my God-story honestly, simply, and confidently—whether in my home, workplace, or classroom. In Jesus' name, amen.

## WORKMANLIKE ATTITUDE

*"I love those who love me; And those who diligently seek me will find me."*

PROVERBS 8:17 • NASB®

The people I know who have the most successful prayer lives approach prayer with a workmanlike attitude. Becoming a person of prayer is a commitment to showing up, doing what you know, doing it with consistency, and understanding that the outcomes are beyond you. It's this notion of rolling up your sleeves and doing your part. For many years now there has been a group of people who are at our campus to pray every morning from 6:30 to 7:30. They've done it without fanfare, but I can tell you that remarkable things have happened because those people have been praying faithfully. I'd like to invite you to approach prayer with a new diligence. When you wake up in the morning, say, "Lord, thank You for giving me this day." When you pull into the parking lot at work, say, "Lord, help me honor You here today." When you come home at night, say, "Lord, help me do well in the roles I have here." Begin with simple prayers like these, and the habit of prayer will begin to change the momentum of your life.

### • THINK ABOUT IT •

Prayer begins with a choice you make to take whatever measure of faith you have and bring it before God. As in any relationship, it can take time to learn how to have a good conversation with Him. Listening to His thoughts in His Word helps.

### *Prayer*

Heavenly Father, override the doubts and hindrances that keep me from praying consistently. Expose the deceptions that have become my own rationale for being prayer-less on so many points. I want to draw nearer to You in prayer. In Jesus' name, amen.

## DON'T STAY NAÏVE

*Once when we were going to the place of prayer, we were met by a female slave who had a spirit by which she predicted the future. She earned a great deal of money for her owners by fortune-telling.*

ACTS 16:16

We don't have to look very hard to see the influence of the occult in our world—that's any kind of spiritual activity that is not under the direction of the Holy Spirit. The idea that you have to be pursuing evil in order for evil to pursue you is very naïve. You say, "I had my palm read, but just for fun. I asked for an influence in my life from a spirit other than the Holy Spirit, but it was just for laughs." Because of our lack of awareness and our stubborn refusal to believe in unholy things, we've been incredibly vulnerable. There are unclean spiritual forces just waiting for you to open a door for them. If you have already done that, ask the Lord to cleanse your heart and mind and fill you with thoughts of Him. He wants you to find joy and direction and purpose in Him alone.

· THINK ABOUT IT ·

Jesus described the Devil as coming only "to steal, kill, and destroy." It is the height of folly, then, to give him any open doors into your life through contact with his realm of the occult.

*Prayer*

Heavenly Father, I renounce all contact with anything occult or satanic. Forgive me and cleanse my heart, soul, mind, and body with the shed blood of Jesus. I thank You, Jesus, that You died on the cross and rose again to purchase my release. In Your name, amen.

# DAY 141

## ORDINARY TURNED HERO

*But the LORD said to Samuel, "Do not consider his appearance or his height, for I have rejected him. The LORD does not look at the things man looks at. Man looks at the outward appearance, but the LORD looks at the heart."*

### 1 SAMUEL 16:7

I learned about Moses and the Exodus with the help of Charlton Heston, whose real name was John Charles Carter. The Bible does not tell us what Moses looked like—we imagine him to be tall, handsome, and articulate because we've seen Charlton Heston's version along with the beautifully animated movie The Prince of Egypt. It's more likely that Moses was not an imposing figure at all, but a rather ordinary man with an ordinary voice. That would explain why Pharaoh was not intimidated by him. I think we would be surprised to see just how normal our Bible heroes were. This verse tells us that God does not choose His workers, even kings, based on their outward appearance. Think about that when you assume that God will not use you because of your ordinariness. He is looking at your heart, not your height.

### • THINK ABOUT IT •

Have you been more impressed with or more greatly valued people based on their outward appearance? Ask the Lord to help you see people through His eyes and the value He places on each one.

### *Prayer*

Heavenly Father, I repent of judging people based on their outward appearance. You alone can judge the heart righteously. Cleanse my heart of all that would disqualify me from Your assignments. I want to be ready to serve You. In Jesus' name, amen.

## DIFFERENCE MAKERS

*Each of you should use whatever gift you have received to serve others, as faithful stewards of God's grace in its various forms.*

1 PETER 4:10

Many years ago, we asked ourselves: "If our church closed its doors, would it matter to anyone other than those of us who worship here?" At the time we asked that question, the answer was, "Probably not." We knew we could not change that overnight, but we determined to become a part of our community and try to enrich the lives of the people who are our neighbors. Many of the things our people do, both as a congregation and as individuals serving the community, make an incredible difference. We want the values of our faith to be broadly shared so that they impact the quality of life in our community. Those things are the assignment of the Church, so we make ourselves available to the Lord and see what doors of opportunity He will open for us. It's a good question for every church to ask itself regularly: "If our church closed its doors, would it matter to anyone other than those of us who worship here?"

· THINK ABOUT IT ·

Consider your role and purpose in the Body of Christ. How could you become increasingly effective in enriching those around you in every area of your influence with your time, talent, and resources?

*Prayer*

Heavenly Father, show me the opportunities in my community to serve and make a good impact. Make my life a blessing to those around me that they might see the good works You have prepared for me to do, and thereby, be drawn to You. In Jesus' name, amen.

## YOUR DAYS ON EARTH

*This is the day the LORD has made; let us rejoice and be glad in it.*

PSALM 118:24

I find it rather amazing that God has invested His spiritual authority under the sun in this age in people. When we needed a Redeemer, God didn't send an angel. He sent the Son of God to live among us as a man. When Jesus recruited helpers, He started with fishermen. When the first disciples began organizing the first churches, where did the leadership come from? Just regular people. Even Paul, the great evangelist, provided for his needs by working as a tentmaker. Our days on the earth are a privileged opportunity to yield ourselves as living sacrifices that in turn give expression to the glory of Almighty God. As you go about your days, see them not as filled with monotonous tasks. See them as opportunities to serve the Lord.

· THINK ABOUT IT ·

It is a tragedy to consume any of our days on the earth for our own self-centered purposes. Ask the Lord to help you see your days not from your vantage point, but His. Then use them to glorify Him.

*Prayer*

Heavenly Father, You are the Lord of my routine. I want to bring an obedient response in conduct and speech to each task, so I can honor You and change the atmosphere around my life for the better. May every part of my day be used for Your glory. In Jesus' name, amen.

## HELP FOR THE DESPERATE

*Praise be to the God and Father of our Lord Jesus Christ, the Father of compassion and the God of all comfort, who comforts us in all our troubles, so that we can comfort those in any trouble with the comfort we ourselves have received from God.*

2 CORINTHIANS 1:3-4

The wonderful news of the gospel is that the power of God was made available through the Person of Jesus Christ to anyone who would receive Him. The power of God is available to deliver you from disease, to comfort your broken heart, to help you overcome the most horrific abuse, to set you free from habits that have dominated your life. In order to receive the benefits you have to acknowledge that you are a sinner, that you are beset by something that you are powerless to overcome by yourself. In my life experience, help comes to the desperate, not to the casual inquirers. The good news is that God is not intimidated or frightened or caught off guard by our desperation. He has made full provision for His people to live victoriously—through the power of the gospel of Jesus Christ. In response, it is our great privilege to tell others what He has done for us.

### • THINK ABOUT IT •

In Scripture, the biggest miracles came to the most desperate people: parents of sick children, blind men, lepers rejected and alone. Desperation made them pursue Jesus without reservation and that was key.

### *Prayer*

Heavenly Father, I am Your child. Jesus is my Lord. I am in desperate need of Your help and grace for: _____. Do not let the enemy's schemes against me succeed. Thank You for hearing my cry for help and giving me hope. In Jesus' name, amen.

## UNBURDENED

*"Come to me, all you who are weary and burdened, and I will give you rest."*

MATTHEW 11:28

We sometimes wonder if Jesus can relate to the conflicts we face, but Jesus' life was marked by conflict. When He was born, Herod heard that there was a baby born in Bethlehem who might have a claim to the throne, so he had every boy there under the age of two slaughtered. Jesus' family fled with Him to Egypt to protect Him. When He began His public ministry in His hometown of Nazareth, He went into the synagogue on the Sabbath as was His custom. He read from the prophet Isaiah, then closed the scroll and said, "Today this scripture is fulfilled in your hearing" (Luke 4:21). He began to offer them some insights, and they became so enraged that they drove Him to the edge of town in order to throw Him off a cliff. Jesus' conflicts with the established religious leaders didn't end until He died on a cross. Don't ever think that Jesus cannot understand your weariness and the burdens you are bearing. His invitation is simple: "Come to me, all who are weary and burdened, and I will give you rest."

### • THINK ABOUT IT •

In the midst of much conflict and rejection, Jesus kept His peace and His capacity to be compassionate, gentle, and patient. Ask the Holy Spirit to work this miraculous response in your life, too.

### *Prayer*

Heavenly Father, You are the source of the true peace and rest that I long for in every part of my being. To that end, I relinquish my burdens to Your care and power. Help me to rest in the finished work of Jesus on the cross. In Jesus' name, amen.

## SALVATION'S SOURCE

*He is the head of the body, the church; he is the beginning and the firstborn from among the dead, so that in everything he might have the supremacy.*

COLOSSIANS 1:18

Jesus is the Head of the Church, and the externals matter little as long as we are committed to Him. We can sing ancient hymns or contemporary praise songs. We can sit on the floor or padded pews. We can celebrate communion every week or every month. At the heart of every true church is a recognition of the deity and work of Jesus. Some of the groups that call themselves a church have veered away from or added to Scripture. Some have minimized the work of Jesus on the cross to the point that they no longer truly believe He is the source of salvation. Some refuse to submit to His authority, and some "churches" were never interested in Him to begin with. He said (John 14:6): "I am the way and the truth and the life. No one comes to the Father except through me." So be careful about the faith group you associate with. No matter what the sign says, if Jesus isn't the Head of a church, it's not a church!

· THINK ABOUT IT ·

Those who trust in and honor Jesus with their lives comprise His true Church, over which He is the Head. Does He take the highest place in your life and faith groups?

*Prayer*

Heavenly Father, thank You for Your true Church and for the opportunity to be a part of the family of God. Help me live in such a way that all around me will know I am committed to Jesus and trust in His sacrifice on the cross. In Jesus' name, amen.

# DAY 147

## CATALYST OF CARE

*The tongue has the power of life and death...*

PROVERBS 18:21

Some people could talk to a rock, and the rock would talk back. Some of us are less verbal, and the rock might need to start the conversation. But words have power—the power of life and death, this verse says—so it is important that we use them. Specifically, I want to encourage you to speak to the people at your church. That sounds obvious, but many of us are in the habit of entering the sanctuary and making a beeline for our seat. Afterward, we leave again without really interacting with the people around us. Most churches have some point in the service to greet one another. Do more than say hello. If you are not acquainted, introduce yourself. Ask a friendly question and listen to their response. Say that you are glad you had the opportunity to meet them and hope to see them again. These simple interactions will do more to make people feel welcome than the sermon or the music, and when you make them feel welcome, you are opening doors for their spiritual growth. We are ambassadors for Jesus, the Bible says, and ambassadors talk.

· THINK ABOUT IT ·

Many come to church seeking to overcome a sense of isolation in their own lives. God promises that He will place the lonely in families. Ask the Lord to help you use your voice to include and bless those around you.

*Prayer*

Heavenly Father, thank You that I can be a representative of Your character. Help me take the initiative to reach out to others as You have reached out to me. May my voice of care and concern make a difference in Your Kingdom. In Jesus' name, amen.

## NO REGRETS

*"Behold, I am coming soon! My reward is with me, and I will give to everyone according to what he has done."*

REVELATION 22:12

There is some confusion in our world between the meanings of success and significance. Success is about fulfilling my plans and my purposes. Significance is serving God in time so that we accrue rewards that will last for all eternity. It is not an either/or thing; God is not against your success, but He invites you to more than just being successful. If all you're focused on is success, when your days under the sun are over your success is over. Significance is what we take with us. Because of the choices Jesus made in time, God gave Him the name that is above every name and seated Him at His right hand in Heaven. You'll never regret the choices you make for significance in the Kingdom of God. The people around you may not understand them. These choices may not land you a promotion or even make you a star on social media. But you will never regret them, and they will bring you great rewards.

· THINK ABOUT IT ·

A consistent daily devotional time with God can tune you more fully into His invitations toward a life of significance that will bring great rewards in eternity.

*Prayer*

Heavenly Father, I desire a fruitful life of significance—thank You that there is an eternal reward for diligently following You. Open my heart and ears each day to hear and obey Your voice, helping me align my perspective with Yours. In Jesus' name, amen.

## WITHOUT APOLOGY

*From one man he created all the nations throughout the whole earth. He decided beforehand when they should rise and fall, and he determined their boundaries.*

ACTS 17:26 • NLT

When I began my academic career, the emphasis of the scientific world was centered on evolution and Darwinian Theory. If you had the boldness to say, "I reject evolution as a theory of origins, and I'm an advocate for creationism or intelligent design," it did not go well with you. I'm happy to report that many advances are being made in the field of genetics, and even the scientific community is stepping toward us. Geneticists have now put forward the idea that after all the study and data analysis there seems to be overwhelming evidence that we all are descended from the same two people. Who knew? Don't ever apologize because you choose to trust in the Lord and believe that His Word is true. If the rest of the world hasn't caught up yet with the truth that God has presented, just quietly stand in your place. God's wisdom will break forth. I promise.

### • THINK ABOUT IT •

Have you ever been embarrassed to stand for the biblical truths in the face of world opinion? If so, ask Almighty God for the grace to stand unflinchingly, knowing His truth will prevail.

### *Prayer*

Heavenly Father, Your every word is true: Through Jesus all things were made (John 1:3); by Your Word Heaven and earth and all that is in it came to be (Psalm 33:6-9). May I never be apologetic for believing in Your presentation of truth. In Jesus' name, amen.

## TRUST GOD'S INTENTIONS

*We have all had human fathers who disciplined us and we respected them for it. How much more should we submit to the Father of our spirits and live!*

HEBREWS 12:9

Each of us has had an earthly father whose DNA caused our earth suit to have his flat feet or crooked smile. Your earth suit serves as a vessel for you to live in while you are here, but it comes with an expiration date. You have a Heavenly Father who is the Father of your spirit, and your spirit is eternal. The Bible says that He knew you and had plans for you before your earthly parents even saw you, and if you are a Jesus-follower, you will live with Him forever when your days on earth are done. Our earthly fathers are fallible people who are usually concerned for our welfare but sometimes make mistakes in their correction. Our Heavenly Father is the all-knowing God who will never make a mistake where we are concerned. We can trust God's intentions for us and learn to respect Him and submit to Him in all things.

• THINK ABOUT IT •

Fear of punishment can discolor our relationship with God as Father and distort our response to His discipline. It might take a process of renewing your thinking, but His steadfast love can cast out that fear and redirect you to a healthy trust in Him.

*Prayer*

Heavenly Father, Your Holy Spirit bears witness with my spirit that I am Your child and You are my "Abba, Father." Forgive me my rebellion and grant me a willing spirit to accept Your correction and obey You. I know Your commands bring life. In Jesus' name, amen.

## SOARING IMAGINATIONS

*"For my thoughts are not your thoughts, neither are your ways my ways,"*
*declares the Lord. "As the heavens are higher than the earth, so are my ways*
*higher than your ways and my thoughts than your thoughts."*

ISAIAH 55:8-9

Most of us who spend our days on the surface of the earth struggle to comprehend "the heavens." Our imaginations are very much earthbound. We look up at the stars and planets and think, "Wow, those are a long way away!" Even skilled astronomers using the world's best telescopes do not know everything about the far reaches of our universe. God says His thoughts and plans are like that: He created and fully understands the universe and everything in it, including us. He will always be God, and we will always be human. He has not left us wandering aimlessly, however, but has blessed us with the example of Jesus and the help of the Holy Spirit. Do not be discouraged as you seek God's plans and purposes. He doesn't always do what we think He should do in the way we think He should do it, but we can rest in the knowledge that His plans are always better than ours.

### • THINK ABOUT IT •

Given the vast distance between God's ways and thoughts and ours, it is all the more amazing that the Son of God would humble Himself so much as to become a man. The incarnation is an ultimate demonstration of humility.

### Prayer

Heavenly Father, I rest in Your perfect love and wisdom, and trust Your plans for me. Direct my steps and choices in the righteous paths You have prepared for me. Thank You, Jesus, for becoming my wisdom from God. In Your name I pray, amen.

## THE GIFT OF OTHERS

*We urge you, brothers and sisters, warn those who are idle and disruptive,*
*encourage the disheartened, help the weak, be patient with everyone.*

1 THESSALONIANS 5:14

This verse hits home, doesn't it? At some point every one of us could be described as idle, disruptive, disheartened, weak, or in need of patience. In my life, that is where the people of God have come through for me time and time again. They have called me to account when necessary—sometimes gently, sometimes firmly. They have prodded me when I was idle. They have encouraged me when I was disheartened. They have picked me up and carried me when I was weak. They have been patient with me many times! If you are not actively engaged with a small group who will love you, challenge you, encourage you, comfort you, and pray for you, you are going through life without the benefit of one of God's great gifts to you. I'd encourage you to get connected with a small group of God's people. They will be far less judgmental and far more understanding than you might imagine, because they are making their way through their imperfect lives as well—with the help of God and each other.

### • THINK ABOUT IT •

In his letters in Scripture, Paul always makes note of the people who were working alongside him in each place to advance the gospel. To live a life of significance, these Kingdom relationships are essential.

### Prayer

Heavenly Father, You have given me spiritual gifts, but not all gifts. Place me in relationships with people whose gifts complement my own, so that together by Your Spirit we can build up the Church and each other. In Jesus' name, amen.

## FULLY INFORMED

*"I no longer call you servants, because a servant does not know his master's business. Instead, I have called you friends, for everything that I learned from my Father I have made known to you."*

JOHN 15:15

Most of us in contemporary western society do not live in the world of masters and servants, but we understand that one of the differences between the two groups is access to information. The masters talk about important things among themselves, but servants are not privy to those things. Friends of the master are invited in to sit down for a leisurely chat about his thoughts, feelings, and plans; servants are told what to do and when. Jesus says that we are His friends because He has shared with us what He has learned from His Father. We live in an era when the concept of friendship has been watered down until it is nearly meaningless. In contrast, the friendship of Jesus is intimate and sincere. It opens the door for us to gain understanding about God and His Kingdom. If nothing else can be said of me, I want to be known as a friend of Jesus.

• THINK ABOUT IT •

Jesus' disciples addressed each other as He had addressed them – friends. What responsibilities can you think of that come with being a friend to others and a friend to Jesus?

*Prayer*

Heavenly Father, it is humbling that Jesus would call me His friend. Forgive any selfish attitudes that have prevented me from being a faithful friend. Help me honor Jesus, giving Him first place in all of my life. In His name I pray, amen.

## TEDDY BEAR THINKING

*Therefore, since we are receiving a kingdom that cannot be shaken, let us be thankful, and so worship God acceptably with reverence and awe, for our "God is a consuming fire."*

HEBREWS 12:28-29

It is important that we understand the character of the God we worship. Some contemporary theologians speak about God as if He is simply a cuddly and comforting teddy bear—listening silently to our every confidence, accepting all of our words as true and our actions as right. God is certainly approachable and loving, but it would be wrong to leave it at that incomplete understanding. We've all seen the aftermath of a raging fire that consumes everything—nothing but ash is left in its path. Such will be the result of God's holiness when it encounters the sin of the world. We don't like to think of God in this way, because it has implications for any ungodly behavior in our lives. But it's important to have the complete picture. This is our God—a God of great love and a God of certain justice. Recognizing this, we want to live in a way that pleases Him and honors Him, so that we can anticipate His rewards rather than His judgment.

### • THINK ABOUT IT •

Have you ever found that your idea of God's character differed from the presentation of Scripture? What safeguards you from any incorrect perceptions you might have?

*Prayer*

Heavenly Father, I want to embrace Your complete character—a loving yet holy God who cannot wink at sin. Help me gratefully and reverently live in such a way that I am neither fearful of Your judgment nor presumptive of Your grace. In Jesus' name, amen.

## GLUED TO GOD

*Serve only the LORD your God and fear him alone. Obey his commands, listen to his voice, and cling to him.*

DEUTERONOMY 13:4 • NLT

We have been given an authority in Christ, but it is a positional authority. It is not related to our family pedigree or our education or how much we have achieved—it is related to our proximity and loyalty to Jesus of Nazareth. Much is made of a person's accomplishments, and there is nothing wrong with working hard to become educated and successful in a career. But those things are put to their best use when we are willing to humble ourselves before the Lord, fear Him, serve Him, listen to Him, obey Him, and even cling to Him. God wants to do something through you and me, and He has given us the authority to do great things for Him. But we will be most effective in every area of life when we determine to walk closely alongside Him and put His plans and desires ahead of our own.

### • THINK ABOUT IT •

The word "cling" has recently been given a derogatory connotation. But that all depends on to what you are clinging. It basically means "to stick to something as if glued" or "to refuse to be separated from." Are you "glued" to God?

### *Prayer*

Heavenly Father, I desire to cling to You and faithfully obey Your commands. I renounce any divided loyalties in my heart that would separate me from You and tempt me to serve another master. Unite my heart in devotion to You. In Jesus' name, amen.

## A GOOD HOST

*He witnessed to them from morning till evening, explaining about the kingdom of God, and from the Law of Moses and from the Prophets he tried to persuade them about Jesus. Some were convinced by what he said, but others would not believe...For two whole years Paul stayed there in his own rented house and welcomed all who came to see him.*

ACTS 28:23-24, 30

God's plan here is fascinating: He had allowed Paul to be arrested, then to survive a perilous voyage, then to live under the watchful eye of the Roman government, but in a house where He could welcome the local Jewish leaders in order to "persuade them about Jesus." Judaism was diverse and fragmented, and Paul made his home a safe place to bring their questions—even their arguments. It is good to show hospitality to those who need to know a Jesus-follower personally. Like Paul's guests, some will not believe that Jesus is the Son of God and our Savior, but some will be convinced. We are not called to dictate the outcome, only to create a welcoming atmosphere where people can share their lives and we in turn can tell what Jesus has done for us.

### • THINK ABOUT IT •

Jesus Himself said that no one could come to Him unless the Father first draws that person (John 6:44). Pray that the Lord would use your God-story to draw people to Jesus, as God's sovereign mercy intersects with the free will of those who listen.

### *Prayer*

Heavenly Father, fill my home with a welcoming atmosphere of hospitality where You can freely do Your work to draw others to Jesus. Holy Spirit, help me combine thoughts with words so that I can honor Jesus in authority and power. In Jesus' name, amen.

## CHANGING FILTERS

*Jews demand miraculous signs and Greeks look for wisdom, but we preach Christ crucified: a stumbling block to Jews and foolishness to Gentiles, but to those whom God has called, both Jews and Greeks, Christ the power of God and the wisdom of God.*

### 1 CORINTHIANS 1:22-24

The Jewish people were looking for a Messiah who would lead them to unseat the Romans and restore their autonomy. A crucified Christ was a stumbling block to them because they couldn't imagine the Messiah allowing Himself to be humiliated that way. The Greeks were on a quest for greater wisdom, and they could not see logic in His words and actions. It's easy to criticize them with the benefit of hindsight, but their lives were so filled with other expectations that it was difficult to see reality. We're no different. We have dreams and ambitions that can make it hard to see what God is doing, particularly if He's inviting us on a path that doesn't line up with what we want. When we humble ourselves and trust Him to save us and lead us on the path that is His best for us, His gifts are extravagant: the power of God and the wisdom of God.

### • THINK ABOUT IT •

Have your desires and expectations ever become the filter of your life-perspective? Ask the Lord to reveal this and help replace that filter with His perspective, aligning you more fully to His plans and purposes.

### *Prayer*

Heavenly Father, forgive me when my own expectations and desires took the lead in my thinking and life-responses. I want Your Holy Spirit to guide me and light the path You have for me. May my perspective always be informed by Your truth. In Jesus' name, amen.

## LIGHTS ON!

*"Your kingdom come, your will be done on earth as it is in heaven."*

MATTHEW 6:10

We cannot fully receive the blessings of God and the abundance of God—all those good things that we talk about—unless we also accept the responsibilities of God. We have to care about His agenda and serve Him if we are going to reap His benefits. Jesus taught us to pray, "Let Your will be done on earth as it is in heaven." Do we think it is someone else's responsibility to do the will of God? Isn't that what most of us think? I'm not watching the news thinking, "How can I be a brighter light for You?" I'm watching the news thinking, "I wish those people would stop that foolishness and be more godly!" The challenge for our lives is to let the light of God in us radiate more brightly. Our one small light may seem rather dim and insignificant, but even one pinprick of light shines brightly in the darkness and brings God's blessings. When the people of God choose to live for the Lord in greater numbers, we will make a difference the world cannot ignore.

## • THINK ABOUT IT •

Our obedience to God increases the spiritual light within us and helps light the path toward God for others. We want to be bright lights in God's Kingdom. No darkness can extinguish His light!

## Prayer

Heavenly Father, help me stop raging against the darkness by grumbling and complaining. Instead, help me focus on turning up Your light in the midst of the darkness. Your Kingdom come, and Your will be done on earth as it is in Heaven. In Jesus' name, amen.

## REALIGNMENT

*Teach me Your way, O Lord; I will walk in Your truth; Unite my heart to fear Your name.*

PSALM 86:11 • NASB®

We live in a season when we are told that truth is subjective, personal: You can't know my truth, and I can't know your truth. Nobody should have the pride and arrogance to suggest that there is such a thing as absolute truth. The Bible clearly tells us that there is truth, and it can be known. Absolute truth. Truth that transcends cultures and generations. Truth that transcends technology and empires. There are things that were true when Moses left Egypt with the slaves of that land that are just as true in the twenty-first century. There are things that were true when Jesus was in a boat on the Sea of Galilee with His disciples that are just as relevant in your community today. If you are a Christ-follower, you are going to have to grapple with the notion of truth. You are going to have to decide for yourself what you believe. To the degree that you will bring alignment between your life and the truth of God, it will bring good things to you.

### • THINK ABOUT IT •

Subjective truth is only opinion. Are you grappling with the notion of truth? Be honest with God, and ask Him to help you in this battle.

### *Prayer*

Heavenly Father, Your Word is truth; Your Son, Jesus, is Truth; Your Spirit is the Spirit of Truth. Bring my family, nation, and generation back to a recognition and love of the truth that we might escape the destruction that lies and deception will bring. In Jesus' name, amen.

## THE GIFT OF PRAYER

*This is the confidence we have in approaching God: that if we ask anything according to his will, he hears us.*

1 JOHN 5:14

We interact with people every day who would greatly appreciate knowing that someone is willing to pray for them. When faced with a problem or crisis, even people who don't think of themselves as spiritual or religious will be open to imagining that there is a God who wants to be involved in their lives. Showing your confidence in God to answer prayer can be a profound step toward faith in the lives of people because they may not have anyone else who is willing to step up and have that conversation. Don't minimize the profound effect you have when you open a door for God to work in someone else's life. Don't ever downplay the influence you can have for Jesus by simply offering to pray.

· THINK ABOUT IT ·

Can you think about a time when someone reached out to you simply because they knew you were a person who prays? Ask God for daily opportunities to pray for others—you may be the difference maker in their faith life.

*Prayer*

Heavenly Father, I do have confidence that You hear and answer my prayers, and I want others to grow in that same confidence. Help me increasingly become one others know they can turn to for prayer. I want to make a difference. In Jesus' name, amen.

## UNDERSTANDING AND ABLE

*We do not have a high priest who is unable to sympathize with our weaknesses, but we have one who has been tempted in every way, just as we are—yet was without sin.*

HEBREWS 4:15

We know that Jesus was the Son of God who lived a perfect, sinless life. Yet we also know that He understands every temptation we can possibly face. It is easy to think of Jesus as a distant deity who is removed from our struggles. How could He, sitting at the right hand of His Father in Heaven, understand the pleasure of drugs or the pull of pornography? How could He possibly understand the lure of chasing another relationship? How could He relate to the temptation to borrow money from petty cash? He does understand. That Jesus could be fully God and fully man is one of the mysteries of our faith, but it is true. Scripture says He was tempted in every way that we are, but He never gave in. Yes, Jesus understands our temptations, and we should trust in His ability to deliver us from them.

### • THINK ABOUT IT •

By the empowering help of the Holy Spirit it is possible to say no to temptation. Through His finished work on the cross, Jesus has set us free from being enslaved to sin. This truth elicits both hope and responsibility in us: Turn to Him for help!

*Prayer*

Heavenly Father, through Jesus I can be delivered from slavery to sin. Strengthen me to make decisions for righteousness and break the patterns of destructive behaviors. Help me walk in the freedom Jesus Christ purchased for me. In Jesus' name, amen.

## NOT ASHAMED!

*We have seen and testify that the Father has sent his Son to be the Savior of the world.*

1 JOHN 4:14

There is a huge amount of messaging today that says, "You should be ashamed of the gospel." We're reminded of bad chapters from the history of the Church and bad actors in the name of the Church. We hear, "How dare you advocate for that. You should be ashamed!" My response is, "How dare you manipulate history and twist the record and deny my heritage. I am not ashamed of the gospel!" I'm not ashamed to say I believe that Jesus of Nazareth is the Messiah, God's Son. I'm not ashamed to say I believe that He was born of a virgin and died on a Roman cross. I'm not ashamed to say I believe God raised Him to life again, and He ascended to Heaven, where He is seated at the right hand of the Father. I'm not ashamed to say He's coming back to the earth to judge the living and the dead. I'm not ashamed to say that every knee will bow and every tongue confess that Jesus is Lord of all. No, I'm not ashamed of the gospel!

### • THINK ABOUT IT •

Grace is free but it is not cheap. Jesus paid the price for our redemption that we might be free to live for Him. No matter the argument or opposition, let's determine to identify with and own the gospel of Jesus Christ.

### Prayer

Heavenly Father, I am not ashamed of the gospel—it is an honor to proclaim that Jesus is my Savior and Lord over all. Help me not be embarrassed and therefore miss opportunities to attest to the grace and truth that come through Him and Him alone. In Jesus' name, amen.

## CLEAR CONFIDENCE

*Such confidence as this is ours through Christ before God. Not that we are competent in ourselves to claim anything for ourselves, but our competence comes from God.*

### 2 CORINTHIANS 3:4-5

Confidence comes from two things: information—when you know the truth—and experience—when you put it into practice. Church people are good at gaining information. We love to study, talk about what we've studied, and study some more. Studying about the things of God is a great habit, but we should not use time spent studying as an excuse to avoid the experiential part of our faith. Truth that is divorced from the realm of experience will always live in that hazy realm of doubt, so I would encourage you to part the curtains and look out into your neighborhood and the community around you. Find people who can benefit from your service in the name of Jesus, and put your faith to work for Him. I have no doubt that He will show you that the truth of the gospel makes a difference in the lives of people. In this way, you will gain the confidence that your faith is real and effective.

### • THINK ABOUT IT •

To gain experience, stand alongside others who have already gained a certain level of experience—whether it be in praying for the sick, ministering to the poor, or encouraging stronger families. They can be a great source of encouragement.

### *Prayer*

Heavenly Father, open my eyes to see my place of service in my community. Connect me with a need and with the people who can help me effectively serve to address it. Equip me to serve with the grace You will supply. In Jesus' name, amen.

## UNWAVERING ADVOCATE

*On the day I called, You answered me; You made me bold with strength in my soul. All the kings of the earth will give thanks to You, O LORD, When they have heard the words of Your mouth. And they will sing of the ways of the LORD, For great is the glory of the LORD.*

PSALM 138:3-5 • NASB®

We in the Church have imagined that inclusivity and tolerance of a broader range of ideas, while we diminish the importance of Jesus, will open doors of opportunity for us. In fact, the opposite has happened. We're not welcome in the marketplace or the halls of government. We're not welcome in public schools at any level. That offends me because if my tax dollars support those schools, Jesus should be welcome there. We're going to have to find a more courageous faith—not an angry faith, not a condemning faith, not a belittling faith—but a faith that says, "I'm an advocate for Jesus of Nazareth. He's brought wonderful things to me, and I believe He would be a blessing to you." I intend to keep praying for boldness to take that message anywhere the Lord opens the door.

### • THINK ABOUT IT •

The early Church prayed for boldness in the face of severe persecution and through His Spirit, the Lord gave it to them. Let's pray the same prayer (Acts 4:29-30) and be empowered with the boldness only He can give.

*Prayer*

Heavenly Father, hostility to You has increased exponentially—forgive Your Church's tolerance of this. Renew our commitment to courageously proclaim Your truth, and help me personally be an unwavering advocate of Jesus of Nazareth. In His name I pray, amen.

## COME AND SEE

*Nothing impure will ever enter it, nor will anyone who does what is shameful or deceitful, but only those whose names are written in the Lamb's book of life.*

REVELATION 21:27

One of our goals as Jesus-followers is to add to the number of people in God's Kingdom. Some folks talk about numbers as if they are distasteful, but numbers are not evil. In Heaven there is a register kept, "the Lamb's book of life," with the names of everyone who will spend eternity there. I don't know whether that list is numbered or not, but I know that the Lord knows exactly how many names are on it! Do you know what would jumpstart an increase to that heavenly list? If everyone who attends church would invite just one person to attend with you. They won't all show up, but some will. They won't all come back, but some will. They won't all accept Jesus as Savior and Lord, but some will. They won't all make your church their own, but some will. My request is really rather simple: I'm asking you to step out of your comfort zone and extend an invitation with the potential to change someone's life.

• THINK ABOUT IT •

The first disciples extended a simple invitation regarding Jesus to their friends: "Come and see." Your invitations to others can be just as simple.

*Prayer*

Heavenly Father, prepare the hearts of the ones I will invite to "come and see." Increase hunger in their souls to seek You, and remove any hostile stereotypes that would prejudice them against accepting my invitation. Draw them to Jesus. In His name, amen.

## VALID AND IN CONTEXT

*"A new command I give you: Love one another. As I have loved you, so you must love one another."*

JOHN 13:34

Few pieces of Scripture have fallen out of favor in American life like the Ten Commandments. The Ten Commandments are not suggestions. They are not heavenly prompts or good ideas or church rules; they are directives from God Himself. Unlike what some would like us to believe, the Ten Commandments have never been revised or rescinded. There is no suggestion in Scripture that when Jesus gave this "new command" to "Love one another," He diminished the significance of the Ten Commandments. He said that the other ten could be put under this umbrella. He didn't say, "It's fine to steal as long as you love one another" or "It's acceptable to worship idols as long as you love one another." He didn't set aside the previous ten; He simply gave them context because they had been twisted by the traditions of people. I would encourage you to familiarize yourself with these ten important rules. Yes, they are ancient, but they are as necessary for a happy and productive life as the day they were written on stone tablets.

· THINK ABOUT IT ·

Acknowledging the authority of the Ten Commandments must begin with the Church and be demonstrated in the lives of His people. One idea is to keep a copy close at hand and commit them to heart.

*Prayer*

Heavenly Father, forgive us for treating the Ten Commandments with selective disregard and disobedience. Reveal any place where I have set these commandments aside in my own thoughts, words, or actions. I know Your commands lead to life. In Jesus' name, amen.

## TRANSFORMED TRADITIONS

*In everything set them an example by doing what is good. In your teaching show integrity, seriousness and soundness of speech that cannot be condemned...*

TITUS 2:7-8

Traditions are an interesting subject. Some of them are healthy and bind people together, and others bind people together but in unhealthy ways! The traditions you keep are a revelation of what you think is important and what you want to hand down to the next generation. That begs the questions: What do we hold valuable? What are we teaching and protecting? What are we handing down? I'd like to encourage you to evaluate the traditions that you and your family are teaching and giving away to your children. Determine if each one adds or takes away from the spiritual health of your family. The most important thing we can demonstrate is that the things of God come first in our lives—before loyalty to sports teams, schools, vacation spots, and hobbies. You've heard the old saying that honoring God with your life is more "caught than taught," and that applies to our traditions too.

· THINK ABOUT IT ·

Our traditions express an identity of values to this and future generations. Ask the Holy Spirit to inform your choices as you examine your traditions and help build traditions that honor Jesus.

*Prayer*

Heavenly Father, may my family traditions align with Your instruction in Psalm 78:4 to "tell the next generation the praiseworthy deeds of the Lord, His power and the wonders He has done." Help me transform them where necessary for Your purposes. In Jesus' name, amen.

## APPLY DAILY

*The LORD himself goes before you and will be with you; he will never leave you nor forsake you.*

### DEUTERONOMY 31:8

I've found that there is a tremendous difference between holding a concept in general and embracing it personally. There are many Scripture verses that encourage me greatly when I say them about myself. I want to invite you to make these statements with me: "The Lord goes before me and will be with me; He will never leave me nor forsake me" (Deuteronomy 31:8). "God showed His great love for me by sending Christ to die for me while I was still a sinner" (Romans 5:8). "By grace I have been saved through faith. This was not my own doing; it was the gift of God" (Ephesians 2:8). "I am God's workmanship, created in Christ Jesus to do good works" (Ephesians 2:10). "The Spirit Himself bears witness with my spirit that I am a child of God" (Romans 8:16). "God has poured out His love into my heart by the Holy Spirit, whom He has given me" (Romans 5:5). God's Word is a great gift to you and me, a message for all of us—and each of us.

### • THINK ABOUT IT •

Being able to appropriate the power and authority of God's Word for your own life is part of the riches of your inheritance as a Christ-follower. To fully experience the abundant life He has for you, try praying His Word.

### *Prayer*

Heavenly Father, Your Word is my life-source. Direct me daily to Your Word that I might internalize it and be prepared for what I will need. Teach me how to hide it in my heart and apply it effectively in order to be my best for You. In Jesus' name, amen.

## IMPERFECT VESSEL

*We have this treasure in jars of clay to show that this all-surpassing power is from God and not from us.*

2 CORINTHIANS 4:7

Paul was an incredibly effective advocate for Christianity. Though his work and witness were bound by the travel and communications available during his era, his teaching has since spread into most of the world and impacted generations for the cause of Christ. Paul, writing to the church in Corinth, surely recognized his weaknesses. He knew that he was an imperfect vessel. That was his message for the Corinthian people: God works through people who are fragile and flawed. He works through people who are broken, whose hearts are not always in the right place, whose attitudes are not always the best. God's purposes emerge in and through our lives in spite of us more than because of us. It is my prayer that we will begin to imagine that God wants to use us for His Kingdom purposes, in spite of our many imperfections. Remember, God works through cracked pots so that the world will know that everything good we accomplish comes from Him!

· THINK ABOUT IT ·

Laying down perfectionism and picking up humility transfers your confidence from your own abilities to God's. His desire is to work through our weaknesses so that He might be glorified.

*Prayer*

Heavenly Father, I am here to display Your greatness, not my own. I repent of my pride which scrambles to hide my imperfections, and step out in faith—just as I am—knowing Your power will be "made perfect in my weakness." In Jesus' name, amen.

## LENS OF TRUTH

*"You say, 'I am rich; I have acquired wealth and do not need a thing.' But you do not realize that you are wretched, pitiful, poor, blind and naked. I counsel you to buy from me gold refined in the fire, so you can become rich; and white clothes to wear, so you can cover your shameful nakedness; and salve to put on your eyes, so you can see."*

REVELATION 3:17-18

How can one be "wretched, pitiful, poor, blind and naked" and imagine oneself to be wealthy and have no need? There's only one way I know—deception. Deception means believing something to be true that in reality is not true. These folks in the Laodicean church are in that camp; they think they have everything, when in reality they have nothing. The nature of deception is the same today. Our enemy wants us to think that material wealth is what we need, when in fact our greatest needs are spiritual. It's worth noting that Jesus doesn't condemn them but gives them a resolution. He says, "Buy from me..." For us, as for the Laodiceans, the only things of any eternal value are not material things, but the things of God.

• THINK ABOUT IT •

The Holy Spirit opens our eyes to the true nature of our spiritual condition. He is the Spirit not only of truth, but also of the love and grace we need to be able to face it.

*Prayer*

Heavenly Father, don't let me live in complacent deception. Show me anywhere I have grieved Your Spirit. I ask for Your grace and power to realign me with Your truth and purposes for me. Open my eyes, Lord, so that I might see. In Jesus' name, amen.

## FIERCE FAITH

*Preach the Word; be prepared in season and out of season; correct, rebuke and encourage—with great patience and careful instruction.*

2 TIMOTHY 4:2

There are some fierce things being unleashed on humanity in this season. Certainly, history has seen terrible things, but there is a bold aggressiveness to the evil we are seeing that is unprecedented in my lifetime. There's a destructive character to it at the fundamental, foundational level of human society. We are opening the doorway to some things that only the power of God can reverse, and what that will mean for the generations who follow us is impossible to know. That is why we must have more than head knowledge of the gospel of Jesus Christ. We must know the message and the power of the gospel on an experiential level and bring it to bear on the issues we face. We must be ready to talk about it and patiently use it to correct, rebuke, and encourage—not just from the pulpits of our country, but in our homes, schools, workplaces, and every other area of our lives.

• THINK ABOUT IT •

It is often hard to stand steady in this age of shaking, especially when things you have depended upon fail. Today, consider a trust transfer in those places, transferring your trust to God and asking Him to help you present the truth of His security to others as well.

*Prayer*

Heavenly Father, You have assigned me to serve You in a unique time and season. Help me be strong and of good courage, devoted to truth, firm in faith. Help me use my voice to speak up for You and declare Your message of life. In Jesus' name, amen.

# DAY 172

## YOUR TIME IN THE ARENA

*"So now, go. I am sending you to Pharaoh to bring my people the Israelites out of Egypt."*

EXODUS 3:10

The world would have us believe that we are random occurrences of nature, sheer accidents of genetic happenstance. Scripture tells us plainly, however, that we are not random occurrences or cosmic accidents. The intricacies of the human body suggest that the God who created everything is a God of order and intentionality, and I don't believe we each happened as a result of some statistical probability. I think that God looked across the span of human history and chose you and me, with our unique combinations of gifts and talents, to be on task for Him at the beginning of the twenty-first century. Just as certainly as God put Moses in Egypt in order to deliver His people from slavery and Peter, James, and John in first-century Israel to walk beside Jesus, He put us in our place in order to fulfill the plans and purposes He has for us in this season. He has recruited us, equipped us, and invited us to participate in His work in the earth. I wonder—what will history say you and I accomplished during our season?

• THINK ABOUT IT •

As Queen Esther was called "for such a time as this" you are here in this position and place. Are there any areas where you can more fully maximize the time you have been given?

*Prayer*

Heavenly Father, I am grateful You have uniquely placed me in this time and season. You have given me every tool to accomplish Your purposes. Help me use them wisely and effectively that You might be glorified in this generation. In Jesus' name, amen.

## POSITION AVAILABLE

*The Lord's hand was with them, and a great number of people believed and turned to the Lord.*

ACTS 11:21

The first people who believed that Jesus of Nazareth was the Messiah seemed an unlikely group to accomplish much. Jesus didn't go around recruiting the rich and famous and powerful; we know He chose several fishermen and a tax collector, and Scripture doesn't note that any of those other first twelve were particularly influential. These people had no access to power. They didn't control any votes on the Sanhedrin. The power brokers in Jerusalem looked at them and said, "They're unschooled and ignorant. What do we have to fear from them? They couldn't even stop their leader from being executed." Yet within forty years, by the end of the book of Acts, they had multiplied and carried their message across a vast area, starting many churches. That was not accomplished only by the sheer willpower of people—that was accomplished by the anointing and empowering work of the Holy Spirit. Do not ever doubt the power of the Holy Spirit to use ordinary people to do what seems improbable. In fact, that is what we should ask and expect Him to do!

· THINK ABOUT IT ·

The world requires verification of qualifications, talents, and references when applying for work. God requires only a willing heart and a spirit submitted to His. He will then equip you for His endeavors.

*Prayer*

Heavenly Father, I am willing to be one of Your "improbable" servants. Fill me with Your Spirit and the ability, wisdom, and strength to carry out Your work. You are the source of my confidence and courage because You have anointed and qualified me. In Jesus' name, amen.

## DAILY DETOX

*Do not conform any longer to the pattern of this world, but be transformed by the renewing of your mind.*

ROMANS 12:2

Many ungodly thoughts will come through your mind, but you don't want to hold onto them and dwell on them. We want to focus our hearts and minds toward the Lord. Paul tells the Roman church that we are transformed when we turn away from the sinful patterns of the world and "renew" our minds with the things of God. This is serious business, because the greatest battles of our lives are in our minds. As you begin to invite God into your thought life, you will start to think differently. You will have a new set of hopes that are grounded in a new set of priorities. As you work toward a godly thought life, think about purposefully detoxing your mind. Some simple ways are giving thanks more than you complain, giving more encouragement than criticism, and giving God glory rather than taking it for yourself. The Holy Spirit wants to help you through this transformation. Lean into Him when you find yourself straying to your old ways of thinking, and He will redirect you toward what will please the Lord.

• THINK ABOUT IT •

Do you struggle with a pattern of thought that you know is holding you back from God's best? Ask the Holy Spirit to give you His sword—His Word—to help you cut off that persistent, entangling thought.

*Prayer*

Heavenly Father, I want to love You with my whole mind. Search me and show me any place where I have constructed my thoughts on assumptions and feelings contrary to Your Word. Help me build my thoughts on the foundation of truth. In Jesus' name, amen.

# DAY 175

## COMPLETE CONFIDENCE

*I always pray with joy because of your partnership in the gospel from the first day until now, being confident of this, that he who began a good work in you will carry it on to completion until the day of Christ Jesus.*

PHILIPPIANS 1:4-6

All around me I see people who are leaders. Some are in the corporate realm, managing large organizations. Some stand at the front of classrooms, teaching with authority. Some oversee jobsites, coordinating multiple contractors. Some step into a surgical suite and save a life. Some walk onto a factory floor and ensure that a product comes off the assembly line. Some are at home, guiding children toward maturity and taking care of their family's needs. All of these roles require preparation, coordination, and responsibility. But when it comes to our faith, and someone asks, "Could you host a small group?" we lose our confidence and say, "Sorry, I'm not qualified." I'd like to invite you to ask the Holy Spirit to help you in this area. He will show you how to use the confidence you exhibit in the world to become a person of faith who is able to invite someone toward the transforming power of God.

· THINK ABOUT IT ·

The work of the gospel is a partnership, and the Lord has promised to give you the skill and confidence to do your part. Think about the leadership skills you use in the world and how you might use those skills to advance the Lord's purposes in the earth.

*Prayer*

Heavenly Father, You have promised to equip me and give me the grace and confidence I need to invite others toward faith in You. Open my eyes, silence my fears, and encourage my heart to walk into opportunities to extend Your Kingdom. In Jesus' name, amen.

## ME FIRST

*Test me, O LORD, and try me, examine my heart and my mind...*

PSALM 26:2

Most of us imagine that serving God is about changing the world. That's a noble idea. But what I have discovered is that even though I start with that idea, the greatest change usually comes to me. It's very easy to see what needs to be different in the people around us, but it's a whole lot harder for me to see in my own heart and my own life where I need God's help to be different. Are you willing to change? If you are willing to say, "Lord, change me," that will begin a ripple effect that will have an impact in the world. Sometimes you will be able to see the changes, and at other times you will never know what good your efforts may bring across time. All you need to do is trust the Lord to work in your own heart and life, and He will bring changes in others as He desires.

### • THINK ABOUT IT •

We are influencing others when we don't even realize they are watching. The more we are conformed to His image, the more we will impact our spheres of influence with His light and truth.

*Prayer*

Heavenly Father, You want to conform me to the image of Your Son, and I want to cooperate with You fully. Your Word declares that I am a new creation in Christ. Bring forward the changes that need to be made in my life to accomplish this promise of Your Word. In Jesus' name, amen.

# DAY 177

## OUT OF THE BOX

*The apostles said to the Lord, "Increase our faith!"*

LUKE 17:5 • NASB®

People place their faith in many things. Some people have faith in their physical strength. Some have faith in their intellect. Some have faith in their education. Some have faith in their ability to generate income. Some have faith in their family and friends. Those expressions of faith are not inherently evil. There are different expressions of faith even in the context of our spiritual lives. Some of us have saving faith, believing that God will deliver us from the bondage of sin and welcome us into the Kingdom of God. But we don't have faith to pray that God will heal someone who is sick. We don't have faith that He is able to transform a person. We don't have faith that He is able to heal a relationship. We don't have faith that the Holy Spirit will equip us for the assignments God has invited us to. I'd like for you to consider taking your faith out of the boxes where you are keeping it and allow it to grow until it fills every corner of your life. Pray the simple prayer of the disciples: "Lord, increase my faith!"

### • THINK ABOUT IT •

God declares that nothing is impossible with Him, but we often have at least one area where we think, "That may be true, but not for me—not in this case." Ask the Holy Spirit to reveal any place where you have resigned yourself to unbelief or low expectations.

### *Prayer*

Heavenly Father, help me more fully understand the depth of Your love and power. I repent of any way I have limited You by unbelief and loss of hope. Increase my faith that I might accomplish Your assignments and glorify Your name. In Jesus' name, amen.

## LIFELONG JOURNEY

*But don't just listen to God's word. You must do what it says. Otherwise, you are only fooling yourselves.*

JAMES 1:22 • NLT

You may have believed in the reality of Jesus enough to accept Him as Lord of your life and make a profession of faith, have your sins forgiven, and be birthed into the Kingdom of God. You may have taken another step and publicly declared your faith in Him through baptism. You may be a regular church attender. I commend you for all of those things, but they are not the terminal point in your journey as a Christ-follower. The goal of being a Christ-follower is not to show up on the weekend and sit and stand and be preached at. The goal of a Christ-follower is to become His faithful disciple who loves Him with a whole heart and serves Him joyfully. To gain knowledge of the Lord but never put it to practical use is to live an incomplete Christian life. I would encourage you to ask the Holy Spirit to help you find a place of service in God's Kingdom. You will be a blessing to others, and you will be abundantly blessed as well.

• THINK ABOUT IT •

We have been created in Christ Jesus for good works which God has already prepared for us "to walk in." Walking implies motion—getting out there, and getting it done on an ongoing basis. Ask the Holy Spirit how you can make serving His purposes a lifestyle more than random events.

*Prayer*

Heavenly Father, thank You that I can find a place of service which You have prepared for me. Help me to recognize Your invitations—especially those beyond my expectations—and fill me with Your Holy Spirit to accomplish all Your will. In Jesus' name, amen.

# DAY 179

## LEARNING TO STRETCH

*Then Peter, filled with the Holy Spirit, said to them: "Rulers and elders of the people!"*

ACTS 4:8

The boldness of Peter in Acts 4 is awesome to behold. It is a boldness based not on bravado or his own ego; it is a boldness based on all he has experienced with Jesus, and then fueled by the filling of the Holy Spirit. He has come a long way from where we first met him—a fisherman hauling in his nets, a faithful but ordinary Jewish man waiting for the Messiah with the rest of his people. Since then he has spent time with Jesus, watching and learning. He has seen miracles and even walked on water. Peter's boldness is growing, and it will continue to grow as he stretches his spiritual muscles and learns what it means to minister without Jesus physically by his side. Like Peter, we are in process. As we invite God into our days and seek the filling of the Holy Spirit, we too will be able to stretch our spiritual muscles and learn what it means to be used of the Lord to advance His Kingdom in the earth.

### • THINK ABOUT IT •

In the "going" is the "growing." Like Abraham, who set out with a promise but no map, learning to minister in the Kingdom involves growing in trust that the Lord will be right there with you. Build your trust by reminding yourself of these heroes of the faith, men and women just like you.

*Prayer*

Heavenly Father, I yield to Your Holy Spirit, knowing You will never leave nor forsake me as I obey Your truth. May I be used for Your purposes and add my stories of Your faithfulness to the testimonies of those who have gone before. In Jesus' name, amen.

## COMBAT TRAINING

*The LORD said to Satan, "Where have you come from?" Satan answered the LORD, "From roaming through the earth and going back and forth in it."*

JOB 1:7

I read a book by a British man who participated in World War II. He said that when Great Britain entered the war, no one asked, "Would you like to join this conflict?" Based upon his citizenship in the United Kingdom, when his country entered the war, he entered the war. When we become participants in the Kingdom of God, we inherit an adversary who is roaming the earth. I find that some Christians are awkward with that idea. "Pastor, I don't know if I want to believe in the Devil or demons. I certainly don't want to talk about that." I understand that, because evil is unpleasant. But that's about as effective as saying, "I don't believe in gravity, so I'm going to jump off this building." If not believing in evil would deliver me from evil, I would be all for it. But it won't, so I will continue to train myself in spiritual warfare and depend on the help of the Holy Spirit as I make my way in this world.

### • THINK ABOUT IT •

Have you reconciled to having inherited an enemy based upon your citizenship in God's Kingdom? Training daily for effective spiritual warfare requires focusing on Jesus' complete victory on the cross over a defeated and lying adversary.

*Prayer*

Heavenly Father, Jesus' sacrifice on the cross redeemed me from sin and defeated death. Thank You that this victory frees me to ask Your Holy Spirit for the help I need to stand on this truth: I am more than a conqueror in the face of evil. In Jesus' name, amen.

# DAY 181

## PRESENT TENSE TRUTH

*Neither the sexually immoral nor idolaters nor adulterers nor male prostitutes nor homosexual offenders nor thieves nor the greedy nor drunkards nor slanderers nor swindlers will inherit the kingdom of God. And that is what some of you were. But you were washed, you were sanctified, you were justified in the name of the Lord Jesus Christ and by the Spirit of our God.*

1 CORINTHIANS 6:9-11

The churches of today are not that different from the congregation at Corinth: Sitting in my seat and yours are the sexually promiscuous, worshipers of other gods, greedy thieves, drunkards and drug addicts, and lying cheaters. That's us! But that is what we were—we've been changed! We've been washed, sanctified, and justified in the name of the Lord Jesus Christ. Through the blood of Jesus we are new creations with new hearts, minds, dreams, and priorities. The Holy Spirit is our friend who leads us along new paths of righteousness, because we now desire to live in a way that honors our God. When you doubt your worthiness to approach the Lord in prayer or minister in His name, remember that who you were is not who you are. That is wonderful news!

### • THINK ABOUT IT •

When you become discouraged about your own ability to follow the Lord obediently and consistently, refocus your confidence on Him. You are His workmanship and He is still working—in you.

### Prayer

Heavenly Father, because of the cross, my past is not my future. Help me walk in Your abundant grace, and let Your power be perfected in my weakness. I will resist every accusing lie with confidence in Your redemption and plan for me. In Jesus' name, amen.

## NO CUTTING IN

*You were running a good race. Who cut in on you and kept you from obeying the truth? That kind of persuasion does not come from the one who calls you.*

GALATIANS 5:7-8

Paul is asking a group of believers what had disrupted their stride and caused them to lose their momentum toward obeying the truth. Picture a line of sprinters as they are waiting for their race to begin. Their faces are filled with concentration as they look down the track toward the finish line in the distance. Everything in them—body, mind, and spirit—is focused on finishing that race well. But they can be thrown off their stride by a noise, a loose shoelace, or another runner cutting into their lane. How can we establish and then sustain momentum that takes us toward godliness? Begin by living with a heightened awareness of spiritual things. Think about it: What strengthens your faith? What causes you to question it? What brings you joy? What diminishes your joy? What is from God, and what is not? Spiritual momentum can be a powerful force for good, so keep your eyes on the finish line and do everything in your power to keep going in the right direction.

### • THINK ABOUT IT •

Scripture repeatedly invites us to not just be interested in God, but to actively pursue Him, and pursuing requires laser-focus on the goal and the One we are seeking. Is your relationship with the Lord marked by this kind of single-mindedness?

*Prayer*

Heavenly Father, I want to diligently honor Your boundaries and pursue Your pathway for my life. Direct my heart and mind away from distractions that indulge selfish desires and break my momentum, interfering with Your purposes. In Jesus' name, amen.

## GIVE GOD THE CREDIT

*Thanks be to God! He gives us the victory through our Lord Jesus Christ.*

1 CORINTHIANS 15:57

Sometimes when I hear stories of spiritual transformation, I wonder if God was involved at all. Some seem to want the world to think that they were able to outwit the evil that touched their lives. Through their extraordinary willpower, they turned their lives around and became godly people. Others try to bury their past and deny that they were ever something different than the person they are today. In both of these situations, people are erasing the power of God from their stories and taking the credit for themselves. The truth is that we all are evil people saved by the blood of Jesus, and we need to get in line with the rest of the sinners God changed and used for His purposes: Moses, the murderer; Rahab, the prostitute; David, the adulterer; Mary, the demon-possessed woman; and Paul, the persecutor. God is in the business of delivering people and transforming their lives. We are victorious only because of what Jesus has done for us. That's my story, and I'm glad to tell it.

### • THINK ABOUT IT •

It is not always easy to rehearse the things from which the Lord has rescued you. When your adversary, the accuser of the brethren, tries to use shame to silence your story, don't let him. There are others who need to hear that Jesus can help them too.

### *Prayer*

Heavenly Father, I want You to receive the full glory for redeeming me through the finished work of Your Son, Jesus, on the cross. Help me, Holy Spirit, make the most of every opportunity to express what Your love and mercy have done for me. In Jesus' name, amen.

## TODAY'S EXPECTATIONS

*Shouts of joy and victory resound in the tents of the righteous: "The Lord's right hand has done mighty things!"*

PSALM 118:15

Christianity is often presented as being pretty front heavy, with all the important God-choices happening near the beginning of the journey. We experience salvation, we make a profession of faith, we are baptized, and then we sit and wait for Heaven. This is a sad way of understanding our faith, because the most important season of our walk with Christ is right now. I will enjoy hearing about your profession of faith when you were twelve, but I really get excited when I hear about a victory God gave you this week. I will rejoice over the way He delivered you from a painful past, but I also am curious about what mighty things you are expecting Him to do today. Don't ever allow your faith journey to become past tense: what Jesus did for you way back when. You want your walk with Jesus to be so current that you can talk about it in the present tense: what Jesus is doing in you and through you today.

### • THINK ABOUT IT •

Christ-followers are "citizens of Heaven," living on earth for God's purposes. If you do not have a habit of asking Him to work in and through you each day, begin to ask Him today. Your God-stories will multiply!

*Prayer*

Heavenly Father, I willingly accept Your assignments and want to continually experience Your transforming power at work in my life and in the lives of others. Enable me to be a faithful ambassador of Your grace and truth today. In Jesus' name, amen.

## FUTURE-SHAPING GENEROSITY

*Let us not become weary in doing good, for at the proper time we will reap a harvest if we do not give up. Therefore, as we have opportunity, let us do good to all people, especially to those who belong to the family of believers.*

GALATIANS 6:9-10

I remember when we stepped out on faith and built our first sanctuary. We borrowed a little money and put up a steel building with a concrete floor. As we could afford to, we built classrooms for children. At one point the remaining debt was weighing on our small group. A family friend called and said, "I've had a burden on my heart for your little church. Is there still a debt on it?" When they answered yes, he said, "I'd like to see that paid off. Would it be OK if I wrote a check?" It wasn't an enormous amount of money, but it was a sizable amount to us at the time. That man gave of his resources and changed the vision of the church. When the Holy Spirit prompts you to be generous, do it. When God blesses you through Spirit-led generosity, praise Him from whom all blessings flow!

### • THINK ABOUT IT •

Today that gentleman's great grandchildren are a part of our congregation. How have you seen the generosity of God's people reap a harvest in future generations?

*Prayer*

Heavenly Father, open my heart and my hand to give as freely as You have given to me, no matter my circumstance. As I do, multiply my seed for sowing toward Your Kingdom purposes, and help me be sensitive to Your promptings to give. In Jesus' name, amen.

## ASTOUNDING INTERVENTION

*Very rarely will anyone die for a righteous man, though for a good man someone might possibly dare to die. But God demonstrates his own love for us in this: While we were still sinners, Christ died for us.*

ROMANS 5:7-8

I wasn't a tremendously gifted athlete, but I enjoyed playing high school basketball. I couldn't jump very high or run very fast, and my shot wasn't that great. My backup button didn't work very well, and sometimes my mouth wrote checks that my body couldn't cash. (I'm still working on that.) On more than one occasion when I had gone too far, I'd hear a deep voice from behind me: "Leave him alone." It was one of my friends who was the opposite of me: strong, quiet, and a gifted athlete. As a young man I thought that God probably breathed a sigh of relief when He recruited me onto His team. Now I have gained enough maturity to realize what a liability He accepted when He welcomed me into His Kingdom. Jesus interceded for us in a very sacrificial way when He died on the cross and exchanged His righteousness for our sin. Let us never forget that, or take it for granted.

• THINK ABOUT IT •

Jesus humbled Himself so completely to win us back to God. Walk with Him in this same spirit of humility, and declare Him worthy of every exaltation Heaven and earth can offer.

*Prayer*

Heavenly Father, You are worthy of all thanksgiving and praise! Lord Jesus, You are worthy of praise and honor—thank You for exchanging Your righteousness for my sin and redeeming me completely. I humbly bow my knee before You. In Your name I pray, amen.

# DAY 187

## SEARCH AND RESCUE

*"For God so loved the world that he gave his one and only Son, that whoever believes in him shall not perish but have eternal life. For God did not send his Son into the world to condemn the world, but to save the world through him."*

JOHN 3:16-17

God initiated the ultimate search and rescue mission so that any person who chooses to follow Him can benefit. The benefit isn't based on anything we have done; it is based on what was done for us by another Person—Jesus of Nazareth. If we will believe that He is the Messiah, the Christ, and choose Him as Lord and serve Him as King, our lives can be transformed for time and eternity. That's the heart of the gospel. There has never been an alternative to it in all of human history. There is no new theology or ideology or technological advance that will ever replace it. Jesus came to save "whoever believes in him" from every nation, race, language, and tribe. It is a wonderful message of hope for the people of the world, and the Church has the privilege of sharing that message with every generation.

### • THINK ABOUT IT •

Our gospel is exclusive: There is only one way to be saved. It's also inclusive: Any person who turns to Jesus can be saved. This is the offense and attractiveness of the gospel to our age. Ask the Holy Spirit for boldness to carry it joyfully.

### *Prayer*

Heavenly Father, thank You for sending Jesus to seek and save me. Fill me with Your Spirit and enable me to declare all Christ has accomplished on the cross. Let my actions and words display the hope and mercy You have given me. In Jesus' name, amen.

# DAY 188

## HOW DID WE GET HERE?

*Who would not fear you, O King of nations? That title belongs to you alone! Among all the wise people of the earth and in all the kingdoms of the world, there is no one like you.*

JEREMIAH 10:7 • NLT

We look at the Israelites and think: How could they have become so hardened and drifted so far from God? I look at our own nation and wonder: When did the name of Jesus become forbidden in our public schools and public places? Why is corporate America so anxious that Jesus not be mentioned in their boardrooms? How have we arrived at this place, when we are a nation with a Christian heritage? Our experiment in democracy was launched by the idea that without representation, we would not pay our taxes. Yet with a Christian community as large as we have, we have gone silently along this path while they have said, "Don't bring Jesus into the public square!" Excuse me? This is not about the ungodly; this is about us. We need a sweeping change in the way we understand our relationship with God. That will begin with a change in our hearts.

### • THINK ABOUT IT •

Are there places in your life and in your sphere of influence where you have been silent about God and His truth and redemptive power? Ask God to help you find your voice and use it in His power and wisdom, for His glory.

### Prayer

Heavenly Father, forgive me for the times I have gone underground with my faith. Help me to be Your servant—faithful to Your character in word and deed—demonstrating Your love and truth to my family, friends, coworkers, and community. In Jesus' name, amen.

## COVERT ENEMY

*"No one can serve two masters; for either he will hate the one and love the other, or he will be devoted to one and despise the other. You cannot serve God and wealth."*

MATTHEW 6:24 • NASB®

The assignment of the Church in every generation is to share the message of Jesus Christ. Some generations have done a better job of that than others. One of the best ways to nullify or at least diminish the effectiveness of the Church is to let us prosper. It seems the more affluent we become, the more options we have, the less aware we are of the goodness and grace of God and our dependence on Him. Our focus seems to be on getting stuff, getting more stuff, getting nicer stuff, figuring out what to do with all our stuff, and then repeating the cycle. My prayer is that the Church in our generation can put an end to this cycle. I pray that we will shake off the sluggishness that comes from the "muchness" of our lives and give the very best of our time, talent, and resources to Jesus of Nazareth.

· THINK ABOUT IT ·

Invitations and commitments can easily bombard a busy household. Ask the Holy Spirit for His help to plan your life so that you can give Him your best first.

*Prayer*

Heavenly Father, You are my first love and priority. Help me examine my schedule, checkbook, and labors that I might give You my very best. Even good things can distract, so help me surrender all to Your Lordship and Your Holy Spirit. In Jesus' name, amen.

## RESCUED!

*For he has rescued us from the dominion of darkness and brought us into the kingdom of the Son he loves, in whom we have redemption, the forgiveness of sins.*

COLOSSIANS 1:13-14

We have become so accustomed to seeing evil in our world that I'm not sure we understand how insidious and destructive it is. Television, movies, and music are filled with examples of evil being justified and glorified and celebrated. Know this: Evil is in exact opposition to the character of God. The "dominion of darkness" is in complete conflict with the "Kingdom of the Son." Apart from Jesus' intervention, we were slaves to evil. Evil owned us and destined us to destruction. Apart from the grace, mercy, kindness, and love of God, we were under the authority and dominion of evil. There was nothing we could do to rectify that situation. God in His kindness sent His Son to rescue us from that "dominion of darkness" and bring us into His Kingdom. We don't gather in our church buildings because we imagine that we are perfect. We gather as an expression of gratitude for what God has done on our behalf in rescuing us from certain destruction.

## • THINK ABOUT IT •

Becoming desensitized to evil fosters complacency and compromise, with attitudes and actions that grieve the Holy Spirit. Ask the Holy Spirit to sensitize you to the things that break His heart.

## Prayer

Heavenly Father, thank You for delivering me from the "dominion of darkness" through Jesus Christ. Forgive me of complacent participation with anything that opposes Your character, that I might be salt and light in this generation. In Jesus' name, amen.

## PRECIOUS FRAGRANCE

*The four living creatures and the twenty-four elders fell down before the Lamb. Each one had a harp and they were holding golden bowls full of incense, which are the prayers of the saints.*

### REVELATION 5:8

I think at some time each of us has wondered if our prayers were being heard. Perhaps God did not answer in the time frame you were expecting. Perhaps He did not answer in the way you wanted, so you assume that He didn't hear your pleas. This verse gives a dramatic picture of just how significant our prayers are. They exist collectively in the presence of God, held in golden bowls by the four living creatures and the twenty-four elders who surround the throne. They rise before God like incense and fill the air. Never again doubt the importance of prayer. Never say that prayer is for other people. You may say, "I don't know how to pray well. I don't feel like an expert in prayer. I'm learning to pray." Even now our prayers are filling the air around the throne of God, so let's determine to become people who are learning to pray.

### • THINK ABOUT IT •

Your prayers make a significant difference in the lives of those around you and in the course of your community and nation. Paul repeatedly asked others to help him with their prayers, and they were people just like you and me.

### *Prayer*

Heavenly Father, thank You for inviting me to talk with You, praying over matters great and small. Increase my belief that You hear me, and open my heart to hear Your response. Surround me with others who can help me grow in prayer. In Jesus' name, amen.

## THE COURAGE TO RESPOND

*"What are you waiting for? Get up, be baptized and wash your sins away, calling on his name."*

ACTS 22:16

Baptism is an event of tremendous significance and celebration in the life of a Jesus-follower. It completes what began with a profession of faith as we are washed clean in body, soul, and spirit—not physically by the water of a pool, but symbolically by the blood of Jesus that redeems and transforms us. Just as in the book of Acts, it takes tremendous courage to be baptized—to take a public stand, be immersed in water, and say, "Jesus is my Savior and Lord. I want to honor Him with my life." If you have been baptized by immersion, thank the Lord for the deliverance and new life He has given you. If you have not taken that step, I would encourage you to do so and publicly acknowledge Jesus as Lord of your life. It will bring a new focus and joy to your relationship with Him, and He will be dearer to you than He has ever been before.

• THINK ABOUT IT •

If you have already been baptized, use your influence to encourage others in that step of obedience. Determine to be an unapologetic advocate for the invitations of Scripture.

*Prayer*

Heavenly Father, Jesus is Lord, and I will publicly acknowledge Him with joy. I want to follow His example with my life. Draw others to You, Lord, through Your life in me. I thank You for freedom and deliverance. In Jesus' name, amen.

## MARVELOUS DESIGN

*Ears that hear and eyes that see—the LORD has made them both.*

PROVERBS 20:12

One of the things that enabled me to serve the Lord more fully was when I realized the marvels that science reveals. What science shows about our Creator and His creation made me want to worship the Lord! Take the human body, for example. God designed the eye with an iris that enlarges and shrinks depending on the light around you. You don't have to tell your iris, "We're going into a darker room now, so open wide." He designed our ears with a funny looking outside part that catches sound waves and funnels them inside, where they vibrate and send signals to our brain. All of that happens even when we are hearing something we don't particularly want to. He designed you with an immune system that works day in and day out to protect you from unseen micro-enemies. You didn't get up this morning and tell your body, "There's a virus going around. Make white blood cells!" Your body is designed so well that if you break a bone, it will heal. Our bodies are incredibly complex creations and great gifts from our amazing God!

### • THINK ABOUT IT •

The discoveries of science are multiplying daily and testify to the wisdom and power of God in His creation. Practice admiration and worship of God as your first response to the wonders of creation.

*Prayer*

Heavenly Father, I am in awe of Your wisdom, power, and understanding displayed in all You have created! I reaffirm my trust in You for every detail of my life. Thank You for Your immeasurably great power exercised daily on my behalf. In Jesus' name, amen.

## ARMED AND READY

*The devil led him to Jerusalem and had him stand on the highest point of the temple. "If you are the Son of God," he said, "throw yourself down from here. For it is written: 'He will command his angels concerning you to guard you carefully; they will lift you up in their hands, so that you will not strike your foot against a stone.'" Jesus answered, "It says: 'Do not put the Lord your God to the test.'"*

LUKE 4:9-12

Did you know that the Devil knows the Bible? When he tried to lure Jesus into sin by twisting words from a psalm of assurance (Psalm 91), Jesus immediately responded by quoting Moses' words to the Israelites (Deuteronomy 6:16). Our enemy is still twisting Scripture and taking it out of context to lead us away from the truth, and even some in positions of Christian leadership have fallen into his sad and destructive trap. That's why it's so important to read your Bible and get to know the character of God. When we know who He is, we will be able to protect ourselves from the deceptive words that swirl around us.

• THINK ABOUT IT •

A casual knowledge of God's Word makes us especially vulnerable to deception. If you have not, begin now to study the Bible methodically and daily. It will make all the difference in your response to temptation.

*Prayer*

Heavenly Father, help me diligently read the Bible and grow in the knowledge of Your character, delivering me from deceptions that seek to discredit Your truth. Direct me to tools that will help me pursue You and Your Word. In Jesus' name, amen.

## TOGETHER WE CAN MAKE A DIFFERENCE

*Let us consider how we may spur one another on toward love and good deeds. Let us not give up meeting together, as some are in the habit of doing, but let us encourage one another...*

HEBREWS 10:24-25

I cannot tell you how many times I have heard something like this: "Pastor, I don't need to sit in church and hear someone preach to be a Christian. I can worship on a creek bank. God is everywhere, isn't He?" Yes, God is everywhere, and it is easy to worship on a creek bank. But that's not really a reason to avoid participating in a local congregation. Our world pushes a constant stream of messaging toward us on many different platforms. Some of it is positive, and some of it is neutral; but much of it contradicts the message of Scripture. We need time together to reinforce, encourage, and push back on all that messaging. We need to read God's Word together, pray together, and be encouraged as we witness God working in one another's lives. So no, sitting in a church building doesn't make you a Christian, but you gain enormous spiritual strength from the fellowship of other believers.

### • THINK ABOUT IT •

Fellowship with other Christ-followers is one of God's primary means of building you up in the faith. Forfeiting that opportunity lessens your effectiveness in the Kingdom of God, because He knits your unique gifts with those of others to accomplish His purposes.

### Prayer

Heavenly Father, thank You for the encouraging and sustaining fellowship You provide within churches. Help me commit to and maintain community with other believers so that, together, we can be more effective in Your service. In Jesus' name, amen.

## YOUR DEEPEST DESIRE

*"Come, let us go up to the mountain of the LORD, to the house of the God of Jacob. He will teach us his ways, so that we may walk in his paths."*

ISAIAH 2:3

What is the deepest desire of your heart? Some of us desire to achieve great things. We want to build companies, construct great buildings, save lives, or design new products. Some of us want to accumulate wealth and possessions. We want to be the wealthiest person in our town, own rare collections, and drive expensive cars. Some of us want to be recognized for our towering intellect. We want to write books and give speeches and be consulted when decisions must be made. Some of us want to be admired for our ability to entertain. We want to stand on a stage before cheering crowds or be recognized as a movie or television or sports star. It is easy to be captivated by these things. But more than I want to achieve or accumulate or be recognized or admired, I want to know the paths of the Lord. My deepest desire is to walk in a way that pleases Him.

### • THINK ABOUT IT •

What do you most want to be known as? What is the legacy you want to leave? Seek the Lord for how He has imagined you, for the purposes He has hardwired into you. His image of you is your true portrait, not the caricature the world would tempt you to be.

### Prayer

Heavenly Father, thank You for designing me with Your loving and merciful purposes in mind. Where my choices have "disfigured" my life, I ask You to restore and conform me to the image of Your Son that I might walk in the way that pleases You. In Jesus' name, amen.

## NO ATTRACTION-NO REACTION

*When he died, he died once to break the power of sin. But now that he lives, he lives for the glory of God. So you also should consider yourselves to be dead to the power of sin and alive to God through Christ Jesus.*

ROMANS 6:10-11 • NLT

When you are dead to something, it has no attraction for you, and it elicits no reaction from you. I like chocolate, and if there is a bowl of M&M's® in front of me today I will be tempted to have a handful...or two. But when I'm dead you can float me in a vat of M&M's® and I won't be tempted. The Bible says we have to learn to reckon ourselves dead to sin and instead remember that we are "alive to God through Christ Jesus." We are sinful humans living in a world filled with temptations, but like Jesus, we want to live "for the glory of God." When we stop and consider that Jesus died to break sin's hold over us, it will be much easier to focus on Him and take our attention away from those things that tempt us.

• THINK ABOUT IT •

Our spirits, souls, and bodies each hunger for something. Jesus said His "food" was to do the will of Him who sent Him. Satisfying spiritual hunger through God's Word and prayer will diminish the junk cravings of temptation.

*Prayer*

Heavenly Father, teach me to satisfy my spirit with the things that give life. I want my time to be marked by hungering to do the will of my Creator and allowing You to break sin's hold on me so that I might serve You in freedom. In Jesus' name, amen.

## UNLIMITED FUTURE

*For this world is not our permanent home; we are looking forward to a home yet to come.*

HEBREWS 13:14 • NLT

We don't need to look any further than our own homes to see that there is great suffering in our fallen world. Job loss, financial stress, prodigal children, marital difficulties, illness and disease—and many times one of these will lead to others. When we listen to the news and hear of the tragedies that are happening on a daily basis in small towns and cities around the globe, it can be overwhelming. The reality is that this present age is evil, and it brings brokenheartedness and mourning and pain. These things place limits upon us, but the promise of Scripture is that in the age to come those limits will be removed. What will the new age look like? I don't know everything, but I can tell you this: There will be no more crying, or mourning, or pain. There will be a new, righteous authority in place, and we will see the Lord in all of His glory and majesty. What a glorious world that will be!

### • THINK ABOUT IT •

Life's cares and discouragements can sometimes keep us from joyful anticipation of the home Jesus promised He is preparing in eternity. This alone gives us a reason to rejoice every day—let's look forward!

*Prayer*

Heavenly Father, thank You that trials and sufferings are not the seal over our lives—that through the cross, I have a great hope that outweighs my troubles. Each day, help me to both remember all that awaits me and faithfully share this hope with others. In Jesus' name, amen.

## IT'S BOTH/AND

*"Do not think that I have come to abolish the Law or the Prophets; I have not come to abolish them but to fulfill them. I tell you the truth, until heaven and earth disappear, not the smallest letter, not the least stroke of a pen, will by any means disappear from the Law until everything is accomplished."*

MATTHEW 5:17-18

Some believers are unusually focused on either the New Testament or the Old Testament, and I find that odd. The New Testament authors assume that the Old Testament narrative is valid, consistently referring to the Old Testament to secure the points they are making about the character and purposes of God. Even Jesus quoted from the Old Testament. The Old Testament writers urged people to live in a way that would please God even as they looked ahead to the Messiah who is revealed in the New Testament. The Old and New Testaments are God's message for us, written long ago but as relevant as today's headlines. Jesus Himself said that the entirety of Scripture is worthy of our attention until it is fulfilled in the coming age, so I will continue to revere it and study it...all of it.

### • THINK ABOUT IT •

Every word from God is living and proves true. In an age and culture when truth is in such short supply, let's incorporate more of Scripture into our lives—reading, studying, and honoring every word.

*Prayer*

Heavenly Father, Your Word is living and active—all of it! Jesus answered the Devil's temptation by saying man lives by every word that proceeds from the mouth of God. Increase my love for Scripture, and grant me an understanding heart. In Jesus' name, amen.

## PROACTIVE HEART

*The word of the LORD came to Samuel: "I am grieved that I have made Saul king, because he has turned away from me and has not carried out my instructions." Samuel was troubled, and he cried out to the LORD all that night.*

1 SAMUEL 15:10-11

Samuel was the last of the Judges, one of the charismatic leaders that God raised up to shepherd His people through times of crisis. God had sent Samuel to anoint Saul as the first king of Israel. When Saul lost his perspective and gained an elevated opinion of himself, he forfeited the blessing of God on his leadership. Samuel had been serving the Lord since he was a very small boy, and he knew the Lord well. When the Lord came to him with the news of Saul's unrepentant heart, Samuel not only prayed about it, he "cried out to the LORD all that night." When we hear news of an unrepentant heart—whether it's a friend, an acquaintance, or even a politician—how do we react? Do we say, "Wow, that's surprising. I hope they come around"? Or do we go to our knees in prayer that the Lord will change them and transform them for His purposes?

### • THINK ABOUT IT •

Gaining a good shepherd's heart—the kind that goes after the lost sheep on the ledge, knowing the labor and hardship that might entail—will birth the prayers that accomplish God's purposes. Seeking His heart for others can train your own.

### *Prayer*

Heavenly Father, I want to learn from the heart of the Good Shepherd, Your Son. Help me persevere in prayer for my family and friends, reminding me that nothing is too hard for the God who saves. May we yield our lives to You. In Jesus' name, amen.

## REDEMPTIVE POTENTIAL

*Jesus said to him, "Today salvation has come to this house, because this man, too, is a son of Abraham. For the Son of Man came to seek and to save the lost."*

LUKE 19:9-10

Zacchaeus was a wealthy chief tax collector in Jericho. Tax collectors were unpopular because they collected taxes from the Jewish people for the Roman government. They were known for taking more money than was due and keeping the extra for themselves. I'm sure he was aware of his unpopularity, and he was probably very surprised when Jesus called to him and invited Himself over for a meal. His transformation was immediate, and he quickly told the Lord he intended to give half of his possessions to the poor and repay those he had cheated fourfold. There are those among us who have done terrible things. In our eyes they seem unredeemable, perhaps even unworthy of God's grace. But the Lord doesn't see people the way we do. He doesn't see people for what they have done; He sees people for what they can be. Let's ask the Lord to give us a fresh vision of the people around us so that we can see them like He does.

• THINK ABOUT IT •

Let's not underestimate the power and willingness of God to turn "Sauls" into "Pauls" and uneducated fishermen into bold witnesses for God's redemptive power. He delights in transforming our lives.

*Prayer*

Heavenly Father, grant me a fresh perspective of Your power to transform and redeem even those who seem beyond Your reach. Help me align myself with Your Word and desire for all to be saved and come to the truth and pray accordingly. In Jesus' name, amen.

# DAY 202

## MOVED TO TEARS

*During the days of Jesus' life on earth, he offered up prayers and petitions with loud cries and tears...*

HEBREWS 5:7

When I think of Jesus praying, I think of Him speaking with great authority. After all, He was the very Son of God who spoke publicly and the sick were healed, the blind could see, demons were cast out, and the dead were raised to life. Yet this verse says He offered up prayers and petitions to His Father with loud cries and tears. Jesus, while fully God, was also fully human, and He was not afraid to show His emotions to His Father. In the account of the death of Lazarus, He was moved to tears. Do we pray like that? Do we care that much? I'm afraid that when we see tragedy unfolding before us, our first reaction is, "Oh, that's too bad." When we do take a situation before the Lord, our prayers are pretty sterile and buttoned down. Don't be afraid to show your emotions before the Lord. He understands what it means to take our desperation to God, and He will hear your prayers and help you.

### • THINK ABOUT IT •

Our tears are important to God. In Psalms God promises He gives them weight and wants to dry them—that He is near to the brokenhearted. Tears unite spirit, soul, and body in a unique way. When you pray for yourself or others, bring all of yourself—including emotions—to Him.

### Prayer

Heavenly Father, help me be willing to be moved to tears when tragedy unfolds and I cry out to You in the midst of great pain. Then may Your healing presence touch every part of my life and the lives of those You have given me to love. In Jesus' name, amen.

# DAY 203

## LET IT GO

*As far as the east is from the west, so far has he removed our transgressions from us.*

PSALM 103:12

It is very difficult to live a fulfilling life as a Jesus-follower if you are in the habit of dragging the weight of your past failures behind you. I think some of us are just inclined to do this because of our personalities. Others of us grew up in families where failures were never relegated to the past but were used as constant reminders of our shortcomings. Whatever the reason, in order to mature spiritually you will need to learn to let go of your guilt because it does not honor the Lord. When you refuse to turn loose of your guilt, you are saying that what Jesus did was not enough. Yes, we understand that Jesus died on the cross, but surely there must be something that I need to do to add to it a little bit. I want you to understand that what Jesus did for you was enough. You cannot do anything to add to the utterly complete and final redemption that He bought for you that day. Believe it, trust in it, and let the guilt go.

### · THINK ABOUT IT ·

Do you hold onto guilt and shame after asking God for forgiveness through the cross? If so, realize the Devil is tricking you into mocking and doubting the efficacy of Jesus' sacrifice. Let the guilt go.

*Prayer*

Heavenly Father, I rejoice in Jesus' finished and complete redemptive work on the cross, determining to daily proclaim Your gift of life and freedom from guilt and paralyzing regret. Thank You I can now live my life by faith in the One who loved me and gave Himself for me. In Jesus' name, amen.

## ASKING THE RIGHT QUESTION

*There is a time for everything, and a season for every activity under heaven: a time to be born, and a time to die, a time to plant and a time to uproot...a time to tear down and a time to build, a time to weep and a time to laugh...*

ECCLESIASTES 3:1-4

Ecclesiastes 3 assures us that there is "a time for everything." But God's timing is often not what we want, and we are prone to ask why. "I thought this would be a season of laughing, but all I can do is weep. Why is this happening, God?" "I have something wonderful here, and I want to keep planting in this place. Why are You asking me to uproot everything?" "Why" questions are debilitating. We don't like our circumstances. We don't like our path. We don't like waiting. We feel targeted and feel like God is punishing us. The fact is that we all are subject to the rhythms of life. Some choices are ours; others are not. The good news is that our God is faithful, and loving, and completely trustworthy to walk with us along life's journey, wherever it may lead.

• THINK ABOUT IT •

When tempted to ask God, "Why?" consider asking, "How should I respond to this, Lord?" or "What will bring about Your best in this situation?" The right question can add momentum to your spiritual journey and keep you moving forward, humbly trusting a faithful God.

*Prayer*

Heavenly Father, You are sovereign, good, and all-powerful. Thank You that You can make even a discouraging, difficult time work for my good. I trust Your ways for my life and submit myself to Your purposes in every season. In Jesus' name, amen.

## GRACE INTERVENTION

*For I am the least of the apostles, and not fit to be called an apostle, because I persecuted the church of God. But by the grace of God I am what I am, and His grace toward me did not prove vain...*

1 CORINTHIANS 15:9-10 • NASB®

When we first meet the Apostle Paul, he is Saul of Tarsus, a Pharisee. He is an orthodox Jewish man with an impressive education, a powerful mind, and a lot of career momentum. He studied at the right schools and has the right connections. But Saul was violent and profane—a murderer and a blasphemer whose goal was to discredit Jesus' followers and destroy the Church. In Acts 9, Jesus found Saul on the road to Damascus and asked, "Saul, what do you think you are doing?" Now Saul is saying to the Corinthians: "I persecuted the Church of God. But by the grace of God I am what I am, and His grace toward me did not prove vain." Brilliant, educated, articulate, influential, and evil—but the grace of God turned his life around and gave him a completely different ending.

### • THINK ABOUT IT •

Be encouraged that the great cloud of witnesses that have gone before us all overcame significant weaknesses through God's grace to accomplish their purposes in the earth.

*Prayer*

Heavenly Father, I readily receive Your abundant, sufficient grace, and I ask for Your perspective on others. Thank You for the significance and meaning You have given my life through the cross. In Jesus' name, amen.

## ALL-SUFFICIENT MEDIATOR

*Because Jesus lives forever, he has a permanent priesthood. Therefore he is able to save completely those who come to God through him, because he always lives to intercede for them.*

HEBREWS 7:24-25

You don't need a pastor, a priest, or a professional religious person as an intermediary between yourself and God because you have One: The man Jesus Christ is your high priest! The Scripture says that Jesus not only is able to save you completely, but He lives to make intercession for you. Your intercessor is the one who took the punishment for your sin and mine and gave His life on the cross so that we could have His life. Now He is at His Father's throne, interceding for us. The name of Jesus conveys authority; that's why I pray in His name. He says that we can approach the throne of grace with confidence and receive mercy and help in our time of need, and I believe Him. I'm not coming before God's throne on the merits of Allen and my own righteousness; that wouldn't get me very far. I'm coming in the name of my high priest who lives forever—Jesus.

• THINK ABOUT IT •

Recognizing Jesus' tireless prayers for His followers can give you confidence to approach Almighty God in His name. You won't be interrupting Him—You are already on His mind, and You have His attention. Let Him have yours.

*Prayer*

Heavenly Father, thank You that Jesus is my Advocate before Your throne. Thank You, Jesus, for pleading my case and fully redeeming me. Align my heart with Yours so that I can join You in establishing God's will on earth. In Jesus' name, amen.

## FILTER OF BELIEF

*Later Jesus appeared to the Eleven as they were eating; he rebuked them for their lack of faith and their stubborn refusal to believe those who had seen him after he had risen.*

MARK 16:14

Jesus' friends had experienced a great deal that day. His tomb was empty, which was shocking enough, but some said they had seen Him and talked to Him. These of His closest friends were not willing to accept it. Now Jesus is in the room, rebuking them "for their lack of faith and their stubborn refusal to believe." Jesus had told them repeatedly about the events that would lead up to His crucifixion, and His burial and resurrection. They had information and evidence, yet they chose not to believe. We imagine that belief is optional. It's true that we have free will. But it's also clear that when Jesus tells us the truth, He doesn't expect us to sift it through our filters of intelligence, wisdom, and life experience and then decide whether or not we will believe. He expects us to hear His words and His truth and treat them with integrity. Believe Jesus. Trust that what He says is true. It will change your life.

### · THINK ABOUT IT ·

The disciples had both eyewitness testimony and the evidence of Jesus' word. Today, we have the same. Responding with belief to Jesus and the absolute authority of His Word will release transforming power into your life.

### *Prayer*

Heavenly Father, forgive me of any doublemindedness and unbelief in my life. I choose to believe in and rest in the finished work of the cross of Jesus Christ. May Your transforming power be at work in me that You might be glorified. In Jesus' name, amen.

## AUTHENTIC WORSHIP

*O nations of the world, recognize the Lord; recognize that the Lord is glorious and strong. Give to the Lord the glory he deserves! Bring your offering and come into his courts.*

PSALM 96:7-8 • NLT

The word "worship" is a generic term that can apply to any religion. The dictionary says that worship is both the feeling of reverence toward a deity and the expression of that reverence. For Christians, worship has two parts: acknowledging who God is and what He has done and has said He will do on our behalf, and then acting on that. Unfortunately, many of us have fallen into the habit of showing up on the weekend to watch what is happening on the platform, and we think we are worshiping. I'm grateful for all that musicians and our production crew do to facilitate worship, but that is not the essence of worship—that's simply an invitation to worship. True worship—acknowledging God for all He is and acting on that—is a very powerful thing. When we choose to focus our hearts, minds, and voices on expressing our love and adoration for God—that is authentic worship.

## • THINK ABOUT IT •

Directing all of our attention on the Lord when we worship involves self-discipline and doesn't come easily. But the Holy Spirit will help us as we concentrate our adoration toward Almighty God.

## *Prayer*

Heavenly Father, I love You, and I want to worship You in spirit and in truth. Help me corral my wandering mind when I come to worship You, whether I am in a church assembly or home alone in my prayer time that I might honor You. In Jesus' name, amen.

## RESTORATION BUSINESS

*Jesus said to Simon Peter, "Simon son of John, do you truly love me more than these?" "Yes, Lord," he said, "you know that I love you." Jesus said, "Feed my lambs."*

JOHN 21:15

For the last three years Peter had listened to Jesus' teaching and seen and experienced His miracles, but in Jesus' time of need he had denied Him three times. Now, when the resurrected Jesus asks Peter, "Do you love Me?" Peter replies, "Lord, You know I do." "Feed my lambs," Jesus tells him. A few days later, the Spirit of God is poured out in Jerusalem, and a crowd gathers to ask what is happening. Who steps forward? Peter, who says, "Let me tell you about Jesus, the Messiah." The power of God can move through our lives, giving us a long resume of God-stories; but we can still need restoration. Those of us who have witnessed the power of God have been entrusted with greater opportunities and have greater responsibilities. But Jesus is in the business of restoring His people and using us to accomplish His purposes—not just in antiquity, but today.

· THINK ABOUT IT ·

Is there a place where you need restoration? Take hope from Peter's story. Tell the Lord you love Him, and allow Him to pour out His Spirit to restore and empower you for the next part of your race. Your God-journey isn't done yet.

*Prayer*

Heavenly Father, I am grateful for Your mercies, and for Your cleansing me through the blood of Your Son. Continually align me with the plans You have for me that I might serve You with increasing effectiveness in the coming seasons. In Jesus' name, amen.

## PERMISSION TO BE DESPERATE

*During the days of Jesus' life on earth, he offered up prayers and petitions with loud cries and tears to the one who could save him from death, and he was heard because of his reverent submission.*

HEBREWS 5:7

Some of us have grown up in homes and churches where the only prayers we heard sounded like they were written centuries ago—because they were! There is nothing wrong with written prayers and corporate prayers—we pray those regularly at our church. But Jesus is our model, and He did not always offer up neat and tidy prayers. He knew that eternity in Heaven or Hell was in the balance for the people around Him. He suffered constant persecution. Sometimes He was desperate, and that gives me permission to be desperate. Sometimes He cried for help, and that gives me permission to cry for help. Desperation is not a sign of weakness or failure, because Jesus was neither of those. Allowing God to see and hear our deepest feelings is an expression of trust and humility toward the One who has promised to hear us and help us, so don't ever feel you cannot show Him your true emotions.

• THINK ABOUT IT •

God's Holy Spirit searches the deepest recesses of your life—your emotions neither surprise nor offend Him. He is eager for you to invite Him to come in with complete healing and comfort.

*Prayer*

Heavenly Father, I bring it all before You: my thoughts, my desperate emotions, my hidden anxieties. I trust You with every open wound and scar. Hear the cry of my heart and deliver me from my fears, bringing Your healing and hope. In Jesus' name, amen.

## TESTED AND STRENGTHENED

*"Simon, Simon, Satan has asked to sift you as wheat. But I have prayed for you, Simon, that your faith may not fail. And when you have turned back, strengthen your brothers."*

LUKE 22:31-32

These verses are thought-provoking for me. Jesus tells Simon Peter that Satan has asked for permission to target him in order to try to disrupt and destroy his faith. Then Jesus tells Simon Peter that He has prayed that his faith won't fail. Frankly, that is not what I'd want to hear. If it were me, I'd rather He say, "Allen, Satan asked if he could come after you. I told him absolutely not. I recruited Allen, and I know he's loyal to Me. Now get out of here." Isn't that what you would want Him to do for you? But Jesus knew what Peter needed in order for his faith to be refined and grow. Jesus knew that Peter would benefit from seeing the power of God at work in his life, and He knew that Peter's testimony would gain strength from the testing. Jesus is always ahead of us, and He knows what is best for us, even if it's not what we would choose for ourselves.

• THINK ABOUT IT •

We tend to define protection as no conflict, no problems. The Lord defines protection in terms of His promised presence as we persevere through life's tests and trials, trusting in Him.

*Prayer*

Heavenly Father, I want to grow in my faith. Forgive me for when I have resented life's trials. Help me to trust Your process, knowing You are training me both to persevere and to declare Your truth in the face of every challenge. In Jesus' name, amen.

## BRAGGING RIGHTS

*"Let him who boasts boast about this: that he understands and knows me, that I am the LORD, who exercises kindness, justice and righteousness on earth, for in these I delight," declares the LORD.*

JEREMIAH 9:24

Receiving the message of the cross of Christ can be difficult in our culture. From our earliest days we are encouraged and rewarded for our accomplishments and achievements, and there is nothing wrong with that. But when an "achievement = reward" mindset takes root in our spiritual lives, the emphasis becomes more about us and what we think we can do for God than about Jesus and what we know He did for us. His gift of salvation, the righteousness that He purchased with His blood on the cross, is a gift. We cannot achieve it or earn it or purchase it. There is nothing about ourselves that is worthy of boasting over because our intelligence, beauty, and sparkling personalities do not matter at all. It seems too simple to be true, but it is. The greatest gift any human can ever receive is free for the asking for anyone who will come to Jesus in repentance and humbly serve Him as Lord and King.

· THINK ABOUT IT ·

Choosing humility in an age that encourages boasting and self-promotion is a counter-cultural choice. Choose to stand apart, humbly acknowledging your need for what only Jesus can provide.

*Prayer*

Heavenly Father, I humbly admit my need, repent of my sin, and put my whole trust in Jesus' blood and finished work on the cross. I rest in the free gift of salvation only Jesus can provide, and serve Him as my Lord and King. In His name I pray, amen.

# DAY 213

## PERFECT POETIC LICENSE

*Let us fix our eyes on Jesus, the author and perfecter of our faith, who for the joy set before him endured the cross, scorning its shame, and sat down at the right hand of the throne of God.*

HEBREWS 12:2

The term "poetic license" means that authors have the creative liberty to let their stories end however they want them to. Authors can change who the characters are and how they interact with each other. The setting, plot, and even the ending of the story can change. Authors just keep writing and rewriting until their desired outcomes are achieved. That's the image here: Jesus is the author of our faith, and He is the one who will perfect it. Our stories are not about our perfect faith; our stories are about our perfect Jesus. Our stories are not about us always making perfect choices; our stories are about His power at work in us and through us to bring us back when we've lost our way or chosen poorly. Jesus is the final author of our stories. He has already bought our salvation with His blood, and He will do whatever is necessary to bring about the outcome He desires for our lives.

### • THINK ABOUT IT •

Dare to believe that Jesus, through His wisdom and power, will at all costs direct our lives toward His good purposes. Let's concentrate our focus on Him.

### Prayer

Heavenly Father, in Your sovereign authority You grant me freedom through Jesus Christ. I am in awe of Your ways and power in my life to direct me into paths of righteousness. Correct my course when I veer to the right or the left. In Jesus' name, amen.

## TICKET TO TRUTH

*If any of you lacks wisdom, he should ask God, who gives generously to all without finding fault, and it will be given to him.*

JAMES 1:5

Some of the world's most popular speakers and writers are so compelling because they seem so sincere. I'm sure that many of them are absolutely convinced of the truth of their position, and I have no doubt that many of them mean well. They are sure of their ability to help you improve your life if you will just believe what they believe and do what they do. I'm all for being sincere, but being sincere is not the same thing as being true. It is easy to mistake sincerity for truth, but you can be sincere and sincerely wrong. The most convincing lies have some truth wrapped up in them, and they can be the most difficult to spot. Don't evaluate everything you hear and read in terms of your life experience, because those feelings and memories are easy to manipulate. The only way to accurately discern the truthfulness and helpfulness of any teaching is to hold it up to the Word of God, which is completely true and never changing.

· THINK ABOUT IT ·

How often do you pray for wisdom? Ask God today for His wisdom and think about reading a chapter a day from the book of Proverbs. Your godly wisdom will increase.

*Prayer*

Heavenly Father, I need the plumb line of Your true and enduring Word. Deepen my time in Your Word so that I can absorb Your truth and be protected from the deceptions of the world. I ask You for Your wisdom to inform my mind and heart. In Jesus' name, amen.

## OWNING OUR STORY

*Your saints will extol you. They will tell of the glory of your kingdom and speak of your might, so that all men may know of your mighty acts and the glorious splendor of your kingdom.*

PSALM 145:10-12

Some of the most interesting people in the Bible were willing—eager, even—to tell what God had done for them. David was so grateful for God's restoration and blessing that he thanked Him throughout his psalms. Daniel was always ready to give God credit for the miracles that occurred in his life. There is perhaps no better example than Paul, who was willing to tell the dramatic story of who he had been and what God had done for him. He shared his story freely in his writings to the New Testament churches. We can only imagine how his testimony would have been diminished if he had not been willing to share that part of his life. In acknowledging the power of God to redeem us, we show other people how to be redeemed. It's time for us to own our truth and tell our stories. When we do, we open doors for the power of God to be seen in our lives.

· THINK ABOUT IT ·

Try to overcome things that cause you to edit your God-story. Others in their own "deep holes" need to know Jesus' love can reach that far.

*Prayer*

Heavenly Father, Jesus is the Author of my faith. Help me tell the God-story He is writing for me, even when it exposes a past I would rather not amplify. I want others to see both what You have done for me and Your power at work in me. In Jesus' name, amen.

## MOST LIKELY TO

*This righteousness from God comes through faith in Jesus Christ to all who believe. There is no difference, for all have sinned and fall short of the glory of God...*

ROMANS 3:22-23

I imagine that all of us had those "Most Likely" pages in our yearbooks: Most Likely to Be President, Most Likely to Become a Millionaire, Most Likely to Win an Olympic Medal, Most Likely to Be a TV Star. One thing you'll never see there is Most Likely to Become Righteous on Your Own. Scripture says that none of us will see the Lord unless we are righteous, but none of us can achieve righteousness on our own. It comes in only one way: from God, through faith in Jesus as the Messiah. There is a universal sin among all humanity: We have fallen short of God's glory, the glory He created us for. No matter what we achieve or accomplish or accumulate, it will fall short of the glory of God reflected in us. For that reason, instead of some worldly acclaim, let's aim for Most Likely to Fall on My Face Before the Lord and Seek His Righteousness.

### • THINK ABOUT IT •

Take time to worship God for the gift of His righteousness through Jesus Christ. Offer the sacrifice of thanksgiving as you consider what His grace has done for you.

*Prayer*

Heavenly Father, I humbly thank You that Jesus did something for me I could not do for myself, receiving all my punishment for sin and granting me Your gift of righteousness. You are worthy, Lord, of all my praise and devotion. In Jesus' name, amen.

# DAY 217

## WAITING FOR OUR INVITATION

*We, who with unveiled faces all reflect the Lord's glory, are being transformed into his likeness with ever-increasing glory, which comes from the Lord, who is the Spirit.*

2 CORINTHIANS 3:18

I am amused when I hear statements like, "This faith stuff must be easier for you because you're a preacher." I don't usually start naming all of my weaknesses, insecurities, and failures; but you can believe that I have them and that I am struggling toward spiritual maturity with everyone else. I am more grateful than you can imagine that there is a power to help us become more like Jesus. If we are truly going to be transformed, we will have to welcome a power greater than ourselves. We don't study our Bible into a point of transformation. We don't pray our way into transformation. We yield to the Spirit of God, who transforms us. We want an outcome that reaches beyond our frailties and inconsistencies. We want our lives to reflect the power of the God we worship, and the Holy Spirit is waiting for an invitation to help us on that journey.

### • THINK ABOUT IT •

Being led by the Holy Spirit frees you from a reliance on your own good works and intentions. Continually seek the transforming power only His Spirit can provide.

### Prayer

Heavenly Father, I want my life to reflect Your power, mercy, and character. I invite You, Holy Spirit, to have Your way with me. Empower me to bear the fruit You seek. Bring my steps in line with Your will. In Jesus' name, amen.

## SWITCH SEATS

*Then he said to Thomas, "Put your finger here; see my hands. Reach out your hand and put it into my side. Stop doubting and believe." Thomas said to him, "My Lord and my God!"*

JOHN 20:27-28

We all know Thomas' nickname: Doubting Thomas. I think that's a little unfair. Thomas had not been present when Jesus appeared to the other disciples, and he wasn't going to believe what he had not seen. He was only asking for what the other disciples had experienced. When Jesus stepped into the room and saw Thomas, there was no criticism or rebuke. He simply said, "See me. Touch me. Stop doubting and believe." Jesus did not want Thomas to spend the rest of his life on the fringe of doubt and disbelief. Jesus wanted Thomas restored to faith in Him. Jesus wants us restored to Him as well. He wants to see us move out of the seat of the skeptic—the casual observer, the indifferent follower. I don't want to be in the crowd that is waiting for more proof. If Jesus is doing something in the earth, I want to be a part of that.

### • THINK ABOUT IT •

Thomas was an honest seeker, willing and quick to acknowledge Jesus as Lord when that was where the evidence led. Even when you can't see it, resolve to be quick in your belief.

### *Prayer*

Heavenly Father, the evidence of Your mighty works in creation, in changed lives, in the truths of Your Word is clear. By faith I will follow You, Lord Jesus. Let Your works in my life have Kingdom impact in my generation. In Your name I pray, amen.

## AWARD-WINNING LOVE

*"What does the LORD your God ask of you but to fear the LORD your God, to walk in all his ways, to love him, to serve the LORD your God with all your heart and with all your soul..."*

DEUTERONOMY 10:12

Many of us are award-winning actors when it comes to playing church. You can show up at the right times and say the right churchy words to your friends. You can participate in worship services, sitting and standing at the right time, singing along with every song. You can wear the right kind of clothes and carry the right kind of Bible. You can volunteer when needed and drop a check in the offering plate. It is pretty easy to craft together a pretense of faith. Or you can determine to be a Christ-follower. They are not the same. The Lord certainly wants you to participate in the life of a local church and give of your time and resources to His Kingdom purposes. But He wants those things to arise from a heart that wants to please Him above all others. He wants you to love Him with "all your heart and with all your soul."

## • THINK ABOUT IT •

There is a difference between "all" and "most of." Submitting your heart, mind, will, and emotions to the Lord without reservation brings abundant blessings.

### *Prayer*

Heavenly Father, help my love for You to mature so I can know the difference between "all" and "most of" my heart and soul. May my love for You be marked by reverence, joy, action, obedience, and service— from all of my being. In Jesus' name, amen.

## FRIEND OF GOD

*You adulterous people, don't you know that friendship with the world is hatred toward God? Anyone who chooses to be a friend of the world becomes an enemy of God.*

JAMES 4:4

James isn't using the word "world" to mean this ball of matter that is hurtling through space; he is referring to the dominant systems of our culture. Jesus has already told us that this world stands in opposition to the purposes of God. Now plain-spoken James is challenging his readers to examine their attitudes and actions: "Don't you understand? If you are a friend of this world, you are an enemy of God. There is no neutral territory—you are either His friend or His enemy!" So each of us has to settle some things for ourselves: Pray that you would be willing to stand apart from the world in order to be a friend of God—to live differently. Be willing to show the people around you that your primary aim in life is to please the Lord.

### • THINK ABOUT IT •

Being a friend of God in your home, classroom, or job takes courage. Ask the Lord for grace to stand firm for Him, one decision at a time, and trust the consequences to God.

*Prayer*

Heavenly Father, grant me the courage and boldness to stand firm for You and not shrink back. I don't want to be an undercover-Christian. Shine through my life clearly, Lord, so others will recognize whose I am and whom I serve. In Jesus' name, amen.

## PRICELESS AND EFFECTIVE

*God made him who had no sin to be sin for us, so that in him we might become the righteousness of God. As God's fellow workers we urge you not to receive God's grace in vain.*

2 CORINTHIANS 5:21-6:1

Grace is the unearned, unmerited, undeserved favor or blessing of God. It is an expression of His goodness and kindness, without respect for who or what we are. It is hard for us to grasp the true nature of His gift of grace because His generosity is so far beyond any of our generous instincts. Here Paul cautions the Corinthians "not to receive God's grace in vain." A more contemporary reading might be, "Don't render God's grace futile or empty, as if it were nothing." How could you make the unearned, undeserved blessing of God be as nothing? Quite simply, by failing to both accept it and live as though you believe it. It is a great tragedy when people turn their backs on God's grace, and Paul urges us to not treat God's grace as if it were nothing.

• THINK ABOUT IT •

Pride and fear can hinder our comprehension of grace. Humility will open up our understanding of it and bring opportunities to grow in the grace and knowledge of our Lord even more.

*Prayer*

Heavenly Father, I receive Your abundant grace, knowing and believing it is sufficient to meet all my needs. Help me to better understand the truth of Your grace that I might more fully rest in Your love and cooperate with Your purposes. In Jesus' name, amen.

## REWIRED TO YIELD

*He said to them, "My soul is overwhelmed with sorrow to the point of death. Stay here and keep watch with me." Going a little farther, he fell with his face to the ground and prayed, "My Father, if it is possible, may this cup be taken from me. Yet not as I will, but as you will."*

MATTHEW 26:38-39

We cannot fully comprehend the struggle that Jesus faced that night on Gethsemane. Yet that night was as much about the disciples, and those of us who would someday be disciples, as it was about Jesus. Jesus, being fully God and fully man, shared His night of sorrow and agony on Gethsemane in order to show His very real struggle with obedience. What happened there is very carefully recorded so that we will understand each of us will eventually have to come to Gethsemane for ourselves. We are hard-wired to say, "I want it my way!" But the heart of being a Christ-follower is a willingness to submit our will to the will of God. Submitting to Him in the small things and the big things—if it was necessary for Jesus, it is necessary for you and me.

### • THINK ABOUT IT •

Submitting to the Lord is easier when we trust His goodness, wisdom, and love. Yielding will still take self-discipline, but the courage and strength to obey will come to those who trust Him.

*Prayer*

Heavenly Father, what You ask of me will always be marked by Your goodness, wisdom, and love. Give me strength and courage to yield to Your choices, and reveal any place where I am saying no to You. Not my will but Yours be done. In Jesus' name, amen.

## EMBRACING THE BEST LIFE

*You have made known to me the path of life; you will fill me with joy in your presence, with eternal pleasures at your right hand.*

PSALM 16:11

It's easy to look around us and see that we have made idols of comfort and convenience. We have been conditioned to believe that other than friends and family, God's greatest blessings are those we can live in, drive, and wear. These are the things we feel entitled to and the goals we work toward. God doesn't seem to think this way, and we will never fulfill what God has called us to if our life goals are leisure and comfort. I'm not opposed to those things, but I will not make them my gods. Because Jesus was willing to accept God's invitation and walk the difficult path that led to the cross, His Father gave Him a name that is above every name and a seat at His throne. God has a purpose for our lives too. He will not call many of His people to give of themselves to the point of death. But when we yield ourselves to the will of God and joyfully walk the path He has set us on, we are not forfeiting the best of life—we are embracing it.

### • THINK ABOUT IT •

Our goals spring from what we value most. Solomon road-tested goals of leisure and comfort, concluding that they were worthless. Let's avoid that outcome by embracing goals that produce treasures in eternity.

### *Prayer*

Heavenly Father, I want the outcome of my life's pursuits to please You, resulting in eternally lasting fruit. Help me align my goals with Your highest purposes. Strengthen me so I can run my life's race with perseverance and joy. In Jesus' name, amen.

## ATTRACTED TO THE LIGHT

*Do not let any part of your body become an instrument of evil to serve sin. Instead, give yourselves completely to God, for you were dead, but now you have new life. So use your whole body as an instrument to do what is right for the glory of God.*

ROMANS 6:13 • NLT

Darkness is all around us, have you noticed? It is on the television, even in shows that are supposed to be funny and family friendly. It is in the music that makes light of sin and celebrates violence. It is in the websites and chat rooms that want us to believe what happens there has no effect once the screen goes dim. I'm not looking for ways to incorporate darkness into my life. I don't want to open doors into my ears, eyes, and heart. I don't want to find ways to excuse it, tolerate it, or accommodate it. I've had too many years of experience and sat with too many people in that place. Where you tolerate it, it will own you. Let's determine to cooperate with the Spirit of God and be delivered from every expression of the dominion of darkness in our lives.

### • THINK ABOUT IT •

Tolerating darkness can have debilitating effects on your spirit. Spending more time in God's light through His Word, prayer, and fellowship with Him results in increased spiritual freedom and health.

### Prayer

Heavenly Father, I need the searchlight of Your Holy Spirit to show me where I have allowed darkness to infiltrate my interests or practices. Forgive me, and help me seek the light of Your presence and Word. Thank You for Your illumination. In Jesus' name, amen.

## CLEARHEADED, PROTECTED, CONFIDENT

*You aren't in the dark about these things, dear brothers and sisters, and you won't be surprised when the day of the Lord comes like a thief...be on your guard, not asleep like the others...let us who live in the light be clearheaded, protected by the armor of faith and love, and wearing as our helmet the confidence of our salvation.*

1 THESSALONIANS 5:4-8 • NLT

God gave an overwhelming amount of prophetic information about what would be happening in the world before Jesus came the first time. With a few exceptions, those prophecies were ignored and people were caught unaware. We have a significant amount of information about what will be happening in the earth before He comes again, and it's in our best interests not to be caught unaware. In multiple ways and at multiple times, Jesus cautioned us to use the information we have been given to prepare ourselves for His return. I don't think He was issuing threats. I think He was imploring us to stand in the confidence of our salvation as we try to understand the season and maximize our opportunities to advance His Kingdom until He returns.

• THINK ABOUT IT •

Rather than responding to the upheaval in our world with fear or denial, have confidence that God has uniquely designed and positioned you for such a time as this to carry His message of unshakable hope.

*Prayer*

Heavenly Father, You are my sure foundation. Help me shift my focus from the darkness around me to Your opportunities to bring the hope of the cross to the nations. May I be clearheaded, protected, and confident of my salvation. In Jesus' name, amen.

## SONGS OF DELIVERANCE

*And they sang a new song: "You are worthy to take the scroll and to open its seals, because you were slain, and with your blood you purchased men for God from every tribe and language and people and nation. You have made them to be a kingdom and priests to serve our God, and they will reign on the earth."*

### REVELATION 5:9-10

This is the Revelation equivalent of John 3:16. Jesus was slain so that with His blood He could purchase all who would believe that He is the Messiah and serve Him as Lord—people "from every tribe and language and people and nation." He rescued us from the dominion of darkness and death. The residents of Heaven are giving glory to the Lord for it today—what a beautiful vision that is! When we worship the Lord, it is not because God's ego is so fragile that He needs us to affirm Him. We worship the Lord because in the midst of the struggle and challenges we face—physically, emotionally, and spiritually—we need to be reminded that greater is He who is for us than all of the things that are against us.

### • THINK ABOUT IT •

Take time today to consider the immensity of what Jesus has done. Paul used words like "immeasurable" and "indescribable." What words can you use to describe His worthiness?

*Prayer*

Heavenly Father, I am in awe of Your love expressed in Christ Jesus, and I tremble when I consider what it cost You to purchase my salvation. I join the chorus of those who sing Your praise, thanking You for turning my mourning into joy! In Jesus' name, amen.

## PLEASING FOR ETERNITY

*We make it our goal to please him, whether we are at home in the body or away from it.*

### 2 CORINTHIANS 5:9

Sometimes we make Christianity too difficult, quibbling about word origins and such. I love this verse because it gives the essence of our faith: Our goal is to please the Lord. What do I want to do with my life? I want to please the Lord. This helps me sort out many of the decisions I make about how I use my words, time, energy, money, etc. Sometimes the answer is apparent. But if it's not, I say, "Lord, I want to please You. Help me with that." The verse has an interesting, unexpected conclusion: "whether I'm in my body or away from it." I think most of us imagine that we can please the Lord during our days under the sun. But our life's journey is about more than that; it is about gaining momentum so that we will be with Him, and pleasing Him, for eternity. Allow the simple objective of pleasing the Lord to guide your days. My experience has shown that to be the happiest and most fulfilling way to live.

### • THINK ABOUT IT •

The Bible is filled with what pleases and what grieves the Lord. When you find them, determine to align yourself with the actions and attitudes that please Him.

### *Prayer*

Heavenly Father, it is my goal to please You always. Thank You for Your Holy Spirit who counsels me in Your good, acceptable, and perfect will. Show me where I have strayed and grieved You that I might repent and realign with You. In Jesus' name, amen.

## ULTIMATE ACCEPTANCE LETTER

*Praise be to the God and Father of our Lord Jesus Christ, who has blessed us in the heavenly realms with every spiritual blessing in Christ. For he chose us in him before the creation of the world...*

EPHESIANS 1:3-4

When I was young, if you were going to play a sport, you played on a school team. We had tryouts at school, and the coaches would post a list of who made the team on the door of the gym. If your name wasn't on the list, you had to deal with disappointment and embarrassment. Sometimes the coach would say, "We only had so many spots, and you weren't quite good enough," or "Maybe next year!" The same was true of school plays, the debate team, certain music groups, and other activities. There was a lot of rejection around my school! God's Kingdom is just the opposite. The New Testament is God's ultimate acceptance letter. It says that no matter who has rejected you, Almighty God, the Creator of Heaven and Earth, has chosen you to be His child. No more rejection—hallelujah!

### • THINK ABOUT IT •

If a message runs through your head incessantly whispering, "You're not good enough. You can't make the cut," receive the scriptural truth that Jesus took all our rejection on Himself on the cross that we might be accepted in the Beloved. Through the blood of Jesus, we are accepted.

### Prayer

Heavenly Father, I praise You that Jesus endured my rejection that I might receive Your acceptance. I receive Your gift of grace, rejoicing that You have chosen me. Renew my thinking that I would see myself and my future as You do. In Jesus' name, amen.

## CHOOSING FRIENDS WISELY

*I am a friend to all who fear you, to all who follow your precepts.*

PSALM 119:63

I had a problem earlier in my life. I wanted to know the Lord, but I didn't like Christians. They got on my nerves, and I certainly didn't want to hang out with them. I finally realized that attitude said more about who I was and what was happening inside me than it did about the Christians I knew. I asked the Holy Spirit to work on my heart, and I began to realign my values and objectives and priorities with His. When I began seeing my situation more clearly, I knew that I was convicted by their desire to yield to the Lord, and I was the one who needed to change. Christians are just imperfect people who are walking life's journey the best way they know, and we are put together for certain times and seasons in order to help each other grow. Friendship is really about choices, and friendships with people who love the Lord will take you down some very fulfilling paths.

### · THINK ABOUT IT ·

It is freeing to know that we are all an imperfect people invited by the Lord to yield to Him. Ask Him for the willingness and ability to choose our friends with His perspective as our priority.

*Prayer*

Heavenly Father, grant me, along with my family members, treasured friendships with those who revere and obey You. Give us a unity of mind and heart in our common pursuit of You that will accomplish much for Your Kingdom. In Jesus' name, amen.

DAY 230

## DON'T KEEP THEM WAITING

*Do this, understanding the present time: The hour has already come for you to wake up from your slumber, because our salvation is nearer now than when we first believed.*

ROMANS 13:11

If I had to give an analysis of the American Church in recent decades, I would suggest that we have been in an extended season of slumber. There is a time and a place for rest, because it is necessary for our physical and mental health. But when we are asleep we are unaware, unconcerned, and uninvolved. We've been in that condition long enough. It's time for the Church of Jesus Christ to awaken to the opportunities of this generation. Not to sit in buildings and sing songs and endure sermons and pretend that morality has transformed us, but to be engaged with the purposes of God—to know there is a reason for us to be here beyond pleasing ourselves, and there are assignments that God has prepared and equipped each of us for. There are people throughout the world who are anxiously awaiting the awakening of the American Church. Let's not keep them waiting any longer.

· THINK ABOUT IT ·

Seek God's assignment for you with the discipline of one who knows time is of the essence and with the gifts and wisdom God has entrusted to you. He intends to accomplish much by your hand.

*Prayer*

Heavenly Father, help Your Church repent of our apathy and disinterest. May we respond in unity through prayer and action, believing You have equipped us to make a difference for the Kingdom of God in this generation. In Jesus' name, amen.

## PERSISTENT PARTICIPANTS

*"Keep on asking, and you will receive what you ask for. Keep on seeking, and you will find. Keep on knocking, and the door will be opened to you. For everyone who asks, receives. Everyone who seeks, finds. And to everyone who knocks, the door will be opened."*

MATTHEW 7:7-8 • NLT

We often have the mistaken idea that achieving a spiritual breakthrough is something God does for us. We picture Him going before us like a huge bulldozer, completely obliterating every obstacle blocking our way, and ourselves walking behind Him on a perfectly level path. From my life experience, and in observing the lives of others, it seems that God accomplishes something in us and through us so that we are participants in breaking through those barriers. Yes, He rolls away that first boulder, but then He hands us a pickax and says, "Let's get to work here." He opens a door and says, "Here's a flashlight. Let's see what we'll find in this room." Breaking through means that we ask and keep asking, seek and keep seeking, and knock and keep knocking—in other words, persistence, hard work, and probably a little sweat.

### • THINK ABOUT IT •

God did something for us through the cross that we could not do for ourselves. But there are things that, empowered by His Spirit, He expects us to accomplish. Our privilege is that He lets us participate with Him in His endeavors.

### *Prayer*

Heavenly Father, persistence in seeking You is a quality You reward. With the energy inspired by Your Holy Spirit, I will pray and work hard, persevering until I see Your breakthrough in my life and in the lives of those around me. In Jesus' name, amen.

## IT'S OUR TURN NOW!

*He said to them, "Go into all the world and preach the good news to all creation."*

MARK 16:15

Jesus' disciples had traveled with Him for three years. They had front row seats to Jesus' teaching and actions. They had seen and experienced things they never could have imagined. They had received training and coaching. Privately, they had opportunities to ask questions and hear explanations. They had seen Him die on a cross, and now He is standing with them, alive. He's no longer saying, "Just follow Me." He's saying, "Now it's your turn. Go!" He's redefining what it means to be a Jesus-follower. It's no longer just a private commitment or a realignment of priorities. It's no longer watching someone else perform miracles and sitting at your teacher's feet; now there is a mission attached to it. I know of no place in Scripture where Jesus' assignment has been amended or rescinded. It is still ringing in the ears of all of us who call ourselves Christ-followers.

### • THINK ABOUT IT •

First responders understand the imperative to "Go!" because they recognize the desperate condition of those they go to help. The Bible describes the condition of those apart from Christ as "those who are perishing," and we are Christ's "first responders" to them.

*Prayer*

Heavenly Father, forgive my reluctance to obey Your assignment to "go"—next door or beyond. May gratitude for the cross of Jesus Christ compel me to boldly declare to those who do not know You all that You have accomplished for them. In Jesus' name, amen.

# DAY 233

## WATCHFUL & AWARE

*The day of the Lord will come like a thief. The heavens will disappear with a roar; the elements will be destroyed by fire, and the earth and everything in it will be laid bare. Since everything will be destroyed in this way, what kind of people ought you to be? You ought to live holy and godly lives as you look forward to the day of God...*

2 PETER 3:10-12

No event in Scripture has more prophecy directed toward it than Jesus' return to the earth. Yet this passage says that He will come like a thief; He will be unexpected by most, and they will be unprepared. Don't be in that group. The Judge of all the earth is coming back in bodily form to have a personal interaction with you and me. So, what kind of people ought we to be? That question deserves more than a shrug of the shoulders. It deserves a better answer than, "Well, I said the sinner's prayer." If we are not prepared, Jesus' second coming is going to be a very sad and regretful day. Let's not be caught unaware. Let's give our lives to serving the Lord and look forward to His coming.

### · THINK ABOUT IT ·

Jesus called the person faithful and sensible who was found carrying out God's assignments when He returned. Great benefit results from maintaining a daily focus on God's agenda and seeking how you can be involved.

### *Prayer*

Heavenly Father, I long for Jesus' return and want to be a faithful and watchful servant, sensibly making choices and committing my time. Help me accomplish Your assignments today and help others in Your Church to do the same. In Jesus' name, amen.

## HIGH BEAMS

*By your words I can see where I'm going; they throw a beam of light on my dark path.*

PSALM 119:105 • THE MESSAGE

God has given us senses to learn about the environment around us, but our awareness is still limited. It's like driving at night: We can see pretty clearly as far as the headlights illuminate, but we cannot see beyond that into the darkness. Driving at night is an exercise in trust—trust that signs are in place and accurate, trust that engineers smoothed out the worst of the curves, trust that there are no obstacles in our path, trust that bridges are in good condition. God, on the other hand, can see it all. He knows the outcome at the beginning of our journey. He knows what challenges we have overcome and what challenges lie ahead. His counsel to us, through His Word and the Holy Spirit, includes an awareness of all those things—and it comes from a Father who loves us with a love beyond our understanding. We have His Word to light the way and His Spirit to help us understand it. Why would we not want to have the benefit of His insight and wisdom?

### • THINK ABOUT IT •

Understanding that God can see things beyond our awareness and then relying on His wisdom to navigate your journey can bring great freedom. God's Word provides the guidance we need. Let's depend on it more today.

### Prayer

Heavenly Father, Your Word is living—full of truth, instruction, and counsel. I ask for not only a deeper understanding of it, but also the grace to obey it in my life. I want to please You by depending upon and honoring Your Word. In Jesus' name, amen.

## SACRIFICIAL CHOICES

*By faith Moses, when he had grown up, refused to be known as the son of Pharaoh's daughter. He chose to be mistreated along with the people of God rather than to enjoy the pleasures of sin for a short time. He regarded disgrace for the sake of Christ as of greater value than the treasures of Egypt, because he was looking ahead to his reward.*

HEBREWS 11:24-26

When you say yes to the Lord, He will put your feet on a path that you could not have imagined. From a secular viewpoint, Moses should have gone back to Pharaoh and said, "Look, I made a bad mistake. If you'll let me back in the palace, I'll be the most faithful servant you'll ever have. The Hebrew slaves trust me, and I'll make sure they do whatever you say." But he chose another, more difficult path, and in the New Testament we see him having a conversation with Jesus on the Mount of Transfiguration. What a reward! It will not always be easy, and the rewards may not be ones that the world values; but if you follow the Lord, you will have opportunities that are beyond what you could have imagined.

· THINK ABOUT IT ·

We all have times where we are confronted with a choice between two paths—one acceptable to your desires and others, another one much more sacrificial. Ask the Lord for His wisdom—He'll guide you in the right direction.

*Prayer*

Almighty God, I wait upon You, my Deliverer and the One who restores. Pour out Your Spirit afresh that Your power and strength might be evident in my life. May everything that opposes Your purposes be brought down and Your Word be fulfilled in my life. In Jesus' name, amen.

# DAY 236

## IN TRAINING

*Physical training is of some value, but godliness has value for all things, holding promise for both the present life and the life to come.*

### 1 TIMOTHY 4:8

This passage is not advising us to avoid exercise and physical training. I'm in favor of both and need to do more than I do. But Paul is reminding Timothy that while training the physical body has value in this life, training our hearts and minds toward godliness has value both in this life and for all eternity. I'm fond of my earth suit. It has served me well for many years. I try to take care of it so that my days under the sun will be as productive as they can be. But no matter how much time and energy I spend toward maintaining it, it is subject to the passage of time and it is going to wear out someday. My spiritual self is the part of me that guides my decision-making processes, and that is the part of me that will live for eternity. So let's use our God-given wisdom to take good care of our earthly bodies, but let's also take time to invest in our spiritual growth and well-being.

### • THINK ABOUT IT •

A great way to build up physical strength and muscle is to work with a trainer, have a dedicated workout location, and a set of exercises to diligently pursue. These three elements, applied devotionally, can help you grow spiritually too.

### Prayer

Heavenly Father, help me establish the disciplined patterns I need to mature in You. Provide and protect my time and place for prayer and Bible study. Give me wise teachers who, by Your Spirit, can open up Your Word to me. In Jesus' name, amen.

## CONNECTING THE DOTS

*O LORD, I will honor and praise your name, for you are my God. You do such wonderful things! You planned them long ago, and now you have accomplished them.*

ISAIAH 25:1 • NLT

A life without faith in God is just a series of random events. There's no texture to it. It's inexplicable. You just exist while going through a series of unexplained occurrences. Depending on the circumstances, you decide if you should feel happiness or sadness, satisfaction or disappointment, pride or humiliation. In contrast, a life with faith is a life with a context. It has a purpose. It has boundaries. It is a life that has a concrete platform for sustainable hope. It has joy at the beginning and joy at the end. Births, deaths, graduations, marriages, moves, career changes—to the world they are just things that happen; but to the person of faith they are blessings and sorrows, all overseen by the God of the universe. Faith will help you connect the dots of your life and write a God-story you will be happy to tell.

### • THINK ABOUT IT •

If things have stopped making sense and you question, "What is the point?" remember that you were created with purpose by the One who spoke the world into existence. He cares about your life.

*Prayer*

Heavenly Father, apart from You my soul is unanchored, tossed about. But in Jesus all things hold together. Thank You for infusing my life with significance and giving me value before I was born. I rest in Your sovereign love. In Jesus' name, amen.

## TRULY RIGHTEOUS AND HOLY

*Let the Spirit renew your thoughts and attitudes. Put on your new nature, created to be like God—truly righteous and holy.*

EPHESIANS 4:23-24 • NLT

Many within the Church have an increasingly casual attitude toward sin. We think it's not such a big deal. Or we use religious language and say, "Just put it under the blood." We don't want to be perceived as harsh or judgmental. Instead, we want to be understanding and inclusive. The reality is that the Bible says some things are sin, and that sin separates us from God. He is the Almighty God who is sovereign over all. He loves you more than any human being does and has a good plan for your life. If you're separated from Him, you are going without all the good things He wants to do for you and through you. The tragic outcome of sin is always the same: destruction. God doesn't hate sin because He's afraid you're going to have too much fun. God hates sin because He knows that sin will destroy you, and He loves you. So "let the Spirit renew your thoughts and attitudes. Put on your new nature, created to be like God—truly righteous and holy."

• THINK ABOUT IT •

Jesus says in John 14:23 that if we love Him we will obey His teachings. As you allow God to renew your mind, He will help you make decisions that honor Him, and strengthen you to resist the temptations of this world. Pursuing life in relationship with God is worth the effort.

*Prayer*

Heavenly Father, thank You for mercifully renewing my heart so that I can more fully cooperate with You. Please forgive me where I have put the things of this world ahead of you. I choose to honor Your Word as truth for my life. In Jesus' name, amen.

# DAY 239

## THE ONGOING GIFT

*For the wages of sin is death, but the gift of God is eternal life in Christ Jesus our Lord.*

ROMANS 6:23

This is such a powerful verse that it makes an obvious line of demarcation for us. There is a wage to be extracted for sin, but there is also a gift of God. We sell this verse short when we think about it only in terms of our initiation into the Kingdom of God. I think about the benefits of the Kingdom of God and the gifts of God in my life, what it means to be fully and completely transformed into the image of Jesus. It's an ongoing process in my life, and I have to consistently choose that gift as opposed to some of the other offerings of the world. Not every temptation that has come to my life has come in the guise of blatant immorality. Most of us are not greatly tempted to rob a bank or murder our neighbors. The real temptations come to us far more subtly, drawing away our allegiance to the primary loves of our life. Let's determine to pass on the wages of sin and focus on the gifts of God.

### • THINK ABOUT IT •

Our ability to recognize subtle temptations can be impaired by poor choices or our environment. With the Holy Spirit's help, you can be sensitive to the entry points of sin and receive grace to avoid them.

### Prayer

Heavenly Father, please give me discernment by Your Holy Spirit to make good choices that reap eternal benefits. Help me build Your Word into my life so I can focus on and embrace the grace, opportunities, and gifts You offer. In Jesus' name, amen.

## PURPOSEFULLY POSITIONED

*Peter stood up with the Eleven, raised his voice and addressed the crowd: "Fellow Jews and all of you who live in Jerusalem, let me explain this to you; listen carefully to what I say...this is what was spoken by the prophet Joel: 'In the last days, God says, I will pour out my Spirit on all people. Your sons and daughters will prophesy, your young men will see visions, your old men will dream dreams.'"*

ACTS 2:14-17

Jesus' followers were caught off guard by the Day of Pentecost. He had told them to wait in Jerusalem, that the Holy Spirit was coming and would empower them to be His witnesses. Now prophecies were being fulfilled in their midst, and even they were surprised. Soon the whole city of Jerusalem was hearing the Jesus-story. People were laying the sick in the street so they could be healed when Peter's shadow fell on them. Peter had planned to spend his life fishing. Now he and the others are fulfilling the words of the prophets and shaking a nation. Stay open to the direction of the Holy Spirit in your life because God has a plan for you too.

## • THINK ABOUT IT •

Peter and the others may have had no clue about what was coming next, but their obedience to Jesus' command—stay in Jerusalem—positioned them to receive God's next step. Your obedience to His Word will position you for Kingdom purposes too.

## *Prayer*

Heavenly Father, keep me aware of simple steps of obedience to You that I might be well-positioned to be entrusted with the next assignment You have for me. Open my eyes and ears to Your direction as You take me forward in Your plan. In Jesus' name, amen.

## A VISION FOR MORE

*"I have come down to rescue them from the hand of the Egyptians and to bring them up out of that land into a good and spacious land, a land flowing with milk and honey..."*

EXODUS 3:8

The Hebrews never asked God to take them to "a good and spacious land, a land flowing with milk and honey"—they did not even know there was such a land. They simply knew they were suffering in slavery, and they cried out to God for His help. I'm confident that they would have signed a contract to stay where they were if the Egyptians had been willing to cut their production quota in half or improve their living conditions. But God had a vision for them that was greater than the vision they had for themselves. God could see their future better than they could see it—a future that included freedom, and provision, and a special place in God's plan. The same is true for us. Don't ever allow yourself to be content with bondage to whatever has enslaved you. God has blessings planned for your future in "a land flowing with milk and honey."

· THINK ABOUT IT ·

"Don't settle for less" is a common advertising phrase, but it can apply to your life in Christ too. God combines His vision for you with the power He wants to exercise on your behalf. So don't stop short, don't give up, and don't settle for less.

*Prayer*

Heavenly Father, may I not settle for less than the full redemptive transformation that Jesus won for me through the cross. Help me trust You through every challenge—undismayed and resolute—as You lead me into the abundant life You desire for me. In Jesus' name, amen.

## TRADING FUTURES

*Just as you used to offer the parts of your body in slavery to impurity and to ever-increasing wickedness, so now offer them in slavery to righteousness leading to holiness.*

ROMANS 6:19

It is hard to imagine offering ourselves up as slaves to wickedness. But the Bible says that is exactly what we do when we allow our earthly, selfish natures to call the shots. We are hard-wired to prefer doing what we want to do, when we want to do it. Our sinful nature would think we are cleverly negotiating our future when in fact we are trading it away for a fleeting pleasure. Surrendering to God and His righteousness is a choice that has the opposite result. He has a vision for our future that is greater than any future we can imagine for ourselves. Even knowing that, it's still not easy to surrender and say, "I am Yours, Lord. Do with me what You will." Following the Lord in humble submission does not come naturally; it is difficult. But I would encourage you to choose the posture of following Him. The holiness that will result will bring you more joy than any of the world's enticements.

### • THINK ABOUT IT •

God has graciously given us clear information in Scripture about the resulting benefits of yielding to and serving Him. The path we choose—short-term gratification or long-term blessings—will make all the difference in our future.

*Prayer*

Heavenly Father, I want joy that lasts and righteousness that brings peace. Direct me in paths leading to holiness. I submit my will to Yours, asking for grace to not resist or turn back. Because You are holy, I will pursue holiness. In Jesus' name, amen.

## BELIEVING FOR THE IMPOSSIBLE

*Jesus looked at them and said, "With man this is impossible, but not with God; all things are possible with God."*

MARK 10:27

We need to believe in the possibilities of God. That's easy to say, but it can be hard to live. It is easy for us to exchange religion and tradition and doctrine and behavior for the imagination of what God is capable of doing. We have in our minds some rather fixed ideas of what God can do, should do, and will do. Think about Noah building a boat, and David eating the showbread in the Tabernacle, and Jesus redefining what was proper to do on the Sabbath. Scripture is full of accounts of God showing that He is not defined or confined by our expectations. I love what Paul wrote to the Romans; it's another one of those "if" verses: "If God is for us, who can be against us?" (8:31). If God is for us, and He is, then He is capable of opening doorways to things that we could not have imagined for ourselves. Believe that God is for you. Believe that He wants good things for you, and that nothing is impossible for Him.

• THINK ABOUT IT •

How does knowing that God is for you influence your belief for the impossible? Allow it give you courage to be bold for His purposes in your life and in the lives of others.

*Prayer*

Heavenly Father, through Jesus You have proven You are for me, not against me. With renewed and confident hope, help me to align my heart with Yours. I trust You to make a way where there seems to be no way. In Jesus' name, amen.

## IF AND THEN

*My son, if you accept my words and store up my commands within you, turning your ear to wisdom and applying your heart to understanding, and if you call out for insight and cry aloud for understanding, and if you look for it as for silver and search for it as for hidden treasure, then you will understand the fear of the LORD and find the knowledge of God.*

PROVERBS 2:1-5

Some think that Christianity is an attempt to escape the real world, a passive retreat for the inept and the weak who cannot manage life on their own. To those people I would respond with a technical term: Baloney! If your spiritual life is of any substance, your greatest efforts will be expended in the pursuit of God. This passage gives eight expressions of effort before understanding comes. You have to accept, store, turn, apply, call out, cry aloud, look for it, and search for it. Then you'll understand. I don't know why there is so much effort required to know the fullness of God, but that is His plan. I not only accept it; I will pursue it with all my being.

## • THINK ABOUT IT •

A casual interest in God will reduce your potential for spiritual understanding. We want to do more than just "read the headlines" to truly know God. If you store His Word into your mind and heart, then it will help you in your search for understanding.

*Prayer*

Heavenly Father, help me discipline my schedule, removing unhelpful and habitual distractions so that I might be still enough to listen to You. I want to live in the reverential fear of You that I might know You and gain Your wisdom. In Jesus' name, amen.

## A NEW BEHAVIOR

*"Remember the words of the Lord Jesus…'It is more blessed to give than to receive.'"*

ACTS 20:35 • NASB®

"It is more blessed to give than to receive." That's an expression we've all heard, and sometimes it's true. Certainly we take great joy in giving gifts, especially to people we know personally or people we know have specific needs. But human nature says it's more fun to get. If you don't believe that, watch the kids at Christmastime. From an early age, they can tell you how many of the presents under the tree have their names on them. If they're very young children, they think they should get to unwrap every present. We are hard-wired to be selfish, and other polite behaviors are taught. So when Jesus said there is a greater blessing in giving than in receiving, He's pointing us toward a new behavior. If we can learn to be generous, we position ourselves to receive from God a greater blessing than anything that we're capable of giving. It takes faith to believe that, but His invitation to cultivate a heart of generosity always leads down a path of great blessings.

### • THINK ABOUT IT •

From the widow who gave her pennies to the woman who poured out the costly perfume, be inspired that it is extravagant love that produces extravagant giving. Full hearts, not bank accounts, are the wellsprings of generosity.

### *Prayer*

Heavenly Father, You have lavished Your grace on me, promising me all sufficiency. Give me the grace to give cheerfully. Turn my resources of time, talents, and finances into encouraging gifts for those You want to help. In Jesus' name, amen.

## HELPFUL TRAVEL TIPS

*"In everything, do to others what you would have them do to you, for this sums up the Law and the Prophets."*

MATTHEW 7:12

If you are taking a road trip, you can use a GPS to get you to your destination. A whole host of websites will give you advice on which hotels are clean, which restaurants have the best food, and which activities are worth your money. But every one of those things can be absolutely wrong. We've all been led astray by a GPS, and those travel sites are full of opinions that are pretty subjective; the reviewer may have been having a bad day when they wrote that their pillow was lumpy. We are on a journey through life, too, and we have a source of very helpful travel tips: Jesus. The Gospels are full of Jesus' recommendations, such as the one above. Imagine the Creator of the universe saying, "Come here for a minute. I have a couple of suggestions on how you can negotiate life." Should we say, "Nah, I'm busy right now, and my friend already gave me some advice on that"? Or should we lean in and hear what He has to say?

### • THINK ABOUT IT •

Have you read the Bible as if it were life's guidebook? If not, turn on that filter today and consider Jesus' counsel as vital as your GPS on a road trip adventure.

*Prayer*

Heavenly Father, I want to be wise and put Your words into practice in my life's journey. Forgive me for the times I have disobeyed, thinking Your instruction wasn't practical. Your Word always proves to be the best counsel. In Jesus' name, amen.

## SHAKEN BUT STEADIED

*"This is what the LORD Almighty says: 'In a little while I will once more shake the heavens and the earth, the sea and the dry land. I will shake all nations, and the desired of all nations will come, and I will fill this house with glory... The silver is mine and the gold is mine,' declares the Lord Almighty."*

### HAGGAI 2:6-8

It has been over ten years since the world experienced perhaps the greatest financial crisis since the Great Depression. In looking back over some of my sermons from that time, I notice that I often reminded people that while God has told us that He will shake the nations, He also reminds us that all the silver and gold is His. I wonder if the dependence we felt on Him then has slipped back into complacency. Is God a family friend or a casual acquaintance, or is He your stability in times of trouble? Is He truly the Strong Tower you look to for provision and protection? Do you trust Him more than you trust your bank balance and retirement account? I suspect that more shaking will come. Is your security found in Wall Street or in the God of all creation?

### • THINK ABOUT IT •

Are anxieties over provisions and security a recurring struggle? Make regular deposits of His Word into your mind to increase the resources of your faith. It will defeat those fears.

### *Prayer*

Heavenly Father, You have given me everything I need through Your precious promises. My security is in You, not uncertain resources. Help me increase the deposit of Your Word into my mind and heart that I might be rich in faith. In Jesus' name, amen.

## REDIRECTION & REFOCUSING

*Throw off your old sinful nature and your former way of life, which is corrupted by lust and deception. Instead, let the Spirit renew your thoughts and attitudes. Put on your new nature, created to be like God—truly righteous and holy.*

EPHESIANS 4:22-24 • NLT

If you've been around Christianity very long you've heard the notion of renewing your mind. Some people think that renewing our minds involves mainly studying and memorizing Scripture, but I think the most important thing we can do to renew our minds is pray. Prayer is a way of redirecting our thoughts away from our own desires and refocusing them on the things of God. If you are following Jesus, you have been given a "new nature...truly righteous and holy." But it takes an honest expression of your heart to God to bring that continuing process of renewal to the surface. The Holy Spirit is always present and ready to assist you as you "throw off your old sinful nature and your former way of life." Call on Him and ask for His help at any time; you may be surprised at the changes He will bring to your heart and mind.

### • THINK ABOUT IT •

Talking honestly to God reminds us that renewing the mind requires relationship, not just intellect. Time with Him gives God an opportunity for your transformation. The Holy Spirit eagerly waits to spend that time with you.

### *Prayer*

Heavenly Father, I welcome Your transforming work in me and want to yield to You. Help me communicate with You openly, honestly, and frequently. Help me trade old mindsets that oppose Your truth for the renewal only You can offer. In Jesus' name, amen.

## GREAT & AWESOME WONDERS

*He is your praise; he is your God, who performed for you those great and awesome wonders you saw with your own eyes.*

DEUTERONOMY 10:21

I think as Christians, and as churches, we should spend more time acknowledging what God has done for us and through us. Parents take time to document their children's first teeth, first steps, and first words. But do we take the time to document our children's spiritual growth and thank Him for it? Adults are conscientious about updating their resumes. Every new accomplishment and skill mastered is carefully added so that our peers and prospective employers can see what we have done to improve ourselves. But what about the things of God? Do we take the time to acknowledge God's invitations into His Kingdom business? Do we thank Him when we see progress in our spiritual lives? As a congregation, do you stop to acknowledge His work among you? Do you thank Him for the increase in attendance, the multiplying of your small groups, the families He enabled you to reach through Vacation Bible School? These are the "great and awesome wonders" we have seen with our own eyes, and they are worthy of our acknowledgment and praise.

· THINK ABOUT IT ·

Looking back with a heart of gratitude on the places where God has intervened on your behalf can embolden you to walk in faith today.

*Prayer*

Heavenly Father, thank You for the privilege of serving You in every area of Your Kingdom. Through You we do not grow weary in well-doing, knowing our labor is not in vain. Lord, multiply Your laborers and build Your Church. In Jesus' name, amen.

## COURAGE TO OBEY

*When Joseph and Mary had done everything required by the Law of the Lord, they returned to Galilee to their own town of Nazareth. And the child grew and became strong; he was filled with wisdom, and the grace of God was on him.*

LUKE 2:39-40

God's plan for Joseph and Mary was joyful but also awkward and disruptive. Gossip and skepticism are not new. I'll bet someone in Nazareth was keeping a calendar of announcements and deliveries. But Joseph put his reputation on the line with Mary's: "I believe you. We'll walk the streets of this village with our heads up." He didn't let any aspersions be cast or do anything to salvage his reputation. He honored Mary in public, and he will be forever known as Jesus' earthly father. I never think about the Christmas story without thinking about the pressures on this young couple. Scripture gives no indication that they did anything other than a fine job of parenting this most unusual boy. Your circumstances may not be perfect, and they may not be what you have dreamed of, but the hand of God can be present to do amazing things if you will invite Him into your life.

### • THINK ABOUT IT •

Has embarrassment over what people might think ever slowed down a positive response to a God-invitation? If you had a do-over, could you accept His invitation now?

*Prayer*

Heavenly Father, I will put my reputation on the line with Jesus'—neither the praise nor the scorn of men will determine my response to Your invitations for me. I want my faith in You to be marked by courage. In Jesus' name, amen.

## PUT IT TO THE TEST

*Test everything. Hold on to the good. Avoid every kind of evil.*

1 THESSALONIANS 5:21-22

This verse is so wonderfully simple that it would take a preacher to mess it up. Test everything against the Word of God. Don't worry about what the talk show hosts say, what the bestselling authors are writing, or even what your family traditions said was acceptable. Hold on to the good; that means what lines up with God's Word. The Holy Spirit will help you make these decisions if they are not obvious to you. Avoid every kind of evil: big evil, little evil, public evil, private evil, spoken evil, written evil, sung evil. Don't go near it, touch it, watch it, listen to it, or think about it. Don't try to find a way to incorporate just a little evil into your life. Don't see how close you can get to evil without getting burned. Don't toy with evil and look around to see if there are consequences. Test everything. Hold on to the good. Avoid every kind of evil—and God's blessings will roll over you so abundantly that you will wonder why you would ever want anything but His best for you.

### • THINK ABOUT IT •

Reading, absorbing, and knowing Scripture protects us from deception. Test everything called truth against the Word of God. Doing so will help you avoid evil and choose the good things that bring God's blessings.

### *Prayer*

Heavenly Father, train me to distinguish good from evil. Forgive me for any neglect or disregard of Your Word and the compromises with evil that resulted. By Your Spirit and Word help me recognize and avoid every kind of evil. In Jesus' name, amen.

## WHAT'S IN YOUR STOREROOM?

*"Do not store up for yourselves treasures on earth, where moth and rust destroy, and where thieves break in and steal. But store up for yourselves treasures in heaven, where moth and rust do not destroy, and where thieves do not break in and steal. For where your treasure is, there your heart will be also."*

MATTHEW 6:19-21

Jesus says that we shouldn't store up treasures on earth, yet we still spend our lives doing what?—storing up treasures on earth. I think we're not sure how to process His teaching, because our imagination is that the most secure way to live is to get all we can, can all we get, and sit on the can. However, Jesus isn't condemning hard work and making financial provisions for ourselves and our families. He is saying that material assets are not where we should put our hope because they can easily become our primary focus and they can be corrupted or taken away. He said there is a better way to spend our lives under the sun, and that's laying up treasure in Heaven. He is inviting us toward a way of life that is counterintuitive and counter-cultural, but far more rewarding in this life and the next.

### • THINK ABOUT IT •

Knowing your labor has lasting results in Heaven produces a satisfaction in this life and a celebration in the next. Find joy in choosing the Lord, knowing that God's reward for you cannot be lost or stolen.

### Prayer

Heavenly Father, I want my primary focus to be pleasing You and my life's labors wisely invested in Heaven's treasures. Help me not let the cares of this world or the deceitfulness of wealth divert me. I fix my hope on You. In Jesus' name, amen.

## ANCHORED IN TRUTH

*God is not a man, so he does not lie. He is not human, so he does not change his mind. Has he ever spoken and failed to act? Has he ever promised and not carried it through?*

NUMBERS 23:19 • NLT

Are your days full of ups and downs? You arrive at work and overhear a coworker taking credit for one of your projects. You were looking forward to a weekend of fun with your family, but your boss says everyone needs to be in the office to get a project finished. You can't wait to get home, but you have a flat tire. If you are a homemaker, your days are full of challenges. We face various but similar situations every day, some serious and some not so much. No matter the setting, it's easy to stay on an emotional roller coaster ride. Emotions are not the best guide for our lives, and our days will be very difficult if we allow our emotions to drive us. I appreciate the texture they bring to my life, but they will not determine my joy. That is anchored in my God who never lies, and always keeps His promises.

### • THINK ABOUT IT •

Emotions can energize or exhaust, but they never lead very well. It is a relief to know that by God's grace we are free to keep the lordship over our lives where it belongs: Jesus, the worthy Prince of Peace.

*Prayer*

Heavenly Father, thank You for the stability and peace being anchored in Christ provides. I submit my emotions to the truth of Your Word, the evidence that always outweighs my circumstances. I declare: Jesus is the Lord of my life! In His name, amen.

## UNIQUELY CHOSEN LINEAGE

*Joseph also went up from the town of Nazareth in Galilee to Judea, to Bethlehem the town of David, because he belonged to the house and line of David.*

LUKE 2:4

God's choice of Joseph to be Jesus' earthly father is critical because Joseph was a descendant of David. God had said that from the line of David would arise a King who would sit on the throne of Israel forever. David was a uniquely chosen person; the Bible says he was a man after God's own heart. But David was human, and thus flawed, and his family tree had a few knots in it as well. One of David's sons led a rebellion in an attempt to remove David as king and take his place. If Absalom could have put his hands on David, he would have murdered his father. Another of David's sons raped his sister. You may sometimes find yourself thinking, "God can't use me. I don't belong to the right family. We're more notorious than noteworthy." Remember that no one would have asked David and his sons to pose for a "perfect family" portrait, yet God used them to change the world—in spite of themselves.

### • THINK ABOUT IT •

Defects in your family tree don't have to define your life. Be encouraged: His immeasurably great ability to redeem and set free—not just individuals, but also families and nations—is available to you through the cross of Jesus.

### Prayer

Heavenly Father, sinful choices of my family past or present will not determine my life's outcome. I believe the blood of Jesus and His work on the cross will have the final word. I repent of all rebellion, either inherited or embraced. In Jesus' name, amen.

## ALL ACCESS PASS

*"When the Helper comes, whom I will send to you from the Father, that is the Spirit of truth who proceeds from the Father, He will testify about Me."*

JOHN 15:26 • NASB®

You may have heard it said, "We just need more of the Holy Spirit!" I understand the sentiment but disagree on the details. We don't need more of the Holy Spirit; we need to allow the Holy Spirit to have more of us. I once read that some of us are wired so that if we had the opportunity to go to a seminar on Heaven or go to Heaven, we'd go to the seminar. I think some of us feel that way about the Holy Spirit. We want to read and study and discuss the Holy Spirit, but we don't have any significant intent of cooperating with Him. We just want to check His credentials and file them away in our understanding box. The Holy Spirit is more than a phenomenon to be studied; He is a divine Helper whom we should listen to and follow. The more we seek Him and cultivate His presence, the easier we will find it to hear His voice and follow His leading.

### • THINK ABOUT IT •

Ask God to remove anything that might be causing a reluctance to seek His presence and His Holy Spirit's help, and look for opportunities that will allow Him to have full access to you.

*Prayer*

Heavenly Father, thank You for the gift of Your Holy Spirit. Forgive me for times when I have quenched or grieved Him by disobedience or indifference to Your voice through Him. Help me honor Your Holy Spirit and carefully listen to Him. In Jesus' name, amen.

## TRUSTED TO OBEY

*An angel of the Lord appeared to Joseph in a dream. "Get up," he said, "take the child and his mother and escape to Egypt..." So he got up, took the child and his mother during the night and left for Egypt...*

MATTHEW 2:13-14

I'm amazed at Joseph's obedience. He had a dream and got up and started packing. When we read the Bible or look at other people, we project onto them a more compliant heart than we have. We think it is easier for them to be godly. It wasn't easy for Joseph to walk away from his home and work and take his young family to a foreign country. He did it on a moment's notice at a prompting from the Lord. We've gotten to know Joseph in Christmas pageants, a boy in a bathrobe with a towel on his head. But that's not the brave young man God recruited. When the angel said, "It's time to go," Joseph didn't hesitate. He said, "Mary, we're moving. The same angel talked to me about you. We've got to go." I believe God trusted Joseph to protect His Son, and he did it very well.

### • THINK ABOUT IT •

The unsung hero of the Christmas story is Joseph. He sets an inspiring example of humility, service, and instant obedience. When teaching young people, be sure to highlight this part of the Christmas story too.

*Prayer*

Heavenly Father, I want to be more like Joseph, obeying You without procrastinating, serving without applause. Help me make the choices now that will mold my character for Your unexpected assignments that may come my way. In Jesus' name, amen.

## HE KNOWS YOUR NAME

*The eyes of the Lord are toward the righteous and His ears are open to their cry.*

PSALM 34:15 • NASB®

The Tomb of the Unknown Soldier in Arlington National Cemetery is a hallowed reminder for Americans of the sacrifices made on our behalf. It is a remarkable place, a somber place. Since 1937, a soldier has stood guard there, all day, every day, regardless of the weather. I was there for about fifteen minutes on a frigid winter day and was frozen solid; the young man standing guard never flinched. I couldn't help but think as I stood there that in the Kingdom of God there are no unknown soldiers. He knows each of us by name. He knows the ways we have served His Kingdom and the sacrifices we have made. He knows the temptations we have turned away from in order to make godly choices and honor Him in our daily lives. Not only does He notice how we honor and serve Him, He promises to reward us for doing those things. Sometimes the world makes us feel as if we are unknown and insignificant, but we are not unknown or insignificant to God.

### • THINK ABOUT IT •

God knows your name. He knows every detail of your life, down to the numbers of hairs on your head and the thoughts of your heart. What you sacrifice in this life will not be forgotten, and will pale in comparison to the rich reward you receive from the Lord Himself.

### *Prayer*

Heavenly Father, thank You that You know every detail of my life, and that You love me. I want my life to honor and serve You. Please help me to see my sacrifices for You in this life as gain, and be glorified in it. In Jesus' name, amen.

## GAIN MOMENTUM

*I thank Christ Jesus our Lord, who has given me strength, that he considered me faithful, appointing me to his service.*

1 TIMOTHY 1:12

I had a meeting a few years ago with a gentleman who was in his late eighties. He was an accomplished man, and I wanted to talk to him about some ideas I had. As he was showing me something on his computer, I inadvertently saw his to-do list. I was embarrassed and very grateful he couldn't see mine. He was working out more than I was, and one of his goals was to raise several billion dollars in the next ten years! He was in a season of his life where his accomplishments were significant enough that dialing it back would not only have been appropriate, but expected. I walked out of that meeting humbled and focused. As we mature in the Lord, temptation can take the form of complacency: "I've done some significant things and can sit back and relax now." Don't allow yourself to settle for that. Let's don't arrive at the pearly gates in our recliners. Let's show up with our running shoes on and sweat on our brows.

· THINK ABOUT IT ·

It was said of the racehorse Secretariat that he amazingly crossed the finish line of his Triple Crown victory still accelerating. Ask the Lord to strengthen you to likewise run your own race for Him.

*Prayer*

Heavenly Father, You never gave me a quota, but a call. Help me remove any complacency toward spiritual growth and service that I might gain momentum in You. Renew my strength that I might spiritually accelerate to finish my course well. In Jesus' name, amen.

# DAY 259

## UNASHAMED ADORATION

*David again gathered all the elite troops in Israel, 30,000 in all. He led them to...bring back the Ark of God, which bears the name of the Lord of Heaven's Armies, who is enthroned between the cherubim. They placed the Ark of God on a new cart and brought it from Abinadab's house, which was on a hill...David and all the people of Israel were celebrating before the Lord, singing songs and playing all kinds of musical instruments—lyres, harps, tambourines, castanets, and cymbals.*

2 SAMUEL 6:1-5 • NLT

The value of worship and praise and thanksgiving before God is of enormous significance in Scripture. Here we see David, the greatest warrior in Israelite history and now their king, leading thousands of his people to worship God without shame. Verse 14 tells us that David, filled with joy, "danced before the Lord with all his might." I don't know of anything that has greater potential to help people take steps towards freedom and deliverance than inviting them to praise and give thanksgiving to God. Something simply remarkable happens when we acknowledge His power and glory and ask for His involvement in our lives.

### • THINK ABOUT IT •

Praising God invites His presence, which releases His power and scatters His enemies. To see His Kingdom come into your life's circumstances, determine to praise Him daily.

### Prayer

Heavenly Father, I offer grateful adoration to You—my Maker, Redeemer, Deliverer, and ever-present help. You have lovingly provided all I need through the cross. Thank You for delivering me from darkness and filling me with Your Spirit. In Jesus' name, amen.

## ABOUT FACE

*"Repent, then, and turn to God, so that your sins may be wiped out, that times of refreshing may come from the Lord..."*

ACTS 3:19

The Church should be filled with the most repentant people in the earth. In fact, we need to practice until we are world-class at repentance. So often we want to stand and wag our finger at the ungodly and say, "Look at them. They really need to repent and get right with God!" But the Scripture is clear from beginning to end, if the people of God will come to Him with hearts of repentance, He will move Heaven and earth in response to them. Repentance carries with it two meanings. In the Hebrew, it means a change of direction, a physical change, an about-face. In the Greek, it means a change of mind. You need both definitions to get the full benefit of repentance in your life: a change of mind, and a change of direction. While Peter was speaking to a crowd of unbelievers in this verse, his message applies to us as well. When we continue to repent and turn to God, He continues to bless us with times of refreshing.

### • THINK ABOUT IT •

Just as your nose will stop sensing a bad smell after prolonged exposure, your soul can be desensitized by habits of sin. Ask the Holy Spirit to make you sensitive again to His promptings and for help to make the needed changes to align more fully with Him.

### *Prayer*

Heavenly Father, reveal to me anywhere I have become accommodating or desensitized to sin in my life. I am willing to repent of it all. Let Jesus' blood cleanse me, and Your Spirit conform me more to the image of Christ. In Jesus' name, amen.

## COUNT IT ALL JOY

*Because of my chains, most of the brothers in the Lord have been encouraged to speak the word of God more courageously and fearlessly.*

PHILIPPIANS 1:14

Comfort and convenience have become idols for Americans, and that includes Christians. When I go to other places in the world I am humbled by the attitudes of the believers. When we were in Kenya, pastors came from all over that region of Africa. They sat all day and all night to hear the Word of God taught, in what we would consider very uncomfortable surroundings. In one meeting, the guitar player had two strings missing and the drums had no heads. It did not seem to hinder their worship at all. Following God has very little to do with comfort and convenience. When I read of Paul's successful ministry from prison, it seems that succumbing to those idols of comfort and convenience has made us sluggish and ineffective. I believe that Jesus loves the American Church. We wouldn't be where we are without His grace and mercy. But I also believe that He would ask us, "Are you prepared to do whatever it takes to follow Me?"

• THINK ABOUT IT •

There is a cost of discipleship. James considered that cost and counseled us in his letter to "count it all joy." When contemplating the cost of following Jesus, remember the joy set before Him on the cross, and follow Him.

*Prayer*

Heavenly Father, by Your grace, may hardships and trials prove me to be steadfast with the courage to not shrink back from following Jesus. So whatever it takes to follow Him, Father, I proclaim ahead of time that He is worth it all. In His name I pray, amen.

## SEEKING TO KNOW

*The Pharisees and Sadducees came to Jesus and tested him by asking him to show them a sign from heaven. He replied, "When evening comes, you say, 'It will be fair weather, for the sky is red,' and in the morning, 'Today it will be stormy, for the sky is red and overcast.' You know how to interpret the appearance of the sky, but you cannot interpret the signs of the times.*

MATTHEW 16:1-3

Jesus had performed many public miracles, but these religious leaders were intent on discrediting Him and maintaining the status quo. Jesus said, "You're more knowledgeable about the weather than you are the Kingdom of God." Are we that different? I think some of us truly are more concerned about the weather than we are the things of God. We need to get on our knees and ask Him to show us who He is and what He is doing. We need to learn to recognize the voice of His Spirit. We go to church, we follow the rules. We learn what "good people" do and don't do in public. But we need to become more in tune with Him and earnestly seek the things of God.

### • THINK ABOUT IT •

These men were invested in their influence and their power, but they were clueless about the Kingdom of God. What is your heart looking for? Revival is when we begin to say, "God, I want to know You. I want to participate in what You are doing in the earth."

### *Prayer*

Heavenly Father, thank You for Your Word, its truth, and how it points us to Your heart. I want to know You, and I want to begin making decisions rooted in love for You. My hope is in You. In Jesus' name, amen.

## UNAPOLOGETIC BELIEF

*He was pierced for our transgressions, he was crushed for our iniquities; the punishment that brought us peace was on him, and by his wounds we are healed.*

ISAIAH 53:5

Hundreds of years ago a faction of theologians emerged who questioned the integrity of Scripture, and the book of Isaiah was under particular assault. Among their theories was that the book was not God's prophecies given to one man, but a collection of prophecies written by several people. Some rabbis chimed in, saying that no Hebrew prophet would have written the Messianic chapter 53, so Christians must have inserted that. In 1948 a shepherd boy looking for a lost sheep near the Dead Sea threw a rock into a cave. He heard a jar break, began exploring, and found a scroll that would be identified as the scroll of Isaiah. It was a thousand years older and identical to the scroll of Isaiah that was considered authoritative; it had been hand copied by Hebrew scribes. One shepherd kid discredited an entire body of scholarship when he found a scroll in a jar in a cave by the Dead Sea. You never have to be embarrassed because you believe in the integrity of Scripture.

• THINK ABOUT IT •

It's popular in our culture to trust scientific theory over the assertions of Scripture. But over the years we've seen many examples of science eventually verifying its claims. Give God's Word the benefit of the doubt.

*Prayer*

Heavenly Father, Your inspired Word has been recorded with integrity and preserved accurately, sometimes at the cost of Your servants' lives. Help me do my part to love and honor Your Word and faithfully present it to this generation. In Jesus' name, amen.

## LIVING PEACEFUL LIVES

*"Do not worry about tomorrow, for tomorrow will worry about itself. Each day has enough trouble of its own."*

MATTHEW 6:34

In our hearts we know that worry doesn't change anything, but it doesn't stop us from trying. God created us and knows exactly what our needs are. His consistent message throughout Scripture is that if you make seeking the Kingdom of God and His righteousness your first priority, the things you need in life will come to you. If you reverse it and make seeking worldly things your first priority, no matter how much you accumulate, no matter how much of your future you think you have under control, those things can change in an instant. "Each day has enough trouble of its own," so He doesn't want us to look too far ahead and worry about things that may happen in the future. Some of us are prone to worry, and others have simply fallen into the habit. I encourage you to put that aside and focus on seeking God's Kingdom. He holds your future in His hands, after all, and He will see that your needs are met.

### • THINK ABOUT IT •

You can't add length to your life by worrying, but medical science warns us you can certainly shorten it by doing so. Trusting God is not only the appropriate thing to do; it's the healthy response too.

### *Prayer*

Heavenly Father, shifting my focus from worrying, I put my trust in Your Word, my confidence in the total provision of Jesus' blood. I give thanks for Your goodness. Let Your Kingdom come as I bear witness to Your faithfulness. In Jesus' name, amen.

## OUR REASONABLE SERVICE

*God demonstrates his own love for us in this: While we were still sinners, Christ died for us. Since we have now been justified by his blood, how much more shall we be saved from God's wrath through him!*

ROMANS 5:8-9

Here's the bargain. God did something extraordinary and miraculous for us. When we were still ungodly and rebellious, God sent His Son to offer Himself as a sacrifice for you and me. We have been completely justified by His blood on the cross. Our reasonable service in return for that is not to offer ourselves as martyrs, but to offer ourselves in serving Him. There was a time in American history when serving was fashionable. Young men and women from the finest families served on the mission field as Christian missionaries, and their journeys were recorded on the front pages of major newspapers. That's almost beyond our imagination today, but that's our history. God has given you gifts, abilities, and a sphere of influence. Don't let the great efforts of your life be for things that are temporary. Let the great passion of your life be to serve the Lord. You'll never regret it.

· THINK ABOUT IT ·

Think about what you could give less time to in order to give more priority to the things of God. Ask the Lord to help you more effectively align your passion and agenda to His.

*Prayer*

Heavenly Father, the life You have given me, I gratefully offer to You in service. Reveal what I need to lay down that I have greater freedom to serve You, and grant me the grace to embrace all that aligns to Your agenda for my life. In Jesus' name, amen.

## NOT UP FOR NEGOTIATION

*Then Samson prayed to the LORD, "O Sovereign LORD, remember me. O God, please strengthen me just once more..."*

### JUDGES 16:28

Before Samson ever drew a breath, God called him for His purposes. God's Spirit would come upon Samson and enable him to do what was impossible apart from the presence of the Lord. Samson recognized that his power was a gift of God, but the undisciplined part of his character was his vulnerability. It was an aspect of his life he wouldn't yield to the Lord, and it was his downfall. He toyed with temptation, and it diminished his ability to hear what God was saying. One of the saddest places in all of Scripture is Samson's prayer at the end of his life. Standing in a pagan temple with his enemies taunting him—led by a child, his eyes burned out—he begs, "Lord, let me feel Your presence one more time." Satan doesn't try to get our cooperation immediately. When he presents us with a temptation, it's a negotiation. His goal is our destruction, of course. But if he can just get us to play around with evil, he has neutralized our effectiveness in the Kingdom of God.

### • THINK ABOUT IT •

The lure of immediate gratification is one way the Devil does his own fishing for men. If you've already been "hooked," be encouraged that the blood of Jesus and repentance can set you free again. Jesus came precisely to rescue, redeem, and restore.

## Prayer

Heavenly Father, make me aware of anything that diminishes my ability to hear and walk closely with You. Help me resist Satan's "negotiations" and guard both my heart and fellowship with You that I might be more effective for Your Kingdom. In Jesus' name, amen.

## TRANQUIL STATE OF CALM

*Then he got into the boat and his disciples followed him. Without warning, a furious storm came up on the lake, so that the waves swept over the boat. But Jesus was sleeping. The disciples went and woke him, saying, "Lord, save us! We're going to drown!" He replied, "You of little faith, why are you so afraid?" Then he got up and rebuked the winds and the waves, and it was completely calm.*

MATTHEW 8:23-26

God wants us to lead peaceful lives. Biblically, peace is not the absence of hardship and conflict, but tranquility and calmness from God in the midst of hardship and conflict. A wonderful example of that is Jesus with His disciples in a boat on the Sea of Galilee. A furious storm blew up, and the disciples thought they were going to drown. What was Jesus doing? Sleeping. They had to wake Him up to tell Him He was about to drown! The picture of Jesus asleep in the midst of the storm is a marvelous portrayal of God's peace. No matter what storms come, you can have that tranquil state of calm knowing that God is watching over you.

### • THINK ABOUT IT •

When we walk in Jesus' peace, we become lighthouses to those around us living in this chaotic age. His peace not only blesses you; it can make you a beacon for others looking for safe harbor.

### *Prayer*

Heavenly Father, You are the keeper of my being, watching over my comings and goings. Let Your peace guard my heart and mind and be evidence to others of Your power to save and give hope. You are my anchor, shelter, and shield. In Jesus' name, amen.

## HIS IMAGE, HIS BREATH

*Then God said, "Let us make man in our image, in our likeness, and let them rule over the fish of the sea and the birds of the air, over the livestock, over all the earth, and over all the creatures that move along the ground."*

GENESIS 1:26

In the twenty-first century, we have to pause and think about the place of humanity in the world. There is a commonly held worldview that says human beings are simply the top of the evolutionary ladder and we don't have any more intrinsic value than an orangutan, a salamander, or a spotted owl. A biblical worldview says we are not only different from the rest of creation, we are the highest form of creation. God fashioned mankind in His image and breathed into Adam the breath of life. He chose to identify with humanity, and the redemptive work of Jesus Christ involved God putting on flesh and blood. We have been given dominion over creation and so have a responsibility to care for it, but make no mistake about the preeminent place of humanity in the world God created.

· THINK ABOUT IT ·

Being made in His image has granted each of us dignity and value. Every worldview that denies this truth will devolve into a system that values neither life nor freedom.

*Prayer*

Heavenly Father, I am made in Your image and purchased by Jesus' blood. Help me exercise authority wisely in Your name to see Your Kingdom come and Your will done. Help me speak into my culture the eternal value of each human life. In Jesus' name, amen.

# DAY 269

## MINISTERS OF DELIVERANCE

*The angel of the LORD encamps around those who fear him, and he delivers them...blessed is the man who takes refuge in him.*

PSALM 34:7-8

Sometimes it can be hard to believe in what we cannot see, but the Bible makes it clear that there are unseen powers that impact our lives. There are spiritual forces of darkness that look for every opportunity to exploit our weaknesses; their goal is our ultimate destruction. However, God's angels are standing guard to deliver us from those evil forces. God has sent these angels to minister on our behalf, and there is no shame in admitting our weaknesses and running to Him for refuge; in fact, this verse says we will be blessed when we take refuge in Him. In our can-do, "I'll take care of this" culture, I find it very reassuring and comforting to know that there are angels camped out around God's people, guarding us and rescuing us from enemies seen and unseen. When you are beset by the snares of the enemy, do not seek refuge in the latest self-help guru. Run to the Lord and cry out to Him, "Lord, I need You! Help me!"

### • THINK ABOUT IT •

Images of angels in art and media have made them look more mythic than real. Consider how, in his psalm, David describes angels as beings: "mighty in strength, who perform His word, obeying the voice of His word!"

### Prayer

Heavenly Father, I need every support You give as I seek to obey Your Word. Thank You for assigning angels to guard me and help me prevail. You are my true Defender and shield, and I run to You alone. Be my help as I seek You now. In Jesus' name, amen.

## SOIL CULTIVATION

*"A farmer went out to plant his seed. As he scattered it across his field, some seed fell on a footpath, where it was stepped on, and the birds ate it. Other seed fell among rocks. It began to grow, but the plant soon wilted and died for lack of moisture. Other seed fell among thorns that grew up with it and choked out the tender plants. Still other seed fell on fertile soil. This seed grew and produced a crop that was a hundred times as much as had been planted!"*

LUKE 8:5-8 • NLT

Jesus describes a man whose harvest had nothing to do with the seed or the sower, but the kind of soil where the seed fell. If you buy seed and throw it out in your yard, you're not going to have a garden. If you want a garden, you'll need to invest time in preparing and tending the soil. The same is true in our spiritual lives. If we just show up on the weekend and expect our lives to bear great fruit for the Kingdom of God, we will be disappointed. We have to prepare and tend the soil of our hearts in order to receive what God has for us.

### • THINK ABOUT IT •

What steps could you take to "prepare the soil" of your heart? What might need to be weeded out? What would enrich your ability to hear His voice?

### *Prayer*

Heavenly Father, help me prepare my heart to follow You. Take out the hard places of unbelief that hinder Your Word rooting firmly in me. Help me pull out any "weeds" that are crowding You out. I desire to be fruitful for You. In Jesus' name, amen.

## ASSIMILATION FOR TRANSFORMATION

*If you listen to the word and don't obey, it is like glancing at your face in a mirror. You see yourself, walk away, and forget what you look like. But if you look carefully into the perfect law that sets you free, and if you do what it says and don't forget what you heard, then God will bless you for doing it.*

JAMES 1:23-25 • NLT

Sometimes we allow ourselves to fall into the mindset that the main objective of being a Christ-follower is to assimilate information about God. I have a computer on my desk that contains dozens of Bible translations, word studies, commentaries, and many other helpful things. If the key to righteousness is having a collection of facts and opinions about God, that computer is the holiest thing in the building. But that computer lacks the ability to put any of that information to practical use. When you and I assimilate information and ideas, but we do not allow them to transform our lives, we are no better than a computer with a full hard drive. I'm an advocate for learning, but I want the knowledge I gain about God to impact my head and my heart.

### • THINK ABOUT IT •

From your heart will come your thoughts, words, and actions (Mark 7:21-22, Luke 6:45), so it is critical that your "head" knowledge about God impact your heart and all that issues from it.

*Prayer*

Heavenly Father, I will love You with all my heart and mind and be a doer, not just a hearer, of Your Word. Make my life evidence of Your transforming power as I apply my knowledge of Your will. Thank You for blessing as I obey. In Jesus' name, amen.

# DAY 272

## DARING TO TRUST

*"If you remain silent at this time, relief and deliverance for the Jews will arise from another place, but you and your father's family will perish. And who knows but that you have come to royal position for such a time as this?"*

ESTHER 4:14

Life has a way of presenting us with choices about the secrets we keep, and Esther was in one of those places. She was Jewish at a time when her people were living in exile, yet through a remarkable set of circumstances she had become the queen of Persia. She had privilege, wealth, and authority—but great deception was required to keep her secret. When the Jewish population was threatened with mass slaying, her cousin, Mordecai, challenged her secret keeping. She had an opportunity to be used in a mighty way, but she would have to trust her future to God. She did, and she and her people were saved. When you learn to trust God, you will open doors of opportunity for Him to take your relationship with Him to new places. There will be times when putting your life in His hands feels like you are putting everything at risk, when in reality you are putting your life in the safest place possible.

· THINK ABOUT IT ·

Choosing courage and obedience as her path, Esther trusted her outcome to God. How has God turned your difficult challenges into good outcomes when you have resolved to trust Him?

*Prayer*

Heavenly Father, hard choices and challenges are my opportunities to trust You more, as Your power works on my behalf. Thank You for turning them into open doors to growth and good outcomes. Your unfailing love keeps me safe. In Jesus' name, amen.

# DAY 273

## ONE CHOICE AT A TIME

*We ask God to give you complete knowledge of his will and to give you spiritual wisdom and understanding. Then the way you live will always honor and please the Lord, and your lives will produce every kind of good fruit. All the while, you will grow as you learn to know God better and better.*

COLOSSIANS 1:9-10 • NLT

In my imagination, life is like a pathway lined with God-choices that we are free to implement or reject. A God-choice looks something like this: We repent of the anger that we have used in order to manipulate people and circumstances to get our way. We repent of giving ourselves permission to behave in an ungodly way. We choose to forgive rather than to hold bitterness or hatred. We choose to read the Word of God on a hectic day. We choose to listen to music that glorifies God. One by one, we take the God-choices off the shelf and say, "I choose this." Do your choices today reflect the desires of your earthly nature, or your desire to please God? It's a very important question to process, because it has a great deal to do with the trajectory of your life.

### • THINK ABOUT IT •

If your choices too often betray divided loyalties between self and God, ask the Holy Spirit's help to move toward an undivided heart one choice at a time.

### *Prayer*

Heavenly Father, I am dismayed by the self-centeredness that runs through so many of my choices. Holy Spirit, help me recognize the God-choices You give me, and strengthen my spirit to choose consistently what pleases You. In Jesus' name, amen.

## CONTINUAL DELIVERANCE

*He has delivered us from such a deadly peril, and he will deliver us. On him we have set our hope that he will continue to deliver us...*

2 CORINTHIANS 1:10

Paul was perhaps the greatest advocate for Jesus that the world will ever know. He worked without the advantages of modern travel or communication, and his influence is still felt two thousand years after his death. But Paul suffered extreme hardship, even as he followed the path that the Lord had set for him. This verse intrigues me because he says that "He delivered us" three times in three different verb forms. God has delivered us: past tense. It happened at a particular point in time. God will deliver us: future tense. We know He's a Deliverer, and He will deliver us if we need it again. Then the perfect tense: God is going to continue to deliver us. So what did Paul want the Corinthians to know about God as a Deliverer? "He did deliver us, He will deliver us, and He is in fact delivering me as I write these words." Our God, who never changes, is just as faithful to deliver us today.

· THINK ABOUT IT ·

Knowing God's deliverance is still available to you today can thwart anxiety and guard your peace. Consider memorizing the above verse as encouragement for yourself and defense against the adversary.

*Prayer*

Heavenly Father, You are a God who still delivers, giving me hope for today and tomorrow. Thank You for Your peace that comes and guards me as I trust You to deliver me again. You remain faithful forever, and I am secure in You. In Jesus' name, amen.

## THE POWER OF REPENTANCE

*Have mercy on me, O God, because of your unfailing love. Because of your great compassion, blot out the stain of my sins. Wash me clean from my guilt. Purify me from my sin. For I recognize my rebellion; it haunts me day and night.*

PSALM 51:1-3 • NLT

Psalm 51 is a psalm of repentance, attributed to David as a confession to God after he had sinned with Bathsheba. At a young age David had been chosen by God for an important role in His Kingdom, and he truly loved his Lord. Yet he was a rebellious sinner just as we are and succumbed to temptation just as we sometimes do. David recognized the life-giving and life-changing power of repentance. He knew that God invites us to come before Him just as we are, to face Him with our sorrows and regrets, shames and burdens, and to be cleansed and know the freedom and blessing of His forgiveness. Sometimes we use theology and doctrine as the spiritual equivalent of make-up that hides our imperfections. But God says simply, "If you'll turn to Me in honesty and humility, I will renew you and bring restoration to your life."

### • THINK ABOUT IT •

Sometimes religion says, "Cover it up. Don't let God see the real you." You can face the Lord and trust Him to bring healing and renewal and restoration and freedom to your life. In Him, you will find the fullest expression for which you were created.

### *Prayer*

Heavenly Father, You know me entirely, and I humbly come to You just as I am, laying my failures and sorrows at the foot of the cross. Forgive my rebellion, cleanse me, and restore me to Your purposes. Thank You for saving and renewing me. In Jesus' name, amen.

## APPLICATION BY PROCLAMATION

*"[The Church] overcame him by the blood of the Lamb and by the word of their testimony; they did not love their lives so much as to shrink from death."*

### REVELATION 12:11

This verse describes the Church's victory over Satan, and the two components that will achieve it. One is the power of God demonstrated in the blood of Jesus. The other is the application of that power through the testimony of those who believe. You can have power, but power that is not applied remains useless. You can have a lot to say, but if there is no power behind your words they are just hot air. The combination of the two will result in victory and freedom in our lives. When we take hold of that most powerful combination and live it out in practical ways, we will walk in the victory and blessing that God has for us.

### • THINK ABOUT IT •

You can be an overcomer today. Gain confidence in the Lord by remembering the victories He has given you in the past. Let that testimony encourage those around you to trust Him as well.

*Prayer*

Heavenly Father, thank You for Jesus' shed blood! Give me greater understanding of its power and greater knowledge of Your Word. Teach me to speak life and declare Your promises so I can have overcoming victory and bring blessing to others. In Jesus' name, amen.

## THE PRICE OF OUR REDEMPTION

*It was not with perishable things such as silver or gold that you were redeemed from the empty way of life handed down to you from your forefathers, but with the precious blood of Christ...*

1 PETER 1:18-19

Peter chooses his words very carefully here to describe the price of our redemption. Silver and gold were very rare and valuable commodities in the first century, and they are still valuable today. Some people see their enduring value as a solid investment in uncertain economic times. Peter says, "You weren't redeemed—you weren't bought out of slavery—with silver or gold. You were bought with something more precious." More precious than silver or gold—what could it be? The blood of Christ. Peter recognizes the value of Jesus' blood because he knows its power, a power far greater than the power of silver and gold. We often look for help in the material resources that the world says are valuable, and those resources can be very helpful. But our ultimate redemption is not something that we can earn—it has been purchased with the powerful blood of Jesus, a free gift to all who will believe in Him as Savior and Lord.

### • THINK ABOUT IT •

The value of Jesus' blood in God's sight is infinite and eternal. Contemplate your worth to God that He has been willing to pay such a costly price to rescue you.

*Prayer*

Heavenly Father, blessed be Your name! Through Jesus' precious blood You have freely given me what I cannot earn. I gratefully receive and trust in the power of His blood to redeem me fully and destroy the works of the Devil. In Jesus' name, amen.

## GOD AND GOD ALONE

*Trust in the LORD always, for the LORD GOD is the eternal Rock.*

ISAIAH 26:4 • NLT

One of the first thoughts a toddler expresses is, "Me do it!" If they can imagine themselves doing it, they don't want to be hindered by your influence, whether it's spreading peanut butter or deciding what to wear. One of the annoying aspects of my character is that I still say to God, "Me do it!" God calls us to a life of faith, but the most difficult places in my life are the places I have to trust the Lord—the places where I am truly dependent upon God, that if God isn't God, I'm seriously in trouble; or the places when I feel awkward, the ones I would like to walk past more quickly. At the heart of our God-story is the fact that God has done something for us that we cannot do for ourselves: He redeemed us and delivered us from the power of darkness. Why do we serve the Lord? Why do we honor God with our lives? It's because we recognize the magnitude of what He has done for us and our utter inability to do it for ourselves.

• THINK ABOUT IT •

Recognizing the magnitude of what God has done for us will be a life-long process of repeatedly coming to the end of ourselves and declaring once again: "Only God!"

*Prayer*

Heavenly Father, I admit I am utterly unable to save myself. I acknowledge my complete dependency on Your Spirit to empower and transform me. Help me honor You with my life as You work in and through me. You are my Rock. In Jesus' name, amen.

## EXPECTATIONS REDEFINED

*He said to Simon, "Put out into deep water, and let down the nets for a catch."*
*Simon answered, "Master, we've worked hard all night and haven't caught*
*anything. But because you say so, I will let down the nets."*

LUKE 5:4-5

The disciples had fished all night because the water was so clear that the fish wouldn't strike in the daytime. After a long night with nothing to show for their work, they were washing their nets. People were crowding around Jesus, and He decided to use Peter's (here called "Simon") boat as a teaching platform. When He was finished He told Peter to head for deep water and let down the nets. Peter knew it was pointless to fish in the daytime, but He did it because His Lord said to. What was the result? Nets so full they began to break and boats so full they began to sink. Peter knew that Jesus was no fisherman; He had grown up in a carpenter's shop. But he recognized Jesus' authority and cooperated with it. Do not allow your expectations to stifle God's work in your life. When we acknowledge the authority of God, we open doorways for Him to move in unexpected ways.

• THINK ABOUT IT •

Recognizing Jesus' authority and cooperating with it honored Jesus, and that gained for Peter a glimpse into what God's power could do. Choosing to act likewise can do the same for you.

*Prayer*

Heavenly Father, I want to honor Your authority always, obeying what You ask of me. Expand my expectations beyond my man-made limits, because with You all things are possible. It is enough to know You said so. In Jesus' name, amen.

## CLEAR PLAN, CLEAR PATH, CLEAR POWER

*They asked him, "Lord, are you at this time going to restore the kingdom to Israel?" He said to them: "It is not for you to know the times or dates the Father has set by his own authority. But you will receive power when the Holy Spirit comes on you; and you will be my witnesses in Jerusalem, and in all Judea and Samaria, and to the ends of the earth."*

ACTS 1:6-8

Some of us act as if God has sent us on a treasure hunt that's like a complicated board game: The keys to the Kingdom are hidden, and to find them we have to unlock secret doors that lead to secret passageways. There are some things God does not intend for us to know, but He has gone out of His way to tell us what we do need to know. He has told us what His plans are and has given us the Holy Spirit power we need to follow through with those plans. Don't spend your life looking for things God has said are not ours to know. Spend your life pursuing the Holy Spirit, and your days telling others about the life-changing power of God.

• THINK ABOUT IT •

Pursuing the Holy Spirit includes making His priorities our priorities. The book of Acts clearly reveals that two of His priorities are making disciples and growing His Church. Are there ways—perhaps unique to you—that you can be involved? The Holy Spirit can show you.

*Prayer*

Heavenly Father, Jesus' commission to us has not changed. Fill me with Your Spirit so I can boldly tell what You have done for me. Equip and empower me to do my part as You build Your Church. Unite me with others doing the same. In Jesus' name, amen.

## UNPACK THE BAGGAGE

*"I am your brother Joseph, the one you sold into Egypt! And now, do not be distressed and do not be angry with yourselves for selling me here, because it was to save lives that God sent me ahead of you."*

GENESIS 45:4-5

Pharaoh had made Joseph prime minister of Egypt and put him "in charge of the whole land" (Genesis 41:41). Now the region was suffering from a famine, and Joseph's brothers went to Egypt where they had heard there was food. These were the same brothers who had debated killing him and finally sold him as a slave. Instead of taking vengeance, Joseph forgave them and provided for them—amazing! In modern terms, I'd say that Joseph had unpacked his baggage. He didn't spend his life harboring bitterness and anger. His brothers had surely lived beneath the burden of guilt and the shame of their secret, but Joseph had done the hard work and forgiven them. It takes some heavy lifting to forgive people who have wounded you, but forgiveness made it possible for Joseph to fulfill his part in God's plan. Trust God. Invite Him in. He rescued Joseph and used him, and He'll do the same for you.

### • THINK ABOUT IT •

Do you sense you might still have "some baggage" to unpack? Unforgiveness can sabotage God's best for you, so ask His help to unpack and forgive. As it did for Joseph, it will bring good to you and others.

### *Prayer*

Heavenly Father, as You have forgiven me, help me forgive others. Show me if I am harboring bitterness or anger. I let go of everything that sabotages Your plan for me. Let Your power bring redemptive purpose to my life-story. In Jesus' name, amen.

# DAY 282

## ATTENTION-PULLING POWER

*The priests and the captain of the temple guard and the Sadducees came up to Peter and John while they were speaking to the people. They were greatly disturbed because the apostles were teaching the people and proclaiming in Jesus the resurrection of the dead.*

ACTS 4:1-2

Before the descent of the Holy Spirit on the day of Pentecost, the disciples couldn't get arrested if they tried. They were in the Temple every day, talking about the death and resurrection of their Lord. They were preaching that Jesus of Nazareth was the Messiah, and no one paid attention. After the day of Pentecost, they couldn't stop getting arrested. The Holy Spirit brought attention to who they were and what they were doing. Their message began to spread throughout Jerusalem and beyond. Lives were changed by the thousands, and the Church began to grow. The Holy Spirit is in the earth to impact people and situations for the purposes of God. Our goal as Christ-followers is not to maintain the status quo. Our goal is to invite the presence of the Spirit of God, and when He comes we should expect that life as we know it will never be the same.

### • THINK ABOUT IT •

Are you ready for the Holy Spirit to bring attention to you and what you are doing? The Holy Spirit has courage, boldness, and wisdom ready for your asking.

*Prayer*

Heavenly Father, prepare me for the attention the Holy Spirit will bring to me and my church in these days ahead. Help me make the heart, mind, and soul preparations I need to serve You well. Holy Spirit, we invite You, come! In Jesus' name, amen.

## MOTIVATED TO ENCOURAGE

*See to it, brothers, that none of you has a sinful, unbelieving heart that turns away from the living God. But encourage one another daily...*

HEBREWS 3:12-13

When I was a young and naïve man, I thought only weak people needed encouragement. This passage tells us that encouragement has a spiritual purpose beyond just making us feel better: If we don't have it, "a sinful, unbelieving heart that turns away from the living God" will overwhelm us. The counterintuitive thing about encouragement is that we are responsible for our own. Because of that, I try not to dwell on the things that make me discouraged. I live in the real world, but I'd rather focus on the victories God has poured out on me and around me. I do not go out of my way to spend time with people who bring me down. Instead, I spend time with people who lift me up. I've found the best way to find encouragement is to be an encourager myself. This is one of the areas where we really do reap what we sow, so look for and point out the best in others and you'll find the same coming back to you.

• THINK ABOUT IT •

Encouragement gives support, confidence, and hope. It fuels perseverance and gives you a beautifully effective way to build up His Church. Be an encourager!

*Prayer*

Heavenly Father, I choose to fix my focus on Your victories, on truth and things worthy of praise. I ask You to highlight these things in the lives of myself and others so I can encourage us all to keep on confidently following You. In Jesus' name, amen.

## PERPETUAL CONFIDENCE AND EXPECTATION

*Whoever dwells in the shelter of the Most High will rest in the shadow of the Almighty. I will say of the LORD, "He is my refuge and my fortress, my God, in whom I trust."*

PSALM 91:1-2

We don't typically go around proclaiming our trust in the Lord when everything is going well, but we should because it will make a difference in our lives. Give thanks to the Lord for what He has done and will do in the future. Don't wait until every bill is paid. Don't wait until your relatives are all getting along. Don't wait for the prison doors to swing open. Thank the Lord that He is faithful and that He loves you. Thank Him that He is your refuge and your fortress. Thank Him that He is your shelter and your tower of strength against your enemies (Psalm 61:3). When we learn to trust in Him and dwell in Him, we will be able to sit down and rest in His shadow—isn't that an amazing thought? Almighty God is worthy of our honor and praise and thanksgiving. Let's begin acknowledging that to ourselves, to others, and to the Lord on a daily basis.

· THINK ABOUT IT ·

To jumpstart your daily praise, just try describing God—His character and deeds—aloud. This will buttress your faith in any circumstance and remind you of all the reasons you can always trust Him.

*Prayer*

Heavenly Father, thank You for being my refuge and fortress in every circumstance. Give me words and open doors to speak of Your praises, strength, and mighty works. You are worthy of highest honor, thanksgiving, and trust. In Jesus' name, amen.

## CREATED FOR COMMUNITY

*They devoted themselves to the apostles' teaching and to the fellowship, to the breaking of bread and to prayer.*

ACTS 2:42

I misread this sentence for many years. I thought it meant that the people devoted themselves to the apostles' teaching and to fellowship—that they liked covered dish dinners. But that's not what it says, is it? It says they devoted themselves to the apostles' teaching and to the fellowship, to the community of faith. Americans are known for our rugged individualism, our tendency to ride in like John Wayne with the reigns in our teeth and a pistol in each hand and say, "I'll handle this, fellas. I don't need any help." One of the things I regret about the American Church is that we have brought that attitude into our congregational life. The truth is that we are created to live in community. We need each other. We strengthen and sharpen one another. We will not finish the course that God has called us to without one another. While you truly may not need help in a given situation, it will only be a matter of time until you do.

· THINK ABOUT IT ·

Isolating yourself will cut you off from the fellowship we all need to give us encouragement, insight, and opportunity to use our gifts for His glory. Can you identify areas where you could incorporate more fellowship with other believers?

*Prayer*

Heavenly Father, I want to walk in Your light, but I cannot do it alone. Make my love for others in Your Body increase and overflow. Help us bear each other's burdens. May the unity You give bear witness to our resurrected Lord. In Jesus' name, amen.

## DARKNESS CANNOT VANQUISH LIGHT

*When Jesus spoke again to the people, he said, "I am the light of the world. Whoever follows me will never walk in darkness, but will have the light of life."*

JOHN 8:12

Life on earth is often described as a journey. It begins at conception and continues until our spirit departs our body. The challenge with any journey is the travel, which is always an invitation toward the unknown. It's leaving the familiar behind, and that often brings with it a sense of uneasiness. God does not want us to fear what lies ahead, but to look to the light that He provides. In Genesis, God spoke light into the darkness. Jesus said He is not only a light, but the Light of life who illuminates our path. We have been given the gift of the Holy Spirit, who shines the light of love and freedom into every corner and onto every dark shadow of our lives. Jesus is the Light of the World. When you take steps toward Him, you give God an opportunity to do in your life what only a Living God can do, so let's determine to walk in His light.

· THINK ABOUT IT ·

The darkness increasing in our days intends to overwhelm, but Jesus has promised that you need never walk in it or be overcome by it if you follow Him. The darkness cannot overcome His light.

*Prayer*

Heavenly Father, thank You that Jesus has come and delivered us from darkness. Help me walk in Jesus' light guided by Your Spirit. Shine light into my heart, bringing freedom and truth, so I can arise and shine for Your glory. In Jesus' name, amen.

# DAY 287

## CONNECT THE CIRCUIT

*"I will pass through Egypt and strike down every firstborn—both men and animals—and I will bring judgment on all the gods of Egypt. I am the LORD."*

EXODUS 12:12

Pharaoh refused to release the Israelite slaves, and God had had enough. He instructed the Israelites to put blood on their doorposts. Where there was blood, death would not come. But where there was no blood, the firstborn would perish. I am sure there were Israelites who chose not to apply the blood because they thought that they were from the right group. They had seen a lot of plagues but no results, so they decided not to go to the trouble. I feel equally certain that there were Egyptians who followed God's instructions. They had blood on their doorposts and were spared the death of their firstborn. Unless you applied the blood to your house, it didn't matter who you were; you had to demonstrate your belief in God's power through your actions. The power of God is present in the earth today to deliver His people from Satan's every challenge. But the presence of that power alone is not the full story. We have to be willing to put that power to work in our lives.

### • THINK ABOUT IT •

Simple obedience to God's instructions—"apply the blood"—demonstrated belief and connected the circuit from God's power to the Israelites' need. Obedience to the simple truth you know can make a profound difference in your life.

### Prayer

Heavenly Father, I choose to follow You today in simple obedience to the truth that You have given me. May Your Word be a lamp to my feet. In Jesus' name, amen.

## PRAYER INVITATIONS

*This salvation, which was first announced by the Lord, was confirmed to us by those who heard him. God also testified to it by signs, wonders and various miracles, and gifts of the Holy Spirit distributed according to his will.*

HEBREWS 2:3-4

It's through the Holy Spirit that the power of God is made known in our world. We say we believe that God will do miracles. So what if we pray and one doesn't happen? Then we humbly admit that we are not God. I have extended altar calls to multiplied thousands of people, and they haven't all come—but I keep extending the invitation. I trust God to know the ones He has called and the ones whose hearts He has prepared for that moment in time. I have the same attitude when I pray for God's supernatural involvement in the lives of people. There's much I don't know and much I can't see. There are many questions to which I don't have the answer, but I will continue to pray for God to act. Sometimes the Holy Spirit works quietly and sometimes His work appears miraculous, but I absolutely trust in Him to act to accomplish His purposes.

### • THINK ABOUT IT •

Keep inviting God to act. Your prayers are invitations that will give Him more open doors to accomplish His work in your life and the world beyond.

### Prayer

Heavenly Father, I trust Your love, wisdom, and timing. I will obey Your command to pray and wait on You in hope. Holy Spirit, inspire my prayers to come alongside the works You want to do. Your Kingdom come; Your will be done. In Jesus' name, amen.

## NOT PERFECT—JUST DEVOTED

*His divine power has given us everything we need for life and godliness through our knowledge of him who called us by his own glory and goodness.*

2 PETER 1:3

The villages on the northern end of the Sea of Galilee were ordinary places filled with ordinary people. This is where Peter lived until one day an itinerant rabbi named Jesus arrived. He said to Peter, "Follow me," and he did. Peter spent three years with Jesus, listening to Him teach and watching Him do things he had never seen anyone do. When his friend needed him the most, Peter denied he knew Him and hid, frightened. When Jesus had risen to life again, He found Peter and gave him a life assignment: "Feed my sheep." Scripture indicates that Peter spent the rest of his life doing everything in his power to strengthen the Church. I can see him when this letter was written, his hair streaked with gray but his passion for Jesus growing with each day. Peter was not perfect, but he knew that we have been given everything we need for a godly life, and he was determined to do his best for his Lord.

### • THINK ABOUT IT •

Peter wasn't perfect, but he was a devoted follower of Jesus, and marked by a singleness of purpose to do his best for Him. Don't let your imperfections stop you from choosing the Lord today.

*Prayer*

Heavenly Father, thank You for giving me everything I need for a godly life. Give me grace to know You better, to put into practice what pleases You. With the grace and strength You give, I commit to doing my best for You. In Jesus' name, amen.

## LIBERTY FOR ALL

*Abraham fell facedown; he laughed and said to himself, "Will a son be born to a man a hundred years old? Will Sarah bear a child at the age of ninety?"*

GENESIS 17:17

We often imagine, as the people of God, that other people are the ones who need to be liberated—the addicts and adulterers, the immoral who sin proudly and publicly, the pagans following false gods, the people who commit horrible acts. Scripture says repeatedly that God's people need His liberating power too if we are going to experience all that He created us to be and do. Abraham was an old man and his wife was beyond her childbearing years when God told him that his descendants would be as numerous as the stars in the sky or the sand on the seashore, and that they would become a mighty nation. Abraham was incredulous and laughed at the idea. But God kept His promise and did the seemingly impossible: He gave Sarah a son and Abraham an heir. God does more than just bail us out of our problems. He rescues us, and He delivers us.

### • THINK ABOUT IT •

Is there a place—either of hopes deferred or wounds unhealed—where you need the Lord's liberating power to rescue you? He is able and willing to do the impossible for you too. You also have a part in His plan.

### *Prayer*

Heavenly Father, You don't just rescue me from problems. You do the impossible, delivering me to live fully, chains broken, and make impact for Your Kingdom. I trust You. Renew my faith on the bedrock of Your promises. In Jesus' name, amen.

## FILLED AND OVERFLOWING

*Jesus stood and said in a loud voice, "If anyone is thirsty, let him come to me and drink. Whoever believes in me, as the Scripture has said, streams of living water will flow from within him." By this he meant the Spirit, whom those who believed in him were later to receive.*

JOHN 7:37-39

Israel is predominantly a desert country. The humidity is low, and the temperature is high. It's very easy to become dehydrated, and Jesus' audience was well aware of their need for water. It was natural for Him to compare their need for the Holy Spirit with their need for water. I do not know how to persevere or overcome without the help of the Holy Spirit. If we are going to finish our courses well and overcome the obstacles that will undoubtedly emerge in our pathways, we will need His help. Get to know Him. Cooperate with Him. Determine to open your life to Him as fully as possible. Do not put up any barriers or make any exceptions. If you will just ask Him in, He will fill you with "streams of living water" and guide you along your life's journey.

• THINK ABOUT IT •

The Holy Spirit is willing to help you and always knows what your next step should be. You can trust Him.

*Prayer*

Heavenly Father, I am thirsty for the living water of Your Spirit. Fill me, Holy Spirit; I invite You in without reservation. You are my trustworthy Helper, leading me into all truth. Thank You for empowering me to live for You. In Jesus' name, amen.

## TOP OF THE LIST

*Jesus was led by the Spirit into the desert to be tempted by the devil. After fasting forty days and forty nights, he was hungry. The tempter came to him and said, "If you are the Son of God, tell these stones to become bread." Jesus answered, "It is written: 'Man does not live on bread alone, but on every word that comes from the mouth of God.'"*

MATTHEW 4:1-4

Do you have imagination in your life that the Holy Spirit would lead you to a point of challenge? That is exactly what happens here as the Spirit leads Jesus into the desert to be tempted by the Devil. When the crafty tempter tells Jesus to satisfy His hunger by turning stones into bread, Jesus rebukes him with a statement we will do well to remember: "Man does not live on bread alone, but on every word that comes from the mouth of God." We often hear the first part as light-hearted advice to "Eat up!" But Jesus reminds us that if we are not in the habit of routinely, systematically, reading the Word of God, we are robbing ourselves of the nutrition that is necessary to thrive spiritually.

· THINK ABOUT IT ·

How far down on your To-Do List is "Reading the Bible"? Take care of yourself spiritually; move it to the top of the list. It's the best way to "eat right."

*Prayer*

Heavenly Father, let the attention I give Your Word reflect the value and authority You give it. I know it is living truth, useful in all respects. Teach me Your will as I read it so I can know and serve You better. In Jesus' name, amen.

## CROSS DIRECTED FUTURE

*David said to God, "I have sinned greatly by doing this. Now, I beg you, take away the guilt of your servant. I have done a very foolish thing." The LORD said to Gad, David's seer, "Go and tell David, 'This is what the Lord says: I am giving you three options. Choose one of them for me to carry out against you.'"*

1 CHRONICLES 21:8-10

David was a remarkable man, but he also was an adulterer and a murderer. When David said, "I have sinned," God didn't wink and say, "No problem, Dave. We're friends. I'll let this one go." He said, "There are consequences for your actions." We are rebellious creatures, and we have made ungodly choices in the past. We wanted to do something, and we did it. If you've never allowed the Spirit of God to address your past, I assure you that your past is your present. The beauty of the cross and the love and mercy of God mean that no matter the rebellion, He wants to set us free. We can be forgiven, redeemed, and justified. Whatever the consequences, He will see us through. That is the power of the cross.

· THINK ABOUT IT ·

Are you still dealing with the consequences of your past ungodly choices? Do not lose heart, because the power of Jesus' cross can set you free to have a blessed and hopeful future.

*Prayer*

Heavenly Father, by Your Spirit help me address the choices I have made. Forgive my rebellion and help me walk out my consequences Your way. Thank You that, through the power of the cross, my past will not control my future. In Jesus' name, amen.

## MORE THAN VICTORIOUS

*Who shall separate us from the love of Christ? Shall trouble or hardship or persecution or famine or nakedness or danger or sword?...No, in all these things we are more than conquerors through him who loved us.*

ROMANS 8:35, 37

The Apostle Paul poses a rhetorical question to the Church in Rome, then lists some things Christ-followers through the ages have experienced: trouble, hardship, persecution, famine, nakedness, danger, and the sword. But then he goes on to assure us that "in all these things we are more than conquerors through him who loved us." How can we be more than conquerors? After we have conquered, what's left? The word that's translated "overcomer" or "more than a conqueror" in English means victory—so we are more than victorious. Even though we may be physically and mentally drained after we have overcome the challenge, we are not left without hope. Through our Lord, we are victorious and filled with the desire and ability to live for Him during our days in the earth. That's what it means to be a Christ-follower. We don't just survive for the moment—we thrive with the future in sight!

• THINK ABOUT IT •

Challenges may drain us, but Christ's strong, unfailing love will replenish us. Victory, not weariness, will have the last word for those who love Him.

*Prayer*

Heavenly Father, I praise You for Your love expressed through Jesus! Through His loving sacrifice we are victorious overcomers, pressing forward to serve and see Your Kingdom come. Thank You for this new life I will live for You. In Jesus' name, amen.

## BE DONE WITH IT

*Get rid of all bitterness, rage, anger, harsh words, and slander, as well as all types of evil behavior.*

EPHESIANS 4:31 • NLT

Paul asks a lot of us in this short verse, doesn't he? He gave these instructions because he knew from experience that these things have the ability to consume our mind and emotions and diminish our capacity for a happy and productive life, a godly life. My life experience has shown that if we don't make an intentional decision to change, we will default to our old way of thinking and do what we have always done. It's not enough just to make an intellectual decision to let these things go; behavior is attached. When Paul says "get rid of," I imagine myself physically opening my hand and turning loose of something. One time will not be enough to retool after years of habit and repetition, so these are decisions that we have to make again and again. It is not simple to choose new responses to familiar triggers, but with the help of the Holy Spirit, it can be done.

· THINK ABOUT IT ·

Think of some things that trigger your impatience, anger, or harsh words. Bring these before the Holy Spirit and ask His help to adopt His response instead.

*Prayer*

Heavenly Father, I have too many triggers and am surrounded by a culture immersed in anger and slander. Holy Spirit, help me stand apart and put away all rage, harsh words, and evil response. Let Christ's response be formed in me. In His name, amen.

## GETTING ONTO THE FIELD

*Glory in his holy name; let the hearts of those who seek the LORD rejoice.
Look to the LORD and his strength; seek his face always.*

PSALM 105:3-4

There's an old hymn that says, "Every day with Jesus is sweeter than the day before. Every day with Jesus, I love Him more and more." Is that true for you? I'm afraid that many of us define our relationship with Jesus by what happened to us "back in the day." We walked an aisle years go and were dunked in a pool sometime after that. Since then, we may have been regular church attenders, but in our hearts we are spiritual spectators. It's good to recall those important times of our lives, but our spiritual wellbeing today is shown by our choices today. I'd like to invite you out of the bleachers. I'd like to invite you to intentionally, purposefully seek the Lord and His strength. Read your Bible. Make prayer a part of your day. Meditate on His name and give Him glory for everything He has done for you. God does not give His best to the casual observer, so seek Him with all your heart.

### • THINK ABOUT IT •

Do you recognize yourself in the phrase "spiritual spectator"? Accept God's invitation in His Word to pursue Him wholeheartedly. He has promised to give you life to the full.

### *Prayer*

Heavenly Father, I will seek You wholeheartedly, giving my best. Draw me closer as I pray. Reveal Yourself to me more fully as I read Your Word. Thank You for opening my heart to understand and rejoice as I look to You always. In Jesus' name, amen.

## PRAYER AND ACTION

*We want each of you to show this same diligence to the very end, so that what you hope for may be fully realized. We do not want you to become lazy, but to imitate those who through faith and patience inherit what has been promised.*

HEBREWS 6:11-12

Sometimes it is difficult to respond promptly to God's invitations. We've all heard the saying, "Ready, aim, fire!" For Christians, that can be more like, "Ready, aim, aim—I'd better pray about aiming—aim, aim—maybe I should stop and read a book about this." I fully understand our need to be still and know that God is God. I hope, however, that in your spiritual life you are remaining diligent to not allow aiming to keep you from doing. If inaction has been your norm, it is very easy to maintain that status quo. The Bible hands us work as a part of our life-assignment, and that includes work on the spiritual aspect of our lives too. Showing diligence and effort is a part of our response to God. Personally, I always want to spend time in prayer and in "aiming." But I also want to follow through with doing what God has invited me to do.

### • THINK ABOUT IT •

There are heroes of the faith—Corrie ten Boom, Eric Liddell, Rees Howells, and many others—whose lives have provided us examples of both effective prayer and action. Do you have any heroes of the faith, past or present, whose diligence and effort inspire you?

### *Prayer*

Heavenly Father, I want to imitate the heroes of the faith who diligently completed the work You gave them to do. Deliver me from any timidity, laziness, or insecurity holding me back from the "doing." I want to follow through. In Jesus' name, amen.

## UNAMBIGUOUSLY HIS

*I will ask the Father, and he will give you another Counselor to be with you forever—the Spirit of truth. The world cannot accept him, because it neither sees him nor knows him. But you know him, for he lives with you and will be in you.*

JOHN 14: 16-17

When it comes to the things of God, it seems to me that many of us try to find a way to straddle the fence. We don't want to be offensive to non-believers. We don't want to be seen as too religious. So we try to find a happy place on the fence and watch the action from there. But when we invite the Holy Spirit to truly work in our lives, He electrifies the fence and makes it a very uncomfortable place to sit. When we give the Holy Spirit more room to work in our hearts, we experience the changes that He brings and have a desire for more of Him. My prayer is that we would express an increasing willingness to embrace the Person of the Holy Spirit. I hope you will climb off the fence and say to the Holy Spirit, "You are welcome in my life."

### • THINK ABOUT IT •

Throughout Scripture, the presence of God and the power of God are almost synonymous. Invite the Spirit of the Lord with no conditions, and allow His power to move on your behalf.

### *Prayer*

Heavenly Father, thank You for giving Your Spirit of Truth to be my Counselor. Holy Spirit, I embrace Your presence and welcome Your work in my life. Bring the changes that make it plain to all that I am unambiguously Yours. In Jesus' name, amen.

## HAVE YOU DECIDED?

*And according to Paul's custom, he went to them, and for three Sabbaths reasoned with them from the Scriptures, explaining and giving evidence that the Christ had to suffer and rise again from the dead, and saying, "This Jesus whom I am proclaiming to you is the Christ."*

ACTS 17:2-3 • NASB®

Many of us assume that Christ is Jesus' family name. Christ is the English equivalent of the Greek Christos, which is the equivalent of the Hebrew Mashiach, from which we get "Messiah." When we say Jesus is the Christ, as Paul did here in the synagogue, we are asserting that Jesus of Nazareth is the Messiah, the Anointed One of God. Some say that Jesus was a good man and a teacher, but He could not be the Messiah— even though He met the prophetic criteria regarding His birth, His life, His death, and His resurrection. Our journey as Christ-followers begins with the decision to accept Him as Messiah because if He was not, He was not a good man; He was a liar and a manipulator. Have you decided for yourself that Jesus is the Christ, the Messiah, and chosen to follow Him as Lord? Think about it carefully, because it is the most important decision you will ever make.

### • THINK ABOUT IT •

In a day when many are attempting to redefine Jesus to justify their own choices, it's important to accept Jesus as He defined Himself: Son of God, Savior, and Lord of All.

### *Prayer*

Heavenly Father, I believe Jesus is the Christ, Your Son, crucified for my sin and raised to life again that I might be blameless in Your sight. I repent of my sin, choose to follow Jesus as Lord, and commit my life to lifting up His name. In Jesus' name, amen.

## A SERIOUS CHOICE

*Take care, brethren, that there not be in any one of you an evil, unbelieving heart that falls away from the living God. But encourage one another day after day...*

HEBREWS 3:12-13 • NASB®

Belief in God is healthy and productive, whereas unbelief is corrosive and destructive. Unbelief isn't about gaining information or having life experience; it is a choice that we make. It's as if belief is offered to us and we push it away like a food we don't want to eat. We have been too accommodating of unbelief and have devised all sorts of ways to soft-sell it. Some people say, "Maybe if I studied more, if I learned more about it..." or "With my education, it's just too difficult for me to believe in something I can't see" or "None of my friends have fallen for this." Unbelief is a serious choice with consequences that affect your days under the sun and your days in eternity. When we choose unbelief, we wall off the invitation to have a relationship with God. If you are living with skepticism and doubt, I invite you to put aside your unbelief and place your life in the hands of Jesus, the Savior of the world.

### • THINK ABOUT IT •

The decision to believe God in the face of doubt is one you can have full confidence in. Faith is the catalyst for much of God's miraculous intervention in the lives of His children, and He is delighted when we put it into action.

### *Prayer*

Heavenly Father, I repent of any doubts about You I have harbored. Please help my unbelief and increase my faith in You. Jesus, I acknowledge You are Lord and put my life in Your saving care. In Jesus' name, amen.

## BUILDING WISELY

*If any man builds on this foundation using gold, silver, costly stones, wood, hay or straw, his work will be shown for what it is, because the Day will bring it to light...If what he has built survives, he will receive his reward.*

1 CORINTHIANS 3:12-14

Did you know that you can buy two chairs that look the same but in reality are very different? The manufacturers of poorly constructed furniture and the manufacturers of finely crafted furniture often buy their upholstery fabrics from the same companies. You can have two chairs that look very similar because they are covered by identical fabric. One will last a year or two, and the other will last a lifetime. Neither is the quality of our spiritual life determined by our external appearance. In fact, its appearance may be quite worn. It is determined by the framework we have built it upon. This passage says we will be rewarded when we make the commitment to build a strong foundation. When you are considering what habits you will form in order to strengthen your spiritual framework, remember that the results will matter not only today, but for your future.

### • THINK ABOUT IT •

To help develop good habits as a Christ-follower, get advice from mature fellow believers whose walk with the Lord you respect. Find out what habits have added momentum to their spiritual journeys, and try to adopt one.

### *Prayer*

Heavenly Father, I want to build wisely, to see my efforts survive and produce good results now and in eternity. Help me be diligent in practicing the habits of godliness and good works that please You and bring lasting rewards. In Jesus' name, amen.

## HE'S LISTENING

*The eyes of the LORD are on the righteous, and his ears are attentive to their cry...The righteous cry out, and the LORD hears them..."*

PSALM 34:15, 17

I think we've all been in situations where we wanted the attention of someone who chose to ignore us. It might have been a parent who was unconcerned about something that seemed terribly important at the time. Perhaps it was a teacher who was unwilling to discuss a grade. It might have been a friend who would not hear our side of a misunderstanding. Maybe it was a coworker who was not interested in hearing anyone else's ideas or opinions. Perhaps it was a spouse with a "my way is the only way" attitude. Life is full of situations where we think, "If you would just listen to me!" Scripture tells us that the Lord is not like that. He wants to know our deepest feelings and concerns. He will never turn a blind eye or grow tired of listening. He wants to see us, hear us, and help us. What a comfort it is to know we are watched over by such a loving and patient God!

### • THINK ABOUT IT •

The gift of righteousness through faith in Jesus Christ has given you access to the throne of Almighty God. You can trust He hears you and know He longs to be gracious to you.

### *Prayer*

Heavenly Father, You hear my voice when I cry to You for help, turning toward me to heal, deliver, and protect. Thank You for the free gift of righteousness through Jesus' blood that reconciles me to You, making all this possible. In Jesus' name, amen.

# DAY 303

## PRECIPICE BRIDGED BY FAITH

*Finally the other disciple, who had reached the tomb first, also went inside. He saw and believed. (They still did not understand from Scripture that Jesus had to rise from the dead.)*

JOHN 20:8-9

What? They still didn't understand? They had spent three years with the best teacher the world has ever seen. Were they not paying attention? I think there is a significant lesson for us here: Being a Christ-follower is not simply about embracing a tradition or memorizing a set of facts. Being a Christ-follower is about entering into a relationship with Jesus of Nazareth. If you follow Jesus, He will lead you to places beyond your resources, beyond your strength, beyond your wisdom, beyond even your imagination. If you will trust Him, you will see time after time expressions of the power of an Almighty God. I suspect that no matter how many times you've seen those expressions, when you come back to that precipice where your own resources, or your own strength, or your own wisdom are limited, you will wonder and struggle to believe again. Do not despair, for I've found that it's in those places that our faith in Him will deepen and grow.

· THINK ABOUT IT ·

Recall a time when, faced with your own limits, you saw an expression of God's power on your behalf. Telling someone else this piece of your God-story will glorify Him, while encouraging both your faith and theirs.

*Prayer*

Heavenly Father, admitting my weakness and limits, I trust Christ's power to rest on me. I believe Your Word that Your abundant grace is sufficient, providing me with all things I need, for all things I face, as I follow You. In Jesus' name, amen.

## LAW OF INCREASE

*Jesus...said, "Go home to your own people and tell them how much the Lord has done for you, and how he has had mercy on you." So the man went away and began to tell in the Decapolis how much Jesus had done for him. And all the people were amazed.*

MARK 5:19-20

If you've been to a Southeastern Conference football game, you'll agree that there is no hesitation to express an opinion there. I've never heard, "Shh. We don't want to offend our visitors." If something matters, we usually are willing to say it out loud. When the subject is our relationship with Jesus, do we have the courage to talk about it? Jesus had cast demons from this man, and he naturally wanted to go with Jesus. Instead, Jesus told him to go and tell what He had done for him. I imagine that the more the man talked about Jesus, the more his life changed for the better. The principle was true then and is true now: If you will become an advocate for Jesus, the Holy Spirit will become more involved on your behalf because the Holy Spirit comes where Jesus' name is lifted up.

### • THINK ABOUT IT •

Our choices create momentum for more of the same types of decisions to be made. Be an advocate for Jesus where you currently have influence— the Holy Spirit will empower you to do it elsewhere.

### *Prayer*

Heavenly Father, I long to be less tongue-tied when it comes to lifting up Jesus' name. Loose my tongue, Holy Spirit, to freely declare the wondrous things Jesus has done for me. Fill me with Your passion to see Him glorified. In Jesus' name, amen.

## I'M READY TO GO!

*Caleb silenced the people before Moses and said, "We should go up and take possession of the land, for we can certainly do it." But the men who had gone up with him said, "We can't attack those people; they are stronger than we are."*

NUMBERS 13:30-31

God had delivered the Israelites from slavery, led them through the wilderness, and brought them to the border of the Promised Land. Moses sent twelve spies into Canaan to bring back a report on the people, their towns, and the land's agricultural potential. After forty days the group returned. Joshua and Caleb said, "It's an extraordinary place, and the Lord is with us. Let's go!" The others said, "The land flows with milk and honey. But the cities are large and fortified, and the people are stronger than we are. They will devour us!" The ten naysayers influenced an entire nation, and they spent forty years wandering in a circle while Joshua and Caleb were allowed to enter the land and enjoy God's blessings. What is your response when God invites you toward His best but doesn't give you all the details? Do you cling to the familiar? Or do you say to God, "I'm ready to go!"

## • THINK ABOUT IT •

Clinging to the familiar can be a way of leaning on your own understanding, rather than trusting God. The details God leaves out of His directives for your life are opportunities to let your faith grow. He won't let you down.

## *Prayer*

Heavenly Father, deepen my understanding of Your goodness and power, and the meaning of: "God is with us!" I anchor my trust in Your Word which does not fail. Give me courage to move forward in faith with You toward Your best. In Jesus' name, amen.

## FULL RESTORATION

*Peter was sitting out in the courtyard, and a servant girl came to him. "You also were with Jesus of Galilee," she said. But he denied it before them all. "I don't know what you're talking about," he said.*

MATTHEW 26:69-70

Peter had not believed Jesus when He said that Peter would deny Him three times, but Scripture confirms that it happened. Scripture also says the resurrected Jesus allowed Peter to reaffirm his love for Him, and then assured Peter of his role in the Kingdom. Peter is not the only Jesus-follower who has denied the Lord. Each of us has failed at times to speak up for the things of God or chosen an ungodly path. Some of us still carry the shame and scars of that, but God is just as eager to bring restoration and renewal to us as He was to Peter. Would you dare to believe that God would forgive you and release you from your shame, then restore you and give you an assignment in His Kingdom? Peter became the bedrock of the Church in the following years. God is calling you to a place of significance too, if you'll allow His restoration to become real in your life.

· THINK ABOUT IT ·

Paul describes two kinds of sorrow, one leading to life and the other bringing on the very destruction Jesus' sacrifice was meant to avoid. Don't let a sorrow not from God bind you to a failed past and keep you from the role He has planned just for you.

*Prayer*

Heavenly Father, may my sorrow in having failed You result in repentance and renewed life. Release me from any sorrow that is binding me to regret, shame, or doubt. Then release me into the full restoration that Jesus' sacrifice offers. In Jesus' name, amen.

## HE CARES

*When Jesus looked up and saw a great crowd coming toward him, he said to Philip, "Where shall we buy bread for these people to eat?" He asked this only to test him, for he already had in mind what he was going to do.*

JOHN 6:5-6

When Jesus fed thousands of people with a boy's lunch of five loaves and two fish, He demonstrated the abundance of God in a very tangible way. This wasn't about giving insight into Scripture or healing a desperate person. Instead, He physically demonstrated the power of God to meet the everyday needs of human lives. It's an aspect of the gospel that we still struggle with: Does God really care if we are hungry, or clothed, or protected from the elements? The resounding answer from this account is, "Absolutely yes." I know there is some reluctance to embrace that because we have seen the teaching misapplied, but it's an unmistakable aspect of Jesus' ministry. God is aware of your circumstances, and you can trust Him for your daily needs. He may not provide exactly what you expect or in the way you expect, but you can depend on Him to provide abundantly for your life.

· THINK ABOUT IT ·

God is aware, God is willing, and God is able to meet your everyday needs. He dearly values and cares for you and, as in the story of the loaves and fishes, He stands ready with a plan to help.

*Prayer*

Heavenly Father, forgive me for times when I worry over my daily needs. You gave up Your Son for us, pouring out grace that provides. You know all the details of my life, and You are well able to multiply. My trust is in You. In Jesus' name, amen.

## KEEN INVESTMENT STRATEGY

*"Sell everything you have and give to the poor, and you will have treasure in heaven. Then come, follow me." When he heard this, he became very sad, because he was a man of great wealth.*

LUKE 18:22-23

A man of position and authority came to Jesus and asked what was required in order for him to gain eternal life. Jesus reminded him of the commandments, and the man told Jesus confidently that he had kept them since he was a boy. Without mocking him for his conceit, Jesus invited the man to follow Him—after he had sold everything he had and given the money to the poor. This made the man sad, because he was very wealthy. We don't know what happened to the man after this conversation, but I imagine that he went back to his home, deep in thought. I imagine that he calculated his worth, thinking about how his life would change if he forfeited all of his material comforts and possessions. How would he live? What would define him? He forfeited far more than he could have imagined, all because he was not willing to allow following Jesus to disrupt his life.

### • THINK ABOUT IT •

If you could calculate the total cost of forfeiting your God-opportunities, is that really a price you can afford to pay? Your best long-term life-investment strategy is to say yes to God's invitations.

*Prayer*

Heavenly Father, I repent of exalting my treasure, goals, and schedules. I do not want to forfeit Your rewards in this life and eternity by preferring my own plans. So I commit my time and resources, my entire life, to follow You. In Jesus' name, amen.

# DAY 309

## LIFE'S LITTLE MOMENTS

*O LORD, you have searched me and you know me. You know when I sit and when I rise; you perceive my thoughts from afar. You discern my going out and my lying down; you are familiar with all my ways.*

PSALM 139:1-3

Whether or not we say it out loud, I think the ultimate question that nags all of us is "Does my life really matter?" The true answer to that question is "Yes, your life matters." That God knows us and cares about us is one of the incredible assertions of Scripture. The Bible makes no attempt to justify His interest and concern; it simply says that it is. He knows when we sit and when we stand, when we come and go, and even what we are thinking. Regardless of what your life assignment and daily tasks may be, when you comprehend His attitude toward you, you will approach those tasks with a totally new perspective. How you go about your daily routine has the power to reflect the character of God to the people around you, so ask the Holy Spirit to guide you through your days with wisdom.

### · THINK ABOUT IT ·

Ask the Holy Spirit to make you sensitive to the moments where you need more of His help to demonstrate His character well. Whether you're in traffic, or on your computer, the little moments matter.

### *Prayer*

Heavenly Father, let my life's little moments demonstrate clearly that You are my Lord, at work in me. Holy Spirit, meet me in my daily routine to give the wisdom I need. Pick me up when I stumble. Help me represent You well. In Jesus' name, amen.

## EXPANDED HORIZONS

*When they saw the courage of Peter and John and realized that they were unschooled, ordinary men, they were astonished and they took note that these men had been with Jesus.*

ACTS 4:13

When Jesus recruited Peter he was a fisherman—a young man with a future that was tied to his boat, his nets, and the lake where he plied his trade. By the end of Peter's life, he had gone to Rome and faced the most powerful persons of his generation. He had confronted the world that he knew. Why? Because he chose to believe Jesus of Nazareth was God's Son, and he wanted to see His Kingdom extended in the earth. Jesus is still looking for men and women who will believe. Not just to be religious or keep rules, but who will serve Him as Lord. In my life, Jesus has extended many invitations to leave my comfort zone and trust Him in new ways. Every time I have said yes to Him, He has expanded my horizons beyond any goal I ever had. Our future holds great promise and potential, and it begins by believing that Jesus has greater plans for us than we can even imagine.

### • THINK ABOUT IT •

Get ready for Jesus to ask you to leave your comfort zone. That zone is not big enough to contain His dreams for you. Expect Him to knock out a few walls as He expands your horizons too.

### Prayer

Heavenly Father, I want to see Your Kingdom extended on earth in my day. Now is my moment to say yes to You. Give me the wisdom, courage, and discernment I need to align with Your plan and go where You lead. You have my trust. In Jesus' name, amen.

## NO SHORTCUTS

*We are instructed to turn from godless living and sinful pleasures. We should live in this evil world with wisdom, righteousness, and devotion to God...*

TITUS 2:12 • NLT

I've thought about writing a book entitled, The Chocolate Diet. It would sell for $19.95 and advise eating three pounds of chocolate a day. I'm sure it would be a bestseller. It would take a month for the reviews to call me out as a fraud, but by then I would have retired and moved to a tropical island. We're all vulnerable to falling for a quick fix that requires little commitment or self-discipline. We take the same approach to the things of God. But the truth is that a healthy Christian life requires commitment and willingness to discipline our worldly selves to say no to ungodliness and yes to godliness. I do not know a shortcut to that. I would like to tell you that with maturity you'll no longer face those temptations, but I find that I still have to govern my heart. Thankfully, the cross represents the power of a living God to deliver us, and the Holy Spirit is here to help us find that freedom.

• THINK ABOUT IT •

The culture has it backwards. Do not believe the lie that saying yes to ungodliness is an expression of freedom or that the self-discipline of saying no to it is unhealthy restraint.

*Prayer*

Heavenly Father, help me be determined to govern my heart to say yes to godliness and no to ungodliness. May I discipline and order my life in full devotion to You, gaining Your wisdom and deliverance for increased spiritual freedom. In Jesus' name, amen.

## FROM OBSCURITY TO OPPORTUNITY

*"Isn't this the carpenter's son? Isn't his mother's name Mary, and aren't his brothers James, Joseph, Simon and Judas?"*

MATTHEW 13:55

It was God's plan that Jesus would enter humanity through humble circumstances and grow up in an ordinary family. Jesus was a carpenter's son. He had not studied with a celebrated rabbi. He had no access to the powerful religious authorities. In the beginning of His ministry, He was simply an itinerant rabbi who was recruiting people to help in His cause. The response to follow Jesus was a step of faith, but it was a transformational step because the men who followed Jesus were not celebrated individuals either. Most of them worked jobs that demanded a great deal of them physically and left them with very little economically. But when they followed Jesus, their lives were changed. Whereas once they were unknown to all but their immediate circle of family and friends, now they have been celebrated around the earth for century after century. I won't promise you that following Jesus will make your name known throughout the world, but it will give you opportunities to serve Him in ways that will bless you and others for eternity.

### • THINK ABOUT IT •

Following Jesus is the transformational step to a meaningful life. If you are looking for meaning in your life, Jesus truly is the way.

*Prayer*

Heavenly Father, I will step out in faith to follow Jesus. Let His be the name that is celebrated, His the fame that is spread. I lay down ambition and status for the honor of serving Him and seeing my generation transformed. In Jesus' name, amen.

## THE ULTIMATE ASSET

*Buy the truth and do not sell it...*

PROVERBS 23:23

The ultimate asset in life is the truth. Expend your time and energy to find it. Expend your resources to acquire it, and when you get it, don't let go of it. Don't release it or trade it for something else. Determine to become a person of truth—not just truth about God, but truth about everything. Choose to live the truth and speak the truth. The Bible talks about giving your word and keeping it, even when it costs you something. That applies to your workplace, your home, your friendships, and your community. Truth is not held in very high esteem today, and I suspect that it will continue to deteriorate. But the Bible says God hates a lie, so don't tell one. You can't be an intentional liar and imagine God will bless you, so choose the truth. It will keep you from having to remember all the lies you have told and allow people to give you the gift of their trust. Most importantly, it will enable the Holy Spirit to move on your behalf in amazing ways.

· THINK ABOUT IT ·

The Devil is the father of lies. Jesus is the truth. These two sides have no common ground. The assumption that real life requires you to incorporate a little of both is itself a lie. Choose to be a person of truth.

*Prayer*

Heavenly Father, fill me with Your Spirit to guide me into all truth. Forgive the lies I have told to gain advantage or avoid consequences. Give me courage to seek for, stand for, and speak up for the truth no matter the cost. In Jesus' name, amen.

## A GREAT TRADE

*May the God of hope fill you with all joy and peace in believing, so that you will abound in hope by the power of the Holy Spirit.*

ROMANS 15:13 • NASB®

"You don't really believe that, do you?" This is typically where I have my biggest battle with cooperating with God. I'll read the Scriptures, and my mind will begin searching for a reason to question what I've read. Some of us tend to be prouder of being skeptics than being people of faith. We show more excitement about discerning a fraud than about our willingness to believe. We all have been duped, and we don't want to be duped again, so we tend to celebrate our skepticism. Then we excuse our skepticism by blaming it on our intellect, our education, and our sophistication. I have a feeling when we see the Lord we will all regret that we didn't believe more fully and yield to the authority of God's Word more readily. As Paul wrote to the Romans, belief brings joy and peace and hope as we are filled by the Holy Spirit. That's a great trade for our skepticism, don't you think?

### • THINK ABOUT IT •

Don't sit in the seat of the skeptic. Skepticism pretends to be a choice of your mind, but it is really a choice of your heart. At every opportunity, choose belief.

### Prayer

Heavenly Father, Your witnesses in history and creation give evidence that You are God and Your Word is true. I declare my faith in Jesus and all that His shed blood purchased. Thank You, Holy Spirit, for filling me with joy and peace as I follow Him. In Jesus' name, amen.

## ALL

*Jesus replied: "'Love the Lord your God with all your heart and with all your soul and with all your mind.' This is the first and greatest commandment."*

MATTHEW 22:37-38

Young children learn quickly that one set of words and behaviors works on the playground and another works at church. Many of us carry that over into adulthood and imagine that God does not see the entirety of our lives. We come to church and pretend that we act and talk that way all the time. We go out with other friends and think God doesn't see what's going on. There is no Sunday morning prayer so sweet that it will cause God to ignore how we act the other six and a half days a week. Jesus did not say to love the Lord with half of your heart, half of your soul, and half of your mind. The commandment says that He wants it all. Begin to integrate Him into your life, every day of your life, and you will be amazed at how the Holy Spirit will make Himself a partner in your life in a greater way.

• THINK ABOUT IT •

Embracing the "all" part of loving God, the early disciples were all-in, and they turned their world toward Christ. Partial commitment to Him— with its partial obedience—puts our generation at risk. They watch to see if we really mean it when we say, "Jesus is Lord of my life."

*Prayer*

Heavenly Father, help me learn to walk with You, to partner humbly with Your Holy Spirit. I have rushed by You, giving You time slots instead of obedient attention. Forgive me for being self-focused, giving You less than all. In Jesus' name, amen.

## HYDRATED & HEALTHY

*"Whoever drinks the water I give him will never thirst. Indeed, the water I give him will become in him a spring of water welling up to eternal life."*

JOHN 4:14

Did you know that water is absolutely necessary for our bodies to function? I saw some interesting statistics about the physical changes that come when a person becomes dehydrated. A one percent deficiency in your body will make you thirsty. An eight percent deficiency causes you to stop producing saliva. With a ten percent deficiency you'll lose the ability to walk. If you reach a twelve percent deficiency, your systems shut down. The bottom line is that without water, you will die. It's true physically, and it's also true spiritually. Jesus said He will give us water that runs from a spring that will never run dry, and when we drink from it, we will be nourished in this life and the next. It is our mission, as the Church, to keep ourselves spiritually hydrated and healthy so that we can help other people find that life-giving water too. The next time you take a sip of refreshing water, thank God for His provision for our physical and spiritual thirst.

### • THINK ABOUT IT •

Do you have a plan in place to stay spiritually hydrated? God's Word and His Spirit supply the living water you need. Make time to drink in by reading the Bible daily and listening to Him in prayer.

### *Prayer*

Heavenly Father, thank You for the gift, through Jesus, of living water, filling me and bringing eternal life. Holy Spirit, let these waters in me overflow to the thirsty around me. Replenish me as I pray and read Your Word. In Jesus' name, amen.

## GOD DRAWS NEAR

*He heals the brokenhearted and binds up their wounds.*

PSALM 147:3

We sometimes imagine that the indicator of God's nearness is when someone's life is climbing upward on a trajectory of success and happiness. But Scripture says that Jesus was the exact representation of the being of God, and one of the reasons Jesus came to earth was so we could see the heart of God toward those who are brokenhearted. In Luke 4, Jesus declared that He had come for the poor, the captives, the blind, and the oppressed. It's important to have it tucked in your heart that God is close to you when you are in a difficult place, when you are wounded or struggling. Sometimes when I am in those places, it feels like God is on a long vacation. My prayers don't feel powerful, and it is hard to feel His presence. In spite of my feelings, I know that God is close to me and loves me. I know that He has promised to bring healing and restoration to the broken places in my life. I often can't see just how He will do that, but I absolutely believe that He will.

### • THINK ABOUT IT •

The One who will heal your heart had His own heart broken; the One who binds up your wounds was Himself wounded. As wonderful as His promise to the brokenhearted is, even more amazing was God's willingness to suffer so much to keep it.

*Prayer*

Heavenly Father, through all Jesus endured, I see Your heart toward me. You intimately understand my pain. I will fix my heart on Your Word and let faith shepherd my feelings toward trust, grateful for the wholeness You bring to me. In Jesus' name, amen.

# DAY 318

## TRULY AT HOME

*"He will wipe away every tear from their eyes; and there will no longer be any death; there will no longer be any mourning, or crying, or pain; the first things have passed away."*

REVELATION 21:4 • NASB®

No matter how rewarding the journey, there's nothing as satisfying as walking into my own home and sitting in my own chair. As joyous and restful as that experience is, it will pale in comparison to the joy and rest we will feel when we reach our eternal home. Revelation describes Heaven as a glorious place, and I am curious about what our physical surroundings will be like. But I also wonder about life in a place where there is no need for a wheelchair or prosthetic limb, hospital or funeral home. Can you imagine the joy and rest we will feel in such a place, even as we are focused on the throne of God and Jesus seated at His right hand? When you feel as if you are being consumed by the cares of this world, think about the peace you feel today in the presence of the Lord and imagine the greater peace we will feel when we are truly at home with Him.

### • THINK ABOUT IT •

When troubles are threatening your peace, keep Paul's perspective in mind: "For our present troubles are small and won't last very long. Yet they produce for us a glory that vastly outweighs them all and will last forever!" (2 Corinthians 4:17, NLT)

*Prayer*

Heavenly Father, thank You for what You have prepared in eternity for those who love You. When troubles distress, help me to remember: Troubles are temporary, my citizenship is in Heaven, and my home is with You. Thank You, Jesus! In Your name, amen.

## CHOOSING WELL

*He raised Him from the dead and seated Him at His right hand in the heavenly places, far above all rule and authority and power and dominion, and every name that is named, not only in this age but also in the one to come.*

EPHESIANS 1:20-21 • NASB®

We live in an age of unprecedented celebrity worship. Athletes and entertainers have influenced the public for a long time. But today, anyone who can create a compelling online persona can become famous and launch a trend from their living room. Who would have dreamed that "influencer" could be an actual job description! In all of life, we should be careful about who we elevate to such lofty pedestals, because people will very often lead us astray. As Jesus-followers, we should look to Him as our role model. His is the name that is greater than every other name, in this age and the next—and the only one worthy of our worship. He has not given us a rule or a recommendation for every situation in life, but His example is the one that we should model our lives after. My advice is that when you are looking for an "influencer," look first to Jesus.

### • THINK ABOUT IT •

The greater the influence of Jesus in your life, the greater influence for good you will have on your environment. The Christ-influenced person is the gateway to the Christ-influenced culture.

*Prayer*

Heavenly Father, Jesus said, "Learn from me," so looking first to Him, I give my attention to Your Word. Reveal any influences in my life that dull me to His voice. Transform me to be one who influences others toward Your good. In Jesus' name, amen.

## INVESTING WISELY

*Don't wear yourself out trying to get rich. Be wise enough to know when to quit. In the blink of an eye wealth disappears, for it will sprout wings and fly away like an eagle.*

PROVERBS 23:4-5 • NLT

Several years ago the United States experienced a financial crisis that revealed a lot about our priorities. The things we trusted in with absolute confidence were shaken to their foundations. Some people we thought to be trustworthy managers were not. Things that we counted on to provide for ourselves and for the generations to follow were suddenly not secure. It became obvious that there was little difference between Christians and non-Christians: We were all invested in the same things, and our investments were failing us. God encourages financial investments, and it is wise to plan for our future. But He invites us to put our greatest trust in Him and depend on Him for our ultimate security. As a result of those uncertain times, I determined to invest my life more fully in Him—my time, my talents, my energy. While this earthly kingdom is fragile and subject to human error, His Kingdom will stand forever—sure and unshaken.

### • THINK ABOUT IT •

Does anxiety over finances rob your peace of mind? Know that God wants to be your ultimate security in this life too, not just in the next. His help is real and His grace all-sufficient.

### *Prayer*

Heavenly Father, Your Kingdom cannot be shaken. I want my life fully invested in You. I trust in Your salvation and have confidence in Your grace to provide and equip me for life. You are the stability and hope of my times. In Jesus' name, amen.

# DAY 321

## WE'VE GOT HELP!

*In the same way, the Spirit helps us in our weakness. We do not know what we ought to pray for, but the Spirit himself intercedes for us with groans that words cannot express.*

ROMANS 8:26

It is very encouraging to me to know that I do not need to comprehend what the will of God is in every situation I encounter. Answers and resolutions regarding things in my immediate sphere of family and friends are not always obvious. Decisions regarding work often have more than one good answer, and I am praying for discernment about what is best. Prayers for health and healing can sometimes feel vague. Asking God to restore and bless misguided people and tragic situations can feel overwhelming. But this verse says that I do not need to know God's will for everything and everybody. Jesus knows, and He is at His Father's side, expressing my feeble attempts at communication in ways that I cannot comprehend. No prayer is wasted, so don't allow your insecurities to dampen your prayer life—that is just what our enemy wants. Approach the throne of grace boldly, knowing that Jesus is there, waiting to intercede for you.

### • THINK ABOUT IT •

You have both Jesus and the Holy Spirit interceding for you to help you. When Jesus said He would never leave you or forsake you, that includes when you are praying. Let His support give you confidence to pray.

### *Prayer*

Heavenly Father, thank You for inviting me in my weakness to partner with You in prayer to see Your will done. I approach Your throne of grace, knowing Jesus prays for me and Your Spirit empowers my prayers with His own. In Jesus' name I pray, amen.

## A TRUSTWORTHY RESPONSE

*Here is a trustworthy saying that deserves full acceptance: Christ Jesus came into the world to save sinners—of whom I am the worst.*

### 1 TIMOTHY 1:15

Here's a response in case you ever hear someone say, "God's never done anything for me!" First, point them to Christmas, a remarkable demonstration of God's extravagant provision for our lives. When you look at the story of the relationship between God and Adam and his descendants, we have consistently been a rebellious and uncooperative lot. Yet God chose to become one of us, to change our futures for time and eternity. That's what Jesus' coming to the earth is all about. It's an expression of God's generosity. Then point them to Easter, another remarkable demonstration of God's love for us. It was on the cross that Jesus exhausted the curse that we deserve for our rebellion so that we might receive all the blessings that were due Him for His perfect obedience. He rose from the dead and was seen by many witnesses before He ascended to Heaven. He has promised that we will live with Him there for eternity. What has God done for us? That is what He has done for us!

### • THINK ABOUT IT •

Don't lose sight of the victories God provided for you, or the comfort He brought during a difficult season. Those testimonies will give you courage to trust His provision for the next step.

### Prayer

Heavenly Father, You have done great things for me! For sending Jesus to share our flesh and blood, to die for us to pay sin's penalty and defeat death; for raising Him to life to redeem us for eternity, I will ever praise You! In Jesus' name, amen.

## STRENGTH IN HUMILITY

*For You do not delight in sacrifice, otherwise I would give it; You are not pleased with burnt offering. The sacrifices of God are a broken spirit; A broken and a contrite heart, O God, You will not despise.*

PSALM 51:16-17 • NASB®

King David had been confronted over his sin with Bathsheba, and this psalm is his heartfelt plea for God's forgiveness and renewal. David was referring to the sacrificial system laid out in the Old Testament. There were specific rules for what sacrifices were able to atone for sin, and the offering of sacrifices was a public display—if you had much to atone for, everyone would know it by the size of your offering! But David knew that a public display of religion was not what God wanted from him. He knew that God wanted to see his "broken spirit" and "contrite heart." I think we have imagined spiritual strength as a show of bravado. In reality, spiritual strength is when we are willing to say, "God, apart from You, I have no options. My life is out of control, and I need Your help." Humility before God is not a sign of failure; it is a sign of remarkable strength.

## • THINK ABOUT IT •

Humility is a sign of strength. Ask the Lord for the strength to admit you need help—His help.

*Prayer*

Heavenly Father, I cannot fix my life, and there are times I cannot see a path forward. I humbly ask for Your mercy and help. Thank You that You do not despise my plea and that my dependence upon You is greatly pleasing. In Jesus' name, amen.

## SOURCE OF CREATIVITY

*Jesus looked at them and said, "With man this is impossible, but with God all things are possible."*

MATTHEW 19:26

I have a friend who enjoys coloring books of patterns, flowers, and birds. She laughingly admits to having no artistic talent and little creativity. She uses colored pencils, but she's afraid to blend colors or venture outside the lines because she's afraid she'll make a mistake. I wonder what God would do with those lines on a page. I imagine that He would blend the colors intricately and even use some surprising new ones, and I don't think He would stay inside the lines. I imagine Him using them as a framework for His own creation, and the end result would be something beautiful and totally unexpected. I imagine that is the difference between the way we see our lives and the way God sees our lives. We see spaces to fill with familiar and expected colors while He sees a canvas to be completed with extravagant strokes and details. God is the source of creativity, so don't allow the limitations of your thinking to limit your hopes and expectations of what He can paint on the canvas of your life.

• THINK ABOUT IT •

God is able to do far more abundantly beyond anything we ask or think, so rejoice in His creative lordship of your life! It brings the promise of beauty, meaning, and significance.

*Prayer*

Heavenly Father, I rejoice in Your lordship, thankful for how You work in me fulfilling Your good purposes. Let faith, not fear, instruct my efforts—anything is possible with a creator like You. Make of me what You dream for me. In Jesus' name, amen.

## COMFORT ZONE EXPANSIONS

*Again Jesus said, "Peace be with you! As the Father has sent me, I am sending you."*

JOHN 20:21

Several years ago I went with a medical mission team to Peru. The people in my church would have enjoyed watching me on this trip. I was not the preacher in the nice suit standing on a stage, with everyone quiet and listening to me. I was the sweaty guy in jeans, hauling bags of supplies and medicines and setting up equipment. The locals pointed at me and laughed, and I will never know exactly why. None of this bothered me because I knew why I was there: God invited me to go. Sometimes God invites us to step away from our familiar surroundings. Sometimes He asks us to be vulnerable enough to endure a laugh and a comment. Jesus left the comforts of Heaven in order to come to the earth and be pointed at, harassed, and ridiculed. When Jesus invites you out of your comfort zone, don't start making a list of all the reasons why you should not go. Thank Him for counting you worthy, then start making a list of all the ways you can serve Him through the opportunity.

### · THINK ABOUT IT ·

Have you ever been invited by God outside of your comfort zone, even if it was across the street? If gratitude and trust was not your initial response, ask God to help you get a change of perspective.

### *Prayer*

Heavenly Father, open doors for me to step out into the places Your love wants to go, even if far outside my comfort zone. Grant me an unselfish vision and sufficient resources that I might serve You wherever You lead. In Jesus' name, amen.

## "I AM WHO I AM"

*Moses said to God, "Suppose I go to the Israelites and say to them, 'The God of your fathers has sent me to you,' and they ask me, 'What is his name?' Then what shall I tell them?" God said to Moses, "I AM WHO I AM."*

EXODUS 3:13-14

That notion that God is Almighty has been diminished in our hearts. It's a bit like the "frog and kettle"; it happened so gradually that we hardly noticed. I find we're apologetic about some of the fundamental assertions of Scripture. We're more willing to accept Darwin's theory of evolution than God's assertion that He is the Creator. We choose not to ponder things like the virgin birth, or that Jesus physically died and God raised Him to life again. We're reluctant to say that Scripture is the authoritative Word of God that guides our faith and practice. We hesitate to state God's perspective on morality. What we're indicating is that we don't really believe that God is Almighty, because if we believed it, we would be less likely to step away from His truth. Although God and His Word can withstand our scrutiny, He has never needed to explain Himself. As He said to Moses, "I AM WHO I AM."

· THINK ABOUT IT ·

If you can recognize that you have drifted away from believing that God is Almighty, I invite you to examine His Word. See who the God of the Bible is, and marvel in His power and majesty.

*Prayer*

Lord, I'm sorry, but my heart and mind have been filled more with the thoughts of the secular world than they have with You and Your perspective. Forgive me for when I have doubted Your greatness. Fill me with Your Holy Spirit, and return me to a right relationship with You. In Jesus' name, amen.

## LORD OF ALL

*For there is one God and one mediator between God and men, the man Christ Jesus, who gave himself as a ransom for all men...*

### 1 TIMOTHY 2:5-6

I feel sure that many of the people who are filling the seats in our church buildings are deceived about their relationship with Jesus of Nazareth. They assume that because they are physically present in a building with a church sign out front, and they are standing and sitting and singing at the right time, that they are followers of Jesus. Following Jesus is not about filling a seat on the weekend or following a moral code or saying the right thing at the right time. It is a personal decision regarding Jesus. To participate in the Kingdom of God, you must believe that Jesus is the Christ, the Messiah, the Son of God. Then choosing Him as Lord of your life and giving Him authority over your priorities, will allow Him to change you from the inside out. Are you an authentic follower of Jesus, who gave Himself as a ransom for all? If not, will you consider yielding your life to Him right now?

### • THINK ABOUT IT •

Read Isaiah 29:13. God doesn't want a superficial reverence that only consists of "traditions learned by rote." He desires a humble heart, willing to yield. Choose Jesus wholeheartedly, and without precondition.

### *Prayer*

Heavenly Father, I believe Jesus of Nazareth is Your Son, and I want Him to be Lord of my life—Lord of all that I am and all that I have. Thank You for accepting me into Your Kingdom through Jesus' precious blood and sacrifice. In His name, amen.

## LIKE IN GALILEE

*Jesus returned to Galilee in the power of the Spirit, and news about him spread through the whole countryside.*

LUKE 4:14

I love to visit Galilee. It was there that Jesus began recruiting His disciples with the simple invitation you've heard so many times: "Come. Follow Me." It was there that He turned water into wine, raised the dead, and fed a multitude with a boy's lunch. It was there that He established His reputation as more than just a teacher of Scripture. It was there that He invited people to believe in Him as the Messiah and enter the Kingdom of God. I invite you today to accept the fullness of Jesus of Nazareth and believe that He is Christ, Lord, and King. In believing, our lives are transformed and our futures are changed. Don't be content to fill a seat on the weekend. Don't be content to know some stories about Jesus. Determine for yourself to believe in Him with your whole heart and mind—to imagine that He can open doors of possibility in your life, just as He opened doors of possibility for the people who encountered Him in Galilee.

· THINK ABOUT IT ·

Do not be content to settle for less than a living faith in Jesus Christ. Ask to know Him "in the power of the Spirit."

*Prayer*

Heavenly Father, draw me to Jesus. Holy Spirit, lift Him up and reveal the fullness of Jesus to me, so like Thomas I will declare, "My Lord and my God!" With all my heart I will follow Him, looking forward to my days to come. In Jesus' name, amen.

## STOP AND CONSIDER

*"He performs wonders that cannot be fathomed, miracles that cannot be counted."*

JOB 5:9

How often do we stop to consider the scope and magnitude of the power of God? He can do whatever He wants. He can create planets and set them in orbit. He can create an ocean and cause dry land to rise up from it. He can create living creatures and the food they need for nourishment. He can bring a plague and then take it away. He can make food fall from the sky. He can shorten a life or lengthen it. He is all-powerful. Scripture says that He created us in His image, but we have turned that around and tried to recreate God in our image. We have limits. We get tired. Our strength fails. We have intellectual limits and emotional limits and resource limits. We come to the end of ourselves and our patience. God has no limits. He is powerful over all things, and to a degree that we cannot begin to comprehend or describe. This is our God, the God who created us, the God we love and serve.

### • THINK ABOUT IT •

Take time today to consider the scope and magnitude of God's power. Your reverence for Him will deepen, and your faith and trust in Him will grow.

### Prayer

Heavenly Father, my mind cannot take in the sum of Your works or the greatness of Your power. When I meditate on You, I am filled with awe. I humbly bow before You and trust in You with my whole heart. You are very great! In Jesus' name, amen.

## REWARD IN ETERNITY

*"Blessed are you when people hate you, when they exclude you and insult you and reject your name as evil, because of the Son of Man. Rejoice in that day and leap for joy, because great is your reward in heaven."*

LUKE 6:22-23

No one enjoys the feeling of being excluded or rejected; we would much rather feel like we are accepted and a part of the group. As long as we are in the cozy confines of our church communities, we will enjoy fellowship and the peace that comes from being with like-minded people. But Jesus is warning us that following Him publicly will not always be pleasant. He is not speaking rhetorically here; He is preparing us to suffer, be rejected, be hated, and perhaps be betrayed. He is inviting us toward an imagination that the reward of our existence is not going to be most fully understood in time. If for a season we suffer, or are rejected or mocked, Jesus is calling us to rejoice, because God is working in us and through us. Does God make a difference in our lives in time? He absolutely does. But the real payoff for our faith is in eternity.

• THINK ABOUT IT •

Remember those suffering around the world for their faith in Christ. Pray for them, and let their faithfulness encourage and challenge your own. There is a reward ahead.

*Prayer*

Heavenly Father, give me a courageous faith for my days, that I would be known as one called by Your name. Give me boldness to never deny You by my silence or my disobedience. I rejoice in the prize of eternity with You! In Jesus' name, amen.

# DAY 331

## A GOOD NAME

*A good name is more desirable than great riches; to be esteemed is better than silver or gold.*

PROVERBS 22:1

We should pay attention to how we conduct ourselves because our words and actions will be attached to our names forever. When you say the name of a person you know or know of, you immediately process a mental image. You also think about some of what you know about that person. That leads you to tag that person with some adjectives, especially if it is someone you know well: friendly or unfriendly, helpful or unhelpful, generous or stingy, good or evil. For example, what comes to mind when you hear the name Corrie ten Boom? What do we want people to think when they hear our name? Do we want them to remember our kindness during a trying time? Our generosity during a difficult season? Our faith when their faith was small? If "a good name is more desirable than great riches," we should do what we can to be the kind of person who causes warm feelings to flow when our name is mentioned.

### • THINK ABOUT IT •

You were created in Christ Jesus for good works (Ephesians 2:10). When it comes to doing the kinds of things that bring a good name, the Christ-follower can honestly say: "I was made for this!"

### *Prayer*

Heavenly Father, give me grace to accomplish the good works You have planned and gain a good name that brings honor to Yours. Holy Spirit, help me bear Your fruit as I follow through on Your invitations to bless and serve others. In Jesus' name, amen.

## THE FULLNESS OF GOD'S KINGDOM

*While we are at home in the body we are absent from the Lord...*

2 CORINTHIANS 5:6 • NASB®

Most of us are "at home" in our bodies. We may not like something about the way ours looks, but we usually come to appreciate what we see in the mirror. We may have some physical problems, but we take medicine and carry on. We are at home in these physical bodies because this physical world is all we know. But Paul says while we are at home in these bodies, we are removed from the Kingdom of God in many respects. The Spirit of God dwells within us, and we can see evidence of His Kingdom around us. But we do not see it in its fullness because we are limited by our physical bodies. This season of being "at home in the body" is very temporary. A time is coming when our earth suits will wear out and we will step out of them. Then we will experience the presence of God and the fullness of His Kingdom. I don't know everything about what that will be like, but I know it will be more glorious than anything I can imagine.

### • THINK ABOUT IT •

Jesus was made sin with our sinfulness so that we could be made righteous with His righteousness. Our anticipation of joy in God's presence rests on Christ Jesus, our hope. Praise Him!

### Prayer

Heavenly Father, I praise You for the hope of eternity with You in Your Kingdom. Jesus, thank You for atoning for my sin, exchanging places with me so I can stand in the presence of a holy God, blameless and with great joy. In Your name I pray, amen.

## OFFERING OUR VERY BEST

*"With such an offering on your part, will He receive any of you kindly?" says the LORD of hosts.*

MALACHI 1:9 • NASB®

In Malachi 1, God reprimands the priests who are offering less than the best to Him. "I have loved you," He says in verse 1, then goes on to detail all the ways the priests have dishonored Him by offering second-rate sacrifices. We no longer offer physical sacrifices on an altar, but God still wants our best and wants to give us His best in return. One thing I consistently lament, that truly grieves me, is the tendency we have to come to God with half a heart. We don't often bring the great passion of our life to the things of God. We save the best part of ourselves for our careers, our sports teams, and our hobbies. I invite you to look at your daily schedule, your monthly calendar, and your expenditures, then think about where in life you are investing your time, your energies, and your resources. Does your life demonstrate that you desire God's best enough to give Him your best?

### • THINK ABOUT IT •

Is there a way your interests and talents could be harnessed for Kingdom purposes? Ask the Holy Spirit to help you re-examine your commitments through His lens for the Kingdom potential they could provide as you seek to give Him your best.

### *Prayer*

Heavenly Father, You are my Designer; I delight myself in You. Redirect my focus to a Kingdom perspective that always honors You with my best. Help me harness my interests, resources, and talents as avenues of service to You. In Jesus' name, amen.

## CHOOSING TO REPENT

*All have sinned and fall short of the glory of God...*

ROMANS 3:23

Here's our fundamental problem. God created us and gave us authority over all of His creation. We are not just at the top of the evolutionary ladder. We are unique and created in God's image, with His Spirit breathed into us. We rebelled and forfeited our place of dominion and authority, and we were subjected to another kingdom. In that fallen state, the basest part of us is given expression. We have had a rather lengthy run now of human civilization. Just a casual glance over our history proves quite conclusively that given enough freedom, we will band together to destroy one another. One genocide after another has ravaged many parts of the globe. Leaders with motivations both religious and secular have implemented evil schemes to persecute and kill. So this fallen nature is a problem, and we will not be able to work for the common good until we admit our sin and unite at the foot of the cross.

· THINK ABOUT IT ·

Repentance is a daily exercise for the follower of Christ. Be sensitive to those promptings of the Holy Spirit as He helps you to put off your "old self" and put on the new.

*Prayer*

Heavenly Father, Your Word promises if I confess my sins that You are faithful and just to forgive them. So I kneel at the foot of the cross and repent of and renounce my sins. I thank You for cleansing me through Jesus' blood. In Jesus' name, amen.

## WISE & PROSPEROUS LIFE

*The fear of the LORD is the beginning of wisdom; all who follow his precepts have good understanding.*

PSALM 111:10

The Bible invites us to cultivate the fear of the Lord. It isn't fear in the sense that you shrink away from Him in terror or dread. The biblical presentation of the fear of God has to do with respect, with reverence, with a sense of awe. It is the recognition that there is a God and He is not like us, that He deserves a unique response from us. There are very few things in Scripture that have more promises attached than the fear of the Lord, yet it seems that it has diminished among the people of God. I'm not saying we've lost it altogether, but I don't think we hold it in the same place that we did even a decade ago. No matter how much education you acquire, how successful you are, or what things you manage to achieve with your life, you will take the first steps toward wisdom and true understanding when you begin to cultivate a fear of the Lord.

### • THINK ABOUT IT •

Blessings accompany the fear of the Lord: The Lord will deliver you (Psalm 33:18), bless your labor (Psalm 128:1-2), and instruct your life choices (Psalm 25:12). Lacking nothing, you will get to experience God's friendship (Psalm 34:9 & 25:14). Cultivating the fear of the Lord is definitely wisdom.

*Prayer*

Heavenly Father, instruct my heart in the fear of the Lord, so I can obey You and avoid evil. The fear of the Lord leads to a wise and prosperous life, so grant me an undivided heart that reveres You and fears Your name alone. In Jesus' name, amen.

## THE GREATEST STRENGTH AVAILABLE

*Finally, be strong in the Lord and in his mighty power.*

EPHESIANS 6:10

Being physically strong seems to be the highest goal of some people. Walk into most gyms in America, and you'll see several of those folks. They are either trying to get pumped up or trying to stay that way. I'm grateful for physical strength—I utilize it every day, and I do what I can to maintain what I have for as long as I can. But it is an inevitably changing thing. Early in life your strength is small, and as you age your strength begins to diminish again. Somewhere in between is about a thirty-minute window when your strength is really good! The greatest strength available to you is not your physical strength. In fact, if you are a believer who is growing in knowledge of the Lord and learning to lean into Him and experience His presence in greater ways, you will gain spiritual strength every day until you leave your earth suit behind, no matter how pumped up it may be. I'm all for taking care of our physical bodies, but I want us to take care of our spiritual selves as well.

### • THINK ABOUT IT •

To grow in the trust and knowledge of the Lord and experience His presence more intimately will require a focused self-discipline on your part. Do you have a daily exercise regimen of Bible study and prayer?

### *Prayer*

Heavenly Father, help me obtain the wisdom and self-discipline needed to take care of my spiritual health. Holy Spirit, strengthen me with power so I can have the faithful stamina to run my life's race well and finish strong. In Jesus' name, amen.

## CONFIDENT & COURAGEOUS

*"The LORD himself goes before you and will be with you; he will never leave you nor forsake you. Do not be afraid; do not be discouraged."*

DEUTERONOMY 31:8

Moses is reminding Joshua that he will not be alone as he leads God's people to the land He had promised them. Here, as throughout Scripture, when God is sending His people in a new direction or commissioning a leader, one of the most common statements is: "Don't be afraid, and don't be discouraged." Humans are very susceptible and vulnerable to fear and discouragement. If we weren't, we wouldn't be consistently warned about them. They will immobilize you and keep you from God's best in your life. We also know that if God said to not be afraid or discouraged, it's possible to lead fearless and courageous lives. I have determined that with the help of the Spirit of God I will not forfeit one of God's invitations in my life because of fear or discouragement. Yes, we will be faced with frightening and discouraging things, but we will have to determine in our hearts that we will depend on His strength and not turn back.

· THINK ABOUT IT ·

Your adversary will always focus on your weaknesses and failures, both past and potential. Be encouraged by God's Word to refocus on God's strength and faithfulness, and go forward with confidence in Him.

*Prayer*

Heavenly Father, I am determined by grace to be mastered by no fear but the fear of the Lord. Thank You for Your Spirit of power and love that casts out my fears and encourages my heart forward in every good work and purpose. In Jesus' name, amen.

## SINCERITY & PURITY

*I am afraid that just as Eve was deceived by the serpent's cunning, your minds may somehow be led astray from your sincere and pure devotion to Christ.*

2 CORINTHIANS 11:3

It staggers me that Eve could be deceived. She lived in the lush Garden of Eden. God met her every need and came in the afternoon to walk with her and Adam. Sin was unknown. She had direct, personal contact with her Creator. If Eve was vulnerable to deception, we are vulnerable too. What is the doorway to deception? Our minds and thoughts. Our minds are linked to our emotions. If we allow momentum to build between our thoughts and emotions, we've got enough momentum to be led astray. Satan's target is your sincerity of faith and your pure devotion to Christ. Sincerity and purity are words that are mocked in the public arena, but I'm more concerned about bringing them back into fashion in the Church. If we do not have the intent to be sincere and pure in our faith, it is improbable that it will happen. That is a personal goal of mine, and I hope you will join me and work toward it in your life as well.

### • THINK ABOUT IT •

The word "pure" contains the idea of not being mixed with anything else. A pure faith is uncompromised by dual loyalties. Is your devotion to Christ mixed in with behaviors, beliefs, or attitudes you have absorbed from popular culture?

### *Prayer*

Heavenly Father, teach me how to guard my heart and be renewed in the spirit of my mind. I desire a sincere and pure faith. Enable me to think clearly and not be deceived by fine-sounding arguments. Purify my devotion to You. In Jesus' name, amen.

## A RIGHT UNDERSTANDING

*Humble yourselves, therefore, under God's mighty hand, that he may lift you up in due time.*

1 PETER 5:6

Humility doesn't always look like you think it would. Humility doesn't say, "I'm insignificant," or "I have no value," or "I have nothing to offer to God." God said you are fearfully and wonderfully made, and He sent His Son to rescue you! Humility is a right understanding of who you are, the strengths God has given you, and the weaknesses you have because you are human. Peter wants us to understand the limits that come with our humanity and the difference between ourselves and God. He had seen that Jesus' sojourn on the earth was marked by humility, and he had learned some valuable lessons in humility by the time he wrote this letter. Peter is inviting us to begin to seek the purposes of God by showing humility before Him and learning obedience to Him. When we do that, we will be lifted up and invited to participate more fully in His Kingdom purposes. In doing so, we will be blessed.

### • THINK ABOUT IT •

A right understanding of God, a right understanding of yourself: These truths will call forth the humility that unlocks your potential in God's Kingdom. Ask the Holy Spirit for deeper understanding of these things.

### Prayer

Heavenly Father, You alone are God. I trust Your goodness and love; I submit my will to Yours. Admitting my total dependency on You for my life and breath and all else, I bow before Your throne. You alone can save and deliver. In Jesus' name, amen.

## UNMATCHED POWER

*Who has measured the waters in the hollow of his hand, or with the breadth of his hand marked off the heavens? Who has held the dust of the earth in a basket, or weighed the mountains on the scales and the hills in a balance?*

ISAIAH 40:12

I'm an advocate for science, but many of us have made it a god. Science is not a collection of all the truth of humanity; science is an emerging discipline. A hundred years ago the finest physicians in the world didn't know to wash their hands between patients. If the Lord tarries, third graders a hundred years from now will be laughing at our scientific expertise. Someone told me that scientists had written a paper about what destroyed Sodom and Gomorrah. They proposed that two asteroids collided and caused things to rain down and destroy the cities. That explanation doesn't offend me at all. Can you imagine a God so talented that He could cause the collision of two asteroids so that debris would fall in the precise place that He wanted destroyed? Our God is the Master of the heavens and the earth. Who would not gladly serve a God like that?

· THINK ABOUT IT ·

The Lord's understanding is unsearchable, His power is immeasurable, and His love is infinite. He keeps the celestial bodies in their courses and calls each of the stars by name. He knows your name too and calls you to His good path for you.

*Prayer*

Heavenly Father, Maker and Master of the heavens and the earth, the fingerprints of Your wisdom are everywhere. Your merciful hand on my life gives me peace. I will gladly serve You and embrace Your path for me. In Jesus' name, amen.

## FOUNDATIONAL WORD

*I will show you what it's like when someone comes to me, listens to my teaching, and then follows it. It is like a person building a house who digs deep and lays the foundation on solid rock. When the floodwaters rise and break against that house, it stands firm because it is well built.*

LUKE 6:47-48 • NLT

Foundations are important. You've probably seen photos of buildings that are still standing after the wind and waves of a fierce hurricane have receded. Those structures might have minor damage, but the surrounding structures have been reduced to rubble. Inevitably, when the owners are asked the reason their buildings survived, the answer is the same: They had dug deep in order to build on a firm foundation. The principle is the same if you're constructing a building, a business, or a life of faith: Its strength and stability are directly related to the strength and the stability of its foundation. Jesus tells us that a wise person of faith builds a spiritual life upon the foundation of His Word. When we have the knowledge of Scripture and its truths undergirding us, we will be able to remember that and stand when storms come.

### • THINK ABOUT IT •

A foundation must be made of quality material that can withstand the stress of the structure to be built upon it. The honor and integrity of the Word of God guarantees it is absolutely reliable. Dig deep and build your life on it.

### *Prayer*

Heavenly Father, You honor and uphold Your Word. I know Your Word can uphold me. Your Word is truth and cannot be broken. I will put Your Word in my heart and build my life on it, choosing to honor and obey what You say. In Jesus' name, amen.

## LIFE ABUNDANT

*"The thief comes only to steal and kill and destroy; I came that they may have life, and have it abundantly."*

JOHN 10:10 • NASB®

Even within the Church, we have modified what Scripture tells us about Satan. We have rewritten his role to create a character that's like the zany uncle who comes to town and wants to have a little fun. He drives a great car, takes us to places we've been warned about, and throws lots of money around when he gets there. We're not sure he is destructive; he just wants us to have more fun than God thinks is a good idea. That is not the presentation of Scripture. The Bible says that the Devil's objective—the purpose for his very existence—is your destruction. He has a plan, and his every effort is focused on stealing from you, killing you, and destroying what is precious to you. To the degree that you invite him in and give him space, you're inviting in destruction. In contrast, Jesus came that we may have not only life, but an abundant life full of good things. I'm so grateful for Jesus, our Savior, who rescues us from Satan's clutches.

### • THINK ABOUT IT •

Proverbs warns about being naïve with choices and behaviors that flirt with sin. Remember, Satan's endgame for you is always your destruction. Jesus' goal is your life fully restored, not diminished.

### *Prayer*

Heavenly Father, forgive me for being casual about things I thought were only "just having a little fun." Give me prudence to consider my steps and avoid all evil. Thank You, Jesus, for rescuing my life from destruction. In Your name I pray, amen.

## FOR HE IS GOOD

*Give thanks to the LORD, for he is good; his love endures forever.*

1 CHRONICLES 16:34

In the deep recesses of your heart, do you really believe that God is good? Or do you believe that He is an indifferent puppet master who has set an obstacle course called life and dared you to complete it? The notion that God is good will define the relationship you will consider with Him. If you believe that He loves you, and that your best interests are His great desire, then you'll be far more inclined to yield to Him, to follow Him, and to cooperate with Him. If you don't believe God is good, you'll always hold a part of yourself back. You'll always be reserved and reluctant to see His love for you. I want to invite you to dive a little deeper and think about how you understand the character of God. Do you really think He has your best interests at heart? If the answer is no, I want you to begin to talk to Him about it. He won't be surprised, and the Holy Spirit will bring you the clarity you have been searching for.

· THINK ABOUT IT ·

If the goodness of God seems distant to you, don't let yourself stay there. God's goodness toward you is personal and compassionate—in the details of your life. He hears the prayers of your heart, and knows exactly what you'll need today.

*Prayer*

Heavenly Father, help my heart put away doubt and understand Your goodness more truly. You have made peace between us through Jesus' blood. Holding nothing back, I want to walk more fully in the joy of being reconciled to You. In Jesus' name, amen.

## EYES FIXED ON THE ETERNAL

*We fix our eyes not on what is seen, but on what is unseen. For what is seen is temporary, but what is unseen is eternal.*

2 CORINTHIANS 4:18

How do we "fix our eyes" on the unseen? We can't, with our physical senses. Unseen things are not strange, however—we interact with them every day. If you use a cellphone or a microwave, you're using something you can't see. It does not violate my desire to be a rational person to believe that something I cannot see or fully comprehend influences my life. If you are basing your spiritual journey solely on the input of your physical senses, you are limiting the Holy Spirit's work in your life. The invitation of Scripture is to make life choices—how we spend our time, our energy, our resources, and how we fashion our dreams—based on things we cannot fully understand with our five senses. We are invited to look beyond the things of this world, to the things of God's Kingdom. Sometimes, in Christian circles, people hear that and think, "You're just trying to get me to be fanatical." No, I'm encouraging you to be a faithful follower of Jesus Christ.

### • THINK ABOUT IT •

Looking beyond the information of your five senses to understand truth is an act of humility, not fanaticism. It is admitting the limits of your physical self, while acknowledging the infinite God.

### *Prayer*

Heavenly Father, thank You for the trustworthy revelation Your Word gives me of things real but unseen. Focusing my faith on its truth, I will fix my eyes on Your Word as I look to the things of Your Kingdom. In Jesus' name, amen.

## ONE TRUTH

*Behold, You desire truth in the inward parts, and in the hidden part You will make me to know wisdom.*

PSALM 51:6 • NKJV®

We've all heard something like this: "You can't judge me. You don't know me, and you don't know my circumstances. You haven't walked in my shoes. You don't know what I have had to endure. You don't know what it is to be me. You don't understand my truth." It's true that nobody can know what it means to be another person. But as a society we've devolved down into this place where the prevailing wisdom is "here a truth, there a truth, everywhere a truth-truth," and you just pick the one you like. It is evidence of utter deception to say there is no ultimate truth. Scripture clearly teaches that there is a God, He is sovereign over all, and His truth can be known. We may not like it or agree with it, but each of us is accountable to Him for our response to it. Ask the Lord to show you His truth. He is a generous teacher, and He will not withhold it from you.

• THINK ABOUT IT •

Because Jesus has declared, "I am the truth," to say that there is no ultimate truth is to attack the very identity and authority of God's Son. Do not let the influences of our culture trick you into elevating any feeling or opinion above Him.

*Prayer*

Heavenly Father, feelings and opinions—my own or others'—are not worthy to be called truth. You are worthy; Your Son is truth. I renounce the lie of making idols of my feelings. Guide me in Your truth and let it live in me. In Jesus' name, amen.

## TRAINING IN RIGHTEOUSNESS

*Discipline yourself for the purpose of godliness...*

1 TIMOTHY 4:7 • NASB®

Paul's letters often mention that he wants his readers to discipline themselves and train themselves in righteousness so that they will gain a reward in this life and the life to come. I think we often try to do those things, but in my mind there is a difference between trying and training. Trying says, "I want a different outcome, and I want to throw my heart into it." So you try, usually with the best of intentions. But trying doesn't get it done, and you fail to make progress. Training, on the other hand, is the day-to-day routine of saying no to self-absorption and yes to godliness. It is submitting to a process whereby you engage in a set of behaviors and thoughts and activities so that weeks and months from now, you can accomplish something that you could not accomplish today, no matter how desperately or sincerely you tried. Training in righteousness begins with behaviors such as reading your Bible, praying, giving, serving, and telling your Jesus-story. I invite you to move beyond trying and begin training.

### • THINK ABOUT IT •

Have you been able to move from good intentions to an established routine of training for righteousness? You'll be more successful maintaining growth if it's incremental. Start small and take manageable steps. A few years from now you will have a strong routine.

### *Prayer*

Heavenly Father, I want to pursue You with my whole heart. Holy Spirit, help me get the discipline I need to train myself for godliness, knowing the promise of Your fruit this brings. In Jesus' name, amen.

## IDENTIFYING THE ENEMY

*Many of those who believed now came and openly confessed their evil deeds. A number who had practiced sorcery brought their scrolls together and burned them publicly. When they calculated the value of the scrolls, the total came to fifty thousand drachmas. In this way the word of the Lord spread widely and grew in power.*

ACTS 19:18-20

The Jesus-story was new in Ephesus, and the people were overwhelmed by the magnitude of their sin. They began to repent publicly, bringing their pagan scrolls and burning them. Today that would be like millions of dollars' worth of Ouija boards, tarot cards, horoscopes, and the like going up in smoke! The result of their repentance was a widespread awareness of the power of the gospel. I would love to see what God would do in my community if every pagan item was sacrificed on an altar of repentance. If you own any of those ungodly items, I urge you to send them not to a charity store but to the trash or to the flames. Ask God to cleanse your heart and fill it with His love and power, then look forward to what He will do in you and through you.

· THINK ABOUT IT ·

Ask the Holy Spirit to make you aware of any items you may have in your home that would give evil an entryway. Take the next step to remove them, and ask the Lord for His cleansing.

*Prayer*

Heavenly Father, I desire a clean heart and home. Show me if there is anything I have collected or participated in that offends or grieves Your Spirit. I repent and ask You to cleanse and fill me with Your love and power. In Jesus' name, amen.

## UNCOMPROMISING VISION

*"We want a king over us. Then we will be like all the other nations, with a king to lead us and to go out before us and fight our battles."*

### 1 SAMUEL 8:19-20

Peer pressure is causing God's people to second-guess His plan and say, "We want to be like everybody else!" "Syncretism" is the fancy word for what's happening, and it means to compromise the integrity of one faith by combining it with another faith. The Israelites said, "We don't want to reject God. We just want to bring in some ungodly things too." That's really at the heart of compromise for God's people. We don't want to be limited or exclusionary. We don't want to be too different. We just want to fit in. We want the blessings of God, but we want to be able to blend in among the ungodly. The desire to compromise and accommodate the world is a very powerful motivation in our lives, but it does not come from the Spirit of God. If you find hints of rebellion bubbling up in you, do not give them room to grow. Determine to seek the Lord only, and find your contentment in Him.

### • THINK ABOUT IT •

Fear of people's reactions is the strong undercurrent of "wanting to blend in." This fear is idolatry and will always oppose the lordship of Jesus, even while claiming devotion to His saving grace. Remember, our confession is: Jesus is Lord!

### *Prayer*

Heavenly Father, Jesus is Lord! Forgive me for fearing to offend the world through public obedience to Christ. Unite my heart to fear You and You alone. I will have no other gods before You. In Jesus' name, amen.

## A GOD WHO CAN BE KNOWN

*By faith Enoch was taken from this life, so that he did not experience death;*
*he could not be found, because God had taken him away. For before he was*
*taken, he was commended as one who pleased God.*

HEBREWS 11:5

Other than being the father of the famous Methuselah, Enoch is known for one thing: He didn't die. God liked him so much that He just came and got him. Can you imagine God liking you so much that He just gets you early? "We're not going to wait for him to expire. I want him with me." Wouldn't you like to be that tight with God? The commentary is in verse 6: "Without faith it is impossible to please God, because anyone who comes to him must believe that he exists and that he rewards those who earnestly seek him." What can we infer from this then about Enoch? One, he earnestly sought the Lord. He must have been in deep and constant prayer. Two, his faith pleased God. I doubt that I will be taken like Enoch was, but that kind of faith is a worthy goal for any of us.

• THINK ABOUT IT •

The book of Genesis records "Enoch walked with God." He had the kind of faith that passionately pursued God just for the joy of being with Him. Ask the Lord for that passion and a greater revelation of the peace His nearness brings.

*Prayer*

Heavenly Father, I earnestly desire a living faith marked by wholehearted love for You. Strengthen me in prayer to seek Your presence continually. Deliver me from unbelief that says such a life of faith is out of reach for me. In Jesus' name, amen.

# DAY 350

## A STRONG KNOWLEDGE

*Then the devil took him to the holy city and had him stand on the highest point of the temple. "If you are the Son of God," he said, "throw yourself down. For it is written: 'He will command his angels concerning you, and they will lift you up in their hands, so that you will not strike your foot against a stone.'" Jesus answered him, "It is also written: 'Do not put the Lord your God to the test.'"*

MATTHEW 4:5-7

If you don't know the Word of God, it is easy to use Scripture to deceive you. The Devil had the audacity to use Scripture to challenge Jesus, and he will challenge what God has said about you and the veracity of your faith: "Do you really believe? Why are you acting so holy?" Jesus answered him with Scripture, and that should be our response too: "I am God's child and Jesus' friend. The Holy Spirit lives within me. I am the salt of the earth and the light of the world." Make a commitment to read and get to know your Bible. It will be your strong foundation when you are faced with doubts planted by the enemy.

### • THINK ABOUT IT •

Eve was vague about what God had said (Genesis 3) and the Devil took her out. Jesus was not (Matthew 4) and He prevailed. Do not be satisfied with vague knowledge of Scripture. Vagueness guarantees a dangerous vulnerability.

### Prayer

Heavenly Father, I will not neglect Your Word; I will apply my heart and mind to learning it. Plant Your Word in my heart, and do not let the enemy twist it or steal it. Give me understanding to know it, do it, and not forget it. In Jesus' name, amen.

## WHO'S NEXT?

*Children are a gift from the LORD; they are a reward from him.*

PSALM 127:3 • NLT

Children are a gift from the Lord, and they are worthy of our time and attention. When I was growing up there were multiple layers that spoke into the character formation of children from a godly point of view. Not only in churches, but in schools, extracurricular activities, and athletics— it was understood that if you participated in any of those things that the leaders would speak into you a biblical worldview and values. Authority figures who did not do that would not be tolerated. It wasn't too long ago that prime-time television programming had a biblical worldview. I recently watched a game show on prime-time television, and I would have been embarrassed if children had been in the room. We no longer have those layers of voices speaking into our little people, so we are going to have to give greater attention to our responsibility. You may not be in a parenting season right now, but parents need your help. We have to work together on this, so I encourage you to find a place where you can serve young people.

## • THINK ABOUT IT •

Mentoring, participating in local schoolboard meetings, focusing intercession on a school, classroom, or neighborhood—opportunities abound to demonstrate a biblical model and serve the young. Ask the Holy Spirit to highlight where He would send you.

*Prayer*

Heavenly Father, we have failed to maintain a biblical worldview in our culture. We need Your help and mercy. Pour out Your Spirit on us. Send me to serve and teach the next generation the truth of Your Word. In Jesus' name, amen.

## TO KNOW THE KING

*The people stood watching, and the rulers even sneered at him. They said, "He saved others; let him save himself if he is the Christ of God, the Chosen One."*

LUKE 23:35

This is an incredibly sad scene. At the foot of the cross we see the Jewish rulers. They were the men who held spiritual authority over the people and oversaw all the activity of the Temple. They were the descendants of Abraham, Isaac, and Jacob. They knew the writings of the prophets and were experts in the Law of Moses. They kept all the holidays and ate all the right foods and made the proper sacrifices. Yet here they were, standing at the foot of the cross, sneering at Jesus and mocking Him. It's a chilling realization that people who think of themselves as religious, who look and act and sound religious, can be so wrong about who Jesus is. This should cause us to pause and take stock of our own spiritual condition. Do our hearts and minds truly reflect the outward presentation of faith that we show to the world?

· THINK ABOUT IT ·

It is the difference between "religion" and relationship. Don't just go through the motions—press in. Our King can be known. How much better to serve a King we can know than a set of rules?

*Prayer*

Heavenly Father, I am not interested in religious ritual or facades. I hunger for genuine relationship with You. I want to know You, even in the fellowship of Your sufferings. Give me courage to be fully aligned with You. In Jesus' name, amen.

## A POWERFUL VICTORY

*Having disarmed the powers and authorities, he made a public spectacle of them, triumphing over them by the cross.*

COLOSSIANS 2:15

Hanging on the cross, Jesus did not make a public spectacle of Rome or the religious establishment. If you were a casual observer of Jesus' crucifixion, it looked like Rome had won because the government was rid of a troublemaker. It certainly appeared that the Temple authorities had triumphed, because He could no longer challenge their authority or push against the status quo. But powers greater than governments and religious rulers have existed across centuries and empires. The Bible says that on the cross, Jesus disarmed those powers and authorities, the spiritual forces of wickedness in the heavenly places that were standing against us and enslaving us. He not only disarmed them; He made a public spectacle of them. That means they have no power over us today because through the cross of Jesus we have been delivered from their arena of influence. It is easy to focus on the physical aspects of the cross and forget the spiritual battle that was won on our behalf that day. Praise be to God and His Son, Jesus, for delivering us!

• THINK ABOUT IT •

Don't let your adversary keep you in a prison cell if Jesus has already opened the door for you. Ask the Holy Spirit for greater comprehension of the extent of Jesus' victory and the implications this has for you.

*Prayer*

Heavenly Father, praise be to You and to Jesus, Your Son! Having disarmed our adversaries at the highest level, You have set the captives free, delivering us from the power of darkness. We rejoice in Your victory, Lord! In Jesus' name, amen.

## SEEING THE PLAN

*Let me hear Your lovingkindness in the morning; For I trust in You; Teach me the way in which I should walk; For to You I lift up my soul.*

PSALM 143:8 • NASB®

Sometimes as I'm watching people make life decisions, I think, "That's a really poor choice. Can't they see how this is going to end?" After many years of observation and conversation I've come to understand that the answer usually is: "No, they are not able to see the results of that choice." Some people are able to look at the pieces and see how things will turn out. They can look at a stack of materials and see the end result before the first nail goes in. They can see something that the rest of us can't. The Holy Spirit wants to bring that kind of discernment to our lives because God's plans and purposes for us are not filled with chaos and confusion. He wants to lead us down safe paths to productive outcomes. When we place our trust in Him, He will guide us with a loving hand and show us the way we should walk. His concern and willingness to teach us are simple but profound characteristics of our Almighty God.

• THINK ABOUT IT •

Determine to invite, trust, and yield more fully to the Holy Spirit's counsel. He sees the end from the beginning and is committed to your life's purpose being fulfilled.

*Prayer*

Heavenly Father, thank You for sending the Holy Spirit to be my Counselor. I trust and yield to You, Holy Spirit; lead me on righteous paths. Give me discernment and guidance to make wise decisions. Help me keep in step with You. In Jesus' name, amen.

## BEHOLD, THE LAMB

*"Behold, the Lamb of God who takes away the sin of the world!"*
JOHN 1:29 • NASB®

The prevailing wisdom is that the greatest existential threat to humanity is climate change, but I believe that is the wrong diagnosis. I believe that the greatest existential threat to humanity is the deterioration of human character. When we see the horrible things that people are doing to one another, even innocent bystanders, and then listen to the reasoning of the talking heads who want to evaluate what is happening, it seems the one thing that is seldom if ever discussed is the necessity of character formation. If we don't do something to interrupt the downward spiral of character deterioration, the future for our children and grandchildren is bleak. The only answer to that problem is Jesus. No legislation and no leader will solve this problem. This will be solved when God's people demonstrate to the world that Jesus is the only solution we have and the only Savior we need. "Behold, the Lamb of God who takes away the sin of the world!"

## • THINK ABOUT IT •

No "ism" or ideology can rescue us from our carnal nature. The only answer to the deterioration of character is Jesus. Only He can make any of us a new creation and then empower us by His Spirit to live it out.

## *Prayer*

Heavenly Father, only Jesus can deal with the problem of sin and make all things new. Help me bear witness to Him by demonstrating in my words and actions a redeemed and transformed life. Let His life in me shine out. In Jesus' name, amen.

## PERFECTLY SOVEREIGN

*"I am God, and there is no other...I say, 'My purpose will stand, and I will do all that I please.'"*

ISAIAH 46:9-10

God is "sovereign," a word we don't hear much these days. It means that He can do what He wants, when He wants, the way He wants, and He doesn't require anyone's permission. God is sovereign over all—things we can see and things we cannot see. He created the world and everything in it. He knew you before your parents ever saw you, before you drew your first breath or squeaked out your first cry. God does not take a vote about what He should do next. He does what He knows will forward His Kingdom purposes, even when we do not agree or understand. He knows the end from the beginning, and He will bring His plan to its fulfillment in His good time. God's sovereignty is one of those things that we will not fully understand in this lifetime, and that's OK. But if you're going to have a relationship with Him, you'll need to acknowledge this part of His character and submit yourself to Him.

• THINK ABOUT IT •

God's sovereignty is our guarantee. His holy, gracious character is our confidence that His good purposes will prevail. No act of rebellion has ever provided a better alternative. No wonder His creation rejoices that our God reigns!

*Prayer*

Heavenly Father, Your sovereignty gives me great joy! Righteousness, justice, and truth will prevail, because Yours is the final word. I rejoice that Your purpose will stand for You are good. I humble myself under Your hand. In Jesus' name, amen.

## NOW GO

*When Jesus had called the Twelve together, he gave them power and authority to drive out all demons and to cure diseases, and he sent them out to preach the kingdom of God and to heal the sick.*

LUKE 9:1-2

I've been in many settings where I heard someone say, "Jesus gave that power and authority to a first-century audience, and those were His twelve disciples. He hasn't given that power and authority to anyone else." These people are trying to add some spin to Scripture that just is not there. They are trying to nullify Jesus' invitation to the very power and authority that He came to the world to demonstrate. They want to convince us that it was a first-century occurrence but not a twenty-first-century occurrence. Jesus' command did not impose a geographical limit, so I don't know why anyone would think it had a time limit. Who got to decide when the clock had run out on it? Jesus simply said, "You have my power. You have my authority. Now go." There is nowhere in my Bible where Jesus' gift of His power and authority was rescinded, so let's take it and go!

• THINK ABOUT IT •

We face the same adversaries the first-century disciples did. We share the same assignments they were given. Praise God, Jesus has made the same power and authority available to us to carry out our mission.

*Prayer*

Heavenly Father, give us faith, wisdom, and boldness to exercise the power and authority Jesus has entrusted to us to preach the gospel, heal the sick, proclaim freedom to the captives, and make disciples of all nations. In Jesus' name, amen.

## OUR BEST GIFTS

*As he looked up, Jesus saw the rich putting their gifts into the temple treasury. He also saw a poor widow put in two very small copper coins. "I tell you the truth," he said, "this poor widow has put in more than all the others. All these people gave their gifts out of their wealth; but she out of her poverty put in all she had to live on."*

LUKE 21:1-4

Jesus does the unexpected and celebrates a woman who gave a very small amount instead of the people who gave gifts of great value. His commentary is that she is giving all she had while they are giving out of their excess. Our best gifts to the Lord are not the ones that come from our abundance. Our best gifts to the Lord, no matter their value, are not the ones we give when we don't really miss it—money far beyond our needs, time that we couldn't do anything else with, things that we didn't care about. Our best gifts are the things that we attach value to. This isn't just about money. It's about our time, our attention, and our efforts. What are you willing to give to God?

· THINK ABOUT IT ·

A gift born of true sacrifice is an act of faith. It puts action to the notion that you desire the Lord more than things. It says you believe the Lord will restore to you what you have given up and more, either here or in eternity. Be encouraged and give generously.

*Prayer*

Heavenly Father, thank You that You see what is given, both publicly and privately. Help me to have a generous heart. Show me opportunities to serve You and Your people with my gifts. In Jesus' name, amen.

## STRENGTHENED TOGETHER

*Let us not give up meeting together, as some are in the habit of doing, but let us encourage one another...*

HEBREWS 10:25

I've been a pastor a long time, and I just have to smile when I hear some of these excuses: "Pastor, it was too cold to come to church. We didn't want to get the kids out in this weather." "Pastor, it was too hot to come to church. We didn't want to get the kids out in the heat." "Pastor, the day was so beautiful. We didn't want to miss the opportunity to be outside." I think of them as Goldilocks Christians: The day can be too cold or too hot or just right, and they all are excuses for doing something else. I'd like for you to approach your day of worship with a different kind of focus. We need to purposefully plan our week so that we will have time to present ourselves to the Lord. We need to be there for the encouragement we give other people, if for nothing else. When you make Him an intentional focus of your schedule, He will surprise you with blessings that you had not anticipated.

### • THINK ABOUT IT •

It may be possible to be a Christ-follower without being a part of a church body, but it would be significantly harder. The Church is where we hear the Word, worship together, teach our children about Jesus, sharpen one another, and get help for life's challenges. Don't let flimsy excuses keep you away from God's best.

### *Prayer*

Heavenly Father, thank You for the Church. I pray You'd strengthen it and help it to be a bright light of truth to the world. Let there be a revival amongst Your people, and be glorified in everything we do. In Jesus' name, amen.

## THE RIGHT DIRECTION

*Do not conform to the evil desires you had when you lived in ignorance. But just as he who called you is holy, so be holy in all you do...*

1 PETER 1:14-15

As Jesus-followers, it is tempting to segment our lives. It is easy to have a church face and a business face. It is easy to have one vocabulary for the locker room and another for the Bible study group. It is easy to watch uplifting television shows and movies when others are around and switch to something else when we are alone. Small choices like these can be challenging because we are human and are tempted in many ways, but a few minutes in church on the weekend will not lessen the impact of making ungodly choices the rest of the week. I encourage you to be intentional about following Jesus' example by disciplining yourself to honor the Lord in those daily, small choices. They may seem insignificant in the moment, but over time you will find that you are gaining spiritual strength. Eventually, although you'll still deal with temptation, your desire to please the Lord will override your desire to please your carnal nature.

### • THINK ABOUT IT •

I like the analogy that says what you feed is what will grow. It's true for our spiritual well-being. An honest assessment of what you're taking in regularly will help you begin to build strength and momentum in the right direction.

### Prayer

Heavenly Father, thank You that You guide me with conviction and mercy. May the words of my mouth and meditations of my heart be pleasing to You. Convict me where I am not in line with Your truth. In Jesus' name, amen.

## OUR PART

*Righteousness exalts a nation, but sin is a disgrace to any people.*

PROVERBS 14:34

Righteousness is a big word that simply means a right standing before God. Ungodliness brings God's judgment against a nation, and it will diminish it. Godliness brings God's blessing, and it lifts a nation up. Righteousness is more important to our future than the person living in the White House. Righteousness is more important to our future than the people populating the halls of Congress. Righteousness is more important to our future than the robed figures sitting on the Supreme Court. I'm grateful for all of those institutions, but it is the choices of the people of a nation that will bring the blessing of God or God's judgment. When a nation's people are in a right place with God, their nation will be exalted. This is not beyond us or out of our hands. This is about you and me—we get to make this choice. Will we be a nation that turns a blind eye or even celebrates ungodliness? Or will we be a nation that values righteousness?

### • THINK ABOUT IT •

It's easy to feel helpless and give up when it comes to shaping our culture. Don't let yourself succumb to that line of thinking. Just as you are dependent on God's strength to bring about change in your own life, You can depend on His strength to heal, guide, and protect our nation as we turn to Him and help others do the same.

### *Prayer*

Heavenly Father, thank You that Your mercies are new every morning. Thank You that You are attentive to the prayers of Your people. Heal our land. Guide us in Your truth. Lead us to repent of our sins. Be glorified above all. In Jesus' name, amen.

## A SECURE REWARD

*For the Son of Man is going to come in his Father's glory with his angels, and then he will reward each person according to what he has done.*

MATTHEW 16:27

When Jesus returns, He will reward each person according to what he or she has done during their days in the earth, and those rewards will stretch into eternity. I've concluded that God isn't going to reward me for what this world might see as my successes and achievements. God doesn't need those things. If I accumulate a billion dollars, God doesn't breathe a sigh of relief and say, "That's good. Their tithe of that will fund My next initiative." If I earn multiple degrees, the hosts of Heaven don't say, "OK, we can relax. Allen has the answers." It isn't my success or my achievements that matter for eternity; it is my faithfulness. Every one of us can be faithful, regardless of how the world sees the circumstances of our lives. When we choose to be faithful, God will respond to that with blessings and rewards in this life and the next. That is an amazing promise, and something to consider as we go about our days.

· THINK ABOUT IT ·

Even more than our sacrifices, God desires our obedience. As you pursue deeper understanding of His Word, be attentive to the truths that you already know. Serve God in the everyday, the quiet places, and the unexpected. He sees everything, and you will not lose your reward.

*Prayer*

Heavenly Father, thank You that You are always watching over my life. I want to serve You wholeheartedly today. Let me see the opportunities that would strengthen Your purposes in the earth. You are worthy of all that I have to give. In Jesus' name, amen.

# DAY 363

## HEAVENLY THINGS

*"I have spoken to you of earthly things and you do not believe; how then will you believe if I speak of heavenly things?"*

JOHN 3:12

Nicodemus was a religious leader, and he was interested in this new rabbi. Jesus had told him, "Very truly I tell you, no one can see the kingdom of God unless they are born again" (v. 3), and Nicodemus was confused. Jesus had just blown apart his whole worldview. Nicodemus was quite certain that he belonged to the right group and worshiped in the right way. His entire life—the clothing he wore, the food he ate, the way he conducted himself—was defined by more than six hundred religious rules. Yet Jesus told him that his spiritual condition mattered more than all those rules. Jesus says there are earthly things and heavenly things, and the heavenly things are of more significance. If your faith journey is bound by religious rules regarding external things, ask the Holy Spirit to help you choose a path that takes into account and makes decisions based on heavenly things and not simply earthly things.

### • THINK ABOUT IT •

In the Christian community, it's easy to lean on rule-keeping as a means of reassuring ourselves that we're right with God. But rules will never make us holy. Spend time in your Bible, pray, worship with other believers, seek Him—You'll begin to walk with a God you know, and experience the true freedom found in Him.

### Prayer

Heavenly Father, I desire to know You. I desire Your wisdom and truth to be what guides me. I yield my earthly pursuits to Your will, and ask for a soft heart, sensitive to Your leading. In Jesus' name, amen.

## IDENTITY PROTECTION

*"Did God really say you must not eat the fruit from any of the trees in the garden?" "Of course we may eat fruit from the trees in the garden," the woman replied. "It's only the fruit from the tree in the middle of the garden that we are not allowed to eat. God said, 'You must not eat it or even touch it; if you do, you will die.'"*

GENESIS 3:1-4 • NLT

If you ever doubt that we are a race of rebels, try this. Tell young children they can do anything they want except open one door. Leave the room, and what is the first thing they'll do? Open that door! Our rebellion started in Genesis, and it continues today. Satan knew very well what God had said, so he questioned God's intentions toward humanity. He invited rebellion against God's good plan, and he succeeded. Until this day, we live with the consequences of that decision. Our enemy continues to ask, "Did God really say?" Yes, God really did say, and that needs to be firmly fixed in your mind in order for you to successfully answer the many tough questions that life will present to you.

• THINK ABOUT IT •

God's Word is not only the truth about how we should live, but also an anchor for understanding who we are in God's eyes. One of the central attacks of the enemy is to obscure our true identity in Christ. You were created with a plan and a purpose—a child of the Most High. As a Christ-follower, no weapon, person, or power can take that away from you.

*Prayer*

Heavenly Father, thank You that my identity is secure in You. I rest in knowing You are with me wherever I go. Give me Your peace. In Jesus' name, amen.

## ONE WAY, ONE GREAT LOVE

*For the wages of sin is death, but the free gift of God is eternal life in Christ Jesus our Lord.*

ROMANS 6:23 • NASB®

Participation in the Kingdom of God is a free gift that God has given us, and each one of us must decide to accept it or reject it. Everyone who participates does so by choice. The gift of salvation is not forced upon us; no one will be in the Kingdom of God on a command performance. We don't inherit it or earn it or qualify for it. You can't be good enough, or generous enough, or kind enough, or loving enough, or moral enough to qualify. You can't get in by joining the right church. You can't buy your way in. You can't attend enough worship services or sit in enough small groups. Our salvation is rooted in a Person; His name is Jesus. If you believe Jesus of Nazareth is the Son of God and you choose to accept Him as Lord of your life and serve Him as King, the Bible says you will be saved. This is the simple yet profound gift of a loving God.

• THINK ABOUT IT •

The penalty due our rebellion is unimaginable, but the sacrifice of the sinless Son of God was enough to cleanse us of all unrighteousness—continually. Never be satisfied to let that gift be hidden away. Wherever you go, bring Jesus with you. He's the answer to every problem you'll ever encounter, and He'll never let you down.

*Prayer*

Heavenly Father, thank You for Your perfect provision that continually cleanses me. Give me a heart of compassion for the people far from You. Help me to impact those around me with Your love. In Jesus' name, amen.

## TOPIC

## DAY

## TOPIC

## DAY

## TOPIC

## DAY

## TOPIC

## DAY

## TOPIC                          ## DAY

## TOPIC

## DAY

## TOPIC

## DAY

## TOPIC

## DAY

## TOPIC                                    ## DAY

# ONE-YEAR BIBLE READING PLAN

- [ ] Matthew 1-2
- [ ] Matthew 3-4
- [ ] Matthew 5-6
- [ ] Matthew 7-8
- [ ] Matthew 9-10
- [ ] Matthew 11-12
- [ ] Matthew 13-14
- [ ] Matthew 15-17
- [ ] Matthew 18-19
- [ ] Matthew 20-21
- [ ] Matthew 22-23
- [ ] Matthew 24-25
- [ ] Matthew 26
- [ ] Matthew 27-28
- [ ] Mark 1-3
- [ ] Mark 4-5
- [ ] Mark 6-7
- [ ] Mark 8-9
- [ ] Mark 10-11
- [ ] Mark 12-14
- [ ] Mark 15-16
- [ ] Luke 1-3
- [ ] Luke 4-5
- [ ] Luke 6-7
- [ ] Luke 8-9
- [ ] Luke 10-11
- [ ] Luke 12-13
- [ ] Luke 14-16
- [ ] Luke 17-18
- [ ] Luke 19-20
- [ ] Luke 21-22
- [ ] Luke 23-24
- [ ] John 1-3
- [ ] John 4-7
- [ ] John 8-10
- [ ] John 11-13
- [ ] John 14-16
- [ ] John 17-19
- [ ] John 20-21
- [ ] Acts 1-2
- [ ] Acts 3-4
- [ ] Acts 5-6
- [ ] Acts 7-8
- [ ] Acts 9-10
- [ ] Acts 11-13
- [ ] Acts 14-15
- [ ] Acts 16-17
- [ ] Acts 18-20
- [ ] Acts 21-23
- [ ] Acts 24-26
- [ ] Acts 27-28
- [ ] Romans 1-3
- [ ] Romans 4-7
- [ ] Romans 8-10
- [ ] Romans 11-13
- [ ] Romans 14-16
- [ ] 1 Corinthians 1-4
- [ ] 1 Corinthians 5-8
- [ ] 1 Corinthians 9-12
- [ ] 1 Corinthians 13-16
- [ ] 2 Corinthians 1-3
- [ ] 2 Corinthians 4-7

- ☐ 2 Corinthians 8-10
- ☐ 2 Corinthians 11-13
- ☐ Galatians 1-2
- ☐ Galatians 3-4
- ☐ Galatians 5-6
- ☐ Ephesians 1-3
- ☐ Ephesians 4-6
- ☐ Philippians 1-4
- ☐ Colossians 1-4
- ☐ 1 Thessalonians 1-5
- ☐ 2 Thessalonians 1-3
- ☐ 1 Timothy 1-6
- ☐ 2 Timothy 1-4
- ☐ Titus 1-3; Philemon 1
- ☐ Hebrews 1-3
- ☐ Hebrews 4-7
- ☐ Hebrews 8-10
- ☐ Hebrews 11-13
- ☐ James 1-5
- ☐ 1 Peter 1-5
- ☐ 2 Peter 1-3
- ☐ 1 John 1-5; 2 John 1
- ☐ 3 John 1
- ☐ Jude 1; Revelation 1-3
- ☐ Revelation 4-7
- ☐ Revelation 8-10
- ☐ Revelation 11-14
- ☐ Revelation 15-18
- ☐ Revelation 19-22
- ☐ Genesis 1-3
- ☐ Genesis 4-7

- ☐ Genesis 8-11
- ☐ Genesis 12-15
- ☐ Genesis 16-18
- ☐ Genesis 19-21
- ☐ Genesis 22-24
- ☐ Genesis 25-26
- ☐ Genesis 27-29
- ☐ Genesis 30-31
- ☐ Genesis 32-34
- ☐ Genesis 35-37
- ☐ Genesis 38-40
- ☐ Genesis 41-42
- ☐ Genesis 43-45
- ☐ Genesis 46-47
- ☐ Genesis 48-50
- ☐ Exodus 1-3
- ☐ Exodus 4-6
- ☐ Exodus 7-9
- ☐ Exodus 10-12
- ☐ Exodus 13-15
- ☐ Exodus 16-18
- ☐ Exodus 19-21
- ☐ Exodus 22-24
- ☐ Exodus 25-27
- ☐ Exodus 28-29
- ☐ Exodus 30-32
- ☐ Exodus 33-35
- ☐ Exodus 36-38
- ☐ Exodus 39-40
- ☐ Leviticus 1-4
- ☐ Leviticus 5-7

# ONE-YEAR BIBLE READING PLAN

- ☐ Leviticus 8-10
- ☐ Leviticus 11-13
- ☐ Leviticus 14-15
- ☐ Leviticus 16-17
- ☐ Leviticus 18-19
- ☐ Leviticus 20-21
- ☐ Leviticus 22-23
- ☐ Leviticus 24-25
- ☐ Leviticus 26-27
- ☐ Numbers 1-3
- ☐ Numbers 4-5
- ☐ Numbers 6-7
- ☐ Numbers 8-10
- ☐ Numbers 11-13
- ☐ Numbers 14-15
- ☐ Numbers 16-17
- ☐ Numbers 18-20
- ☐ Numbers 21-22
- ☐ Numbers 23-25
- ☐ Numbers 26-27
- ☐ Numbers 28-30
- ☐ Numbers 31-33
- ☐ Numbers 34-36
- ☐ Deuteronomy 1
- ☐ Deuteronomy 2
- ☐ Deuteronomy 3-4
- ☐ Deuteronomy 5-7
- ☐ Deuteronomy 8-10
- ☐ Deuteronomy 11-13
- ☐ Deuteronomy 14-16

- ☐ Deuteronomy 17-19
- ☐ Deuteronomy 20-22
- ☐ Deuteronomy 23-25
- ☐ Deuteronomy 26-27
- ☐ Deuteronomy 28-30
- ☐ Deuteronomy 31-32
- ☐ Deuteronomy 33-34
- ☐ Joshua 1-4
- ☐ Joshua 5-8
- ☐ Joshua 9-12
- ☐ Joshua 13-16
- ☐ Joshua 17-20
- ☐ Joshua 21-22
- ☐ Joshua 23-24
- ☐ Judges 1-4
- ☐ Judges 5-7
- ☐ Judges 8-10
- ☐ Judges 11-14
- ☐ Judges 15-18
- ☐ Judges 19-21
- ☐ Ruth 1-4
- ☐ 1 Samuel 1-4
- ☐ 1 Samuel 5-10
- ☐ 1 Samuel 11-14
- ☐ 1 Samuel 15-17
- ☐ 1 Samuel 18-21
- ☐ 1 Samuel 22-25
- ☐ 1 Samuel 26-31
- ☐ 2 Samuel 1-4
- ☐ 2 Samuel 5-8

| | |
|---|---|
| ☐ 2 Samuel 9-12 | ☐ 2 Chronicles 3-4 |
| ☐ 2 Samuel 13-15 | ☐ 2 Chronicles 5-6 |
| ☐ 2 Samuel 16-18 | ☐ 2 Chronicles 7-8 |
| ☐ 2 Samuel 19-21 | ☐ 2 Chronicles 9-10 |
| ☐ 2 Samuel 22-24 | ☐ 2 Chronicles 11-12 |
| ☐ 1 Kings 1-3 | ☐ 2 Chronicles 13-14 |
| ☐ 1 Kings 4-6 | ☐ 2 Chronicles 15-16 |
| ☐ 1 Kings 7-8 | ☐ 2 Chronicles 17-18 |
| ☐ 1 Kings 9-11 | ☐ 2 Chronicles 19-20 |
| ☐ 1 Kings 12-15 | ☐ 2 Chronicles 21-22 |
| ☐ 1 Kings 16-19 | ☐ 2 Chronicles 23-24 |
| ☐ 1 Kings 20-22 | ☐ 2 Chronicles 25-26 |
| ☐ 2 Kings 1-4 | ☐ 2 Chronicles 27-29 |
| ☐ 2 Kings 5-8 | ☐ 2 Chronicles 30-31 |
| ☐ 2 Kings 9-11 | ☐ 2 Chronicles 32-33 |
| ☐ 2 Kings 12-15 | ☐ 2 Chronicles 34-36 |
| ☐ 2 Kings 16-18 | ☐ Ezra 1-3 |
| ☐ 2 Kings 19-22 | ☐ Ezra 4-7 |
| ☐ 2 Kings 23-25 | ☐ Ezra 8-10 |
| ☐ 1 Chronicles 1-2 | ☐ Nehemiah 1-4 |
| ☐ 1 Chronicles 3-5 | ☐ Nehemiah 5-7 |
| ☐ 1 Chronicles 6-7 | ☐ Nehemiah 8-10 |
| ☐ 1 Chronicles 8-10 | ☐ Nehemiah 11-13 |
| ☐ 1 Chronicles 11-13 | ☐ Esther 1-5 |
| ☐ 1 Chronicles 14-16 | ☐ Esther 6-10 |
| ☐ 1 Chronicles 17-19 | ☐ Job 1-5 |
| ☐ 1 Chronicles 20-22 | ☐ Job 6-9 |
| ☐ 1 Chronicles 23-25 | ☐ Job 10-13 |
| ☐ 1 Chronicles 26-29 | ☐ Job 14-18 |
| ☐ 2 Chronicles 1-2 | ☐ Job 19-22 |

- ☐ Job 23-28
- ☐ Job 29-32
- ☐ Job 33-36
- ☐ Job 37-39
- ☐ Job 40-42
- ☐ Psalms 1-9
- ☐ Psalms 10-17
- ☐ Psalms 18
- ☐ Psalms 19-22
- ☐ Psalms 23-29
- ☐ Psalms 30-34
- ☐ Psalms 35-39
- ☐ Psalms 40-46
- ☐ Psalms 47-54
- ☐ Psalms 55-61
- ☐ Psalms 62-68
- ☐ Psalms 69-73
- ☐ Psalms 74-77
- ☐ Psalms 78-80
- ☐ Psalms 81-87
- ☐ Psalms 88-91
- ☐ Psalms 92-100
- ☐ Psalms 101-104
- ☐ Psalms 105-106
- ☐ Psalms 107-110
- ☐ Psalms 111-118
- ☐ Psalms 119:1-88
- ☐ Psalms 119:89-176
- ☐ Psalms 120-125
- ☐ Psalms 126-132
- ☐ Psalms 133-139
- ☐ Psalms 140-145
- ☐ Psalms 146-150
- ☐ Proverbs 1-3
- ☐ Proverbs 4-6
- ☐ Proverbs 7-10
- ☐ Proverbs 11-14
- ☐ Proverbs 15-17
- ☐ Proverbs 18-20
- ☐ Proverbs 21-23
- ☐ Proverbs 24-26
- ☐ Proverbs 27-29
- ☐ Proverbs 30-31
- ☐ Ecclesiastes 1-4
- ☐ Ecclesiastes 5-8
- ☐ Ecclesiastes 9-12
- ☐ Song of Solomon 1-4
- ☐ Song of Solomon 5-8
- ☐ Isaiah 1-3
- ☐ Isaiah 4-6
- ☐ Isaiah 7-9
- ☐ Isaiah 10-12
- ☐ Isaiah 13-15
- ☐ Isaiah 16-18
- ☐ Isaiah 19-21
- ☐ Isaiah 22-25
- ☐ Isaiah 26-29
- ☐ Isaiah 30-33
- ☐ Isaiah 34-37
- ☐ Isaiah 38-41
- ☐ Isaiah 42-45
- ☐ Isaiah 46-48

- ☐ Isaiah 49-51
- ☐ Isaiah 52-54
- ☐ Isaiah 55-57
- ☐ Isaiah 58-60
- ☐ Isaiah 61-63
- ☐ Isaiah 64-66
- ☐ Jeremiah 1-4
- ☐ Jeremiah 5-9
- ☐ Jeremiah 10-13
- ☐ Jeremiah 14-17
- ☐ Jeremiah 18-22
- ☐ Jeremiah 23-25
- ☐ Jeremiah 26-29
- ☐ Jeremiah 30-31
- ☐ Jeremiah 32-34
- ☐ Jeremiah 35-37
- ☐ Jeremiah 38-41
- ☐ Jeremiah 42-45
- ☐ Jeremiah 46-49
- ☐ Jeremiah 50-52
- ☐ Lamentations 1-2
- ☐ Lamentations 3-5
- ☐ Ezekiel 1-2
- ☐ Ezekiel 3-5
- ☐ Ezekiel 6-8
- ☐ Ezekiel 9-12
- ☐ Ezekiel 13-15
- ☐ Ezekiel 16-17
- ☐ Ezekiel 18-20
- ☐ Ezekiel 21-22
- ☐ Ezekiel 23-24
- ☐ Ezekiel 25-27
- ☐ Ezekiel 28-30
- ☐ Ezekiel 31-33
- ☐ Ezekiel 34-36
- ☐ Ezekiel 37-39
- ☐ Ezekiel 40-42
- ☐ Ezekiel 43-45
- ☐ Ezekiel 46-48
- ☐ Daniel 1-3
- ☐ Daniel 4-6
- ☐ Daniel 7-9
- ☐ Daniel 10-12
- ☐ Hosea 1-4
- ☐ Hosea 5-9
- ☐ Hosea 10-14
- ☐ Joel 1-3
- ☐ Amos 1-5
- ☐ Amos 6-9
- ☐ Obadiah 1; Jonah 1-4
- ☐ Micah 1-3
- ☐ Micah 4-7
- ☐ Nahum 1-3
- ☐ Habakkuk 1-3
- ☐ Zephaniah 1-3
- ☐ Haggai 1-2
- ☐ Zechariah 1-7
- ☐ Zechariah 8-14
- ☐ Malachi 1-4

# NOTES

# NOTES

# NOTES

# NOTES

# NOTES

# NOTES

# ONE-YEAR DAILY DEVOTIONAL

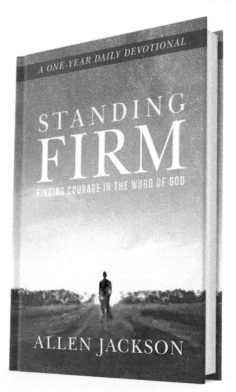

# STANDING FIRM

It's impossible to avoid the shaking that life brings. It's only by anchoring ourselves in the immovable things of God that we can be truly stable—able to stand when the storms come. This book is a tool for you, giving you a moment each day with Scripture and prayer. Use it alongside your Bible-reading time, or look up the daily Scripture in your Bible to find the full story. Resolve to intentionally know God through His Word better today than you did yesterday. He will be a firm foundation for you in every season.

# THREE-VOLUME SMALL GROUP VIDEO STUDY & GUIDE

# THE WHITEBOARD BIBLE™

The Bible tells a story, and these small group studies will help you more fully understand it. The three volumes of *The Whiteboard Bible* develop a twelve-point timeline that serves as the framework for all the characters and events in the Bible, beginning with Creation and concluding with Jesus' return.

For more from Allen Jackson—including sermons, books, and small group materials—visit:

allenjackson.com

# About The Author

Allen Jackson is passionate about helping people become more fully devoted followers of Jesus Christ, who respond to God's invitations for their life.

He has served World Outreach Church since 1981, becoming senior pastor in 1989. Under his leadership, WOC has grown to a congregation of over 15,000 through outreach activities, community events and worship services designed to share the Gospel.

Through Allen Jackson Ministries™, his messages reach people across the globe—through television, radio, Sirius XM, and online streaming. His teachings are also available in published books and other resources.

With degrees from Oral Roberts University and Vanderbilt University, and additional studies at Gordon-Conwell Theological Seminary and Hebrew University of Jerusalem, Jackson is uniquely equipped to help people develop a love and understanding of God's Word.

Pastor Jackson's wife, Kathy, is an active participant in ministry at World Outreach Church.